THE PENGUIN FREUD LIBRARY
VOLUME 8

·

CASE HISTORIES I

'DORA' AND 'LITTLE HANS'

Sigmund Freud

·

*Translated from the German
by Alix and James Strachey*

*Edited by James Strachey
assisted by Angela Richards and Alan Tyson*

*The present volume
edited by Angela Richards*

PENGUIN BOOKS

PENGUIN BOOKS

Published by the Penguin Group
Penguin Books Ltd, 27 Wrights Lane, London W8 5TZ, England
Viking Penguin, a division of Penguin Books USA Inc.
375 Hudson Street, New York, New York 10014, USA
Penguin Books Australia Ltd, Ringwood, Victoria, Australia
Penguin Books Canada Ltd, 2801 John Street, Markham, Ontario, Canada L3R 1B4
Penguin Books (NZ) Ltd, 182–190 Wairau Road, Auckland 10, New Zealand

Penguin Books Ltd, Registered Offices: Harmondsworth, Middlesex, England

Bruchstück einer Hysterie-Analyse first published 1905
First English translation by Alix and James Strachey published 1925
Analyse der Phobie eines fünfjährigen Knaben first published 1909
First English translation by Alix and James Strachey published 1925

Present English translations first published in
The Standard Edition of the Complete Psychological Works of Sigmund Freud
Volumes VII and X
by the Hogarth Press and the Institute of Psycho-Analysis, 1953 and 1955

'Sigmund Freud: A Sketch of His Life and Ideas' first published in
Two Short Accounts of Psycho-Analysis in Pelican Books 1962

This collection, *Case Histories I*, first published in Pelican Books 1977
Reprinted in Penguin Books 1990
1 3 5 7 9 10 8 6 4 2

Translation and Editorial Matter copyright © Angela Richards and the
Institute of Psycho-Analysis, 1953, 1955, 1962

Additional Editorial Matter copyright © Angela Richards, 1977
All rights reserved

Printed and bound in Great Britain by
Cox & Wyman Ltd, Reading
Set in Monotype Bembo

Except in the United States of America,
this book is sold subject to the condition
that it shall not, by way of trade or otherwise,
be lent, re-sold, hired out, or otherwise circulated
without the publisher's prior consent in any form of
binding or cover other than that in which it is
published and without a similar condition
including this condition being imposed
on the subsequent purchaser

CONTENTS

FRAGMENT OF AN ANALYSIS OF
A CASE OF HYSTERIA
('DORA')
(1905 [1901])

ANALYSIS OF A PHOBIA IN
A FIVE-YEAR-OLD BOY
('LITTLE HANS')
(1909)

INTRODUCTION TO
THE PENGUIN FREUD LIBRARY

The Penguin Freud Library (formerly *The Pelican Freud Library*) is intended to meet the needs of the general reader by providing all Freud's major writings in translation together with an appropriate linking commentary. It is the first time that such an edition has been produced in paperback in the English language. It does not supplant *The Standard Edition of the Complete Psychological Works of Sigmund Freud*, translated from the German under the general editorship of James Strachey in collaboration with Anna Freud, assisted by Alix Strachey and Alan Tyson, editorial assistant Angela Richards (Hogarth Press, 24 volumes, 1953–74). The *Standard Edition* remains the fullest and most authoritative collection published in any language. It does, however, provide a large enough selection to meet the requirements of all but the most specialist reader – in particular it aims to cater for students of sociology, anthropology, criminology, medicine, aesthetics and education, all of them fields in which Freud's ideas have established their relevance.

The texts are reprinted unabridged, with corrections, from the *Standard Edition*. The editorial commentary – introductions, footnotes, internal cross-references, bibliographies and indexes – is also based upon the *Standard Edition*, but it has been abridged and where necessary adapted to suit the less specialized scope and purposes of the *Penguin Freud Library*. Some corrections have been made and some new material added.

Selection of Material

This is not a complete edition of Freud's psychological works – still less of his works as a whole, which included important contributions to neurology and neuropathology dating from the early part of his professional life. Of the psychological writings, virtually all the major works have been included. The arrangement is by subject-matter, so that the main contributions to any particular theme will be found in one volume. Within each volume the works are, for the main part, in chronological sequence. The aim has been to cover the whole field of Freud's observations and his theory of psychoanalysis: that is to say, in the first place, the structure and dynamics of human mental activity; secondly, psychopathology and the mechanism of mental disorder; and thirdly, the application of psychoanalytic theory to wider spheres than the disorders of individuals which Freud originally, and indeed for the greater part of his life, investigated – to the psychology of groups, to social institutions and to religion, art and literature.

In his 'Sigmund Freud: A Sketch of his Life and Ideas' (p. 11 ff. below), James Strachey includes an account of Freud's discoveries as well as defining his principal theories and tracing their development.

Writings excluded from the Edition

The works that have been excluded are, (1) The neurological writings and most of those very early works from the period before the idea of psychoanalysis had taken form. (2) Writings on the actual technique of treatment. These were written specifically for practitioners of psychoanalysis and for analysts in training and their interest is correspondingly specialized. Freud never in fact produced a complete text on psychoanalytic treatment and the papers on technique only deal with selected points of difficulty or theoretical interest. (3) Writings which cover the same ground as other major works which have been included; for example, since the *Library* includes the *Introductory Lectures on Psychoanalysis* and the *New Lectures*, it was decided to leave out several of the shorter expository works in which Freud surveys the whole subject. Similarly, because the

Interpretation of Dreams is included, the shorter writings on this topic have been omitted. (4) Freud's private correspondence, much of which has now been published in translation[1]. This is not to imply that such letters are without interest or importance though they have not yet received full critical treatment. (5) The numerous short writings such as reviews of books, prefaces to other authors' works, obituary notices and little *pièces d'occasion* – all of which lose interest to a large extent when separated from the books or occasions to which they refer and which would often demand long editorial explanations to make them comprehensible.

All of these excluded writings (with the exception of the works on neurology and the private letters) can be found in the *Standard Edition*.

Editorial Commentary

The bibliographical information, included at the beginning of the Editor's Note or Introduction to each work, gives the title of the German (or other) original, the date and place of its first publication and the position, where applicable, of the work in Freud's *Gesammelte Werke*, the most complete edition at present available of the works in German (published by S. Fischer Verlag, Frankfurt am Main). Details of the first translation of each work into English are also included, together with the *Standard Edition* reference. Other editions are listed only if they contain significant changes. (Full details of all German editions published in Freud's lifetime and of all English editions prior to the *Standard Edition* are included in the *Standard Edition*.)

The date of original publication of each work has been added to the half-title page, with the date of composition included in square brackets wherever it is different from the former date.

Further background information is given in introductory notes and in footnotes to the text. Apart from dealing with the

1. [See the list, pp. 23–4 *n*. below, and the details in the Bibliography, p. 307ff.]

time and circumstances of composition, these notes aim to make it possible to follow the inception and development of important psychoanalytic concepts by means of systematic cross-references. Most of these references are to other works included in the *Penguin Freud Library*. A secondary purpose is to date additions and alterations made by Freud in successive revisions of the text and in certain cases to provide the earlier versions. No attempt has been made to do this as comprehensively as in the *Standard Edition*, but variants are given whenever they indicate a definite change of view. Square brackets are used throughout to distinguish editorial additions from Freud's text and his own footnotes.

It will be clear from this account that I owe an overwhelming debt to the late James Strachey, the general editor and chief translator of the *Standard Edition*. He indeed was mainly responsible for the idea of a *Pelican Freud Library*, and for the original plan of contents. I have also had the advantage of discussions with Miss Anna Freud and the late Mrs Alix Strachey, both of whom gave advice of the greatest value. I am grateful to the late Mr Ernst Freud for his support and to the Publications Committee of the Institute of Psycho-Analysis for help in furthering preparations for this edition.

ANGELA RICHARDS

SIGMUND FREUD

A SKETCH OF HIS LIFE AND IDEAS

SIGMUND FREUD was born on 6 May 1856 in Freiberg, a small town in Moravia, which was at that time a part of Austria-Hungary. In an external sense the eighty-three years of his life were on the whole uneventful and call for no lengthy history.

He came of a middle-class Jewish family and was the eldest child of his father's second wife. His position in the family was a little unusual, for there were already two grown-up sons by his father's first wife. These were more than twenty years older than he was and one of them was already married, with a little boy; so that Freud was in fact born an uncle. This nephew played at least as important a part in his very earliest years as his own younger brothers and sisters, of whom seven were born after him.

His father was a wool-merchant and soon after Freud's birth found himself in increasing commercial difficulties. He therefore decided, when Freud was just three years old, to leave Freiberg, and a year later the whole family settled in Vienna, with the exception of the two elder half-brothers and their children, who established themselves instead in Manchester. At more than one stage in his life Freud played with the idea of joining them in England, but nothing was to come of this for nearly eighty years.

In Vienna during the whole of Freud's childhood the family lived in the most straitened conditions; but it is much to his father's credit that he gave invariable priority to the charge of Freud's education, for the boy was obviously intelligent and was a hard worker as well. The result was that he won a place in the 'Gymnasium' at the early age of nine, and for the last six of the eight years he spent at the school he was regularly top of his class. When at the age of seventeen he passed out of school his career was still undecided; his education so far had been of the most general kind, and, though he seemed in any case destined for the University, several faculties lay open to him.

Freud insisted more than once that at no time in his life did he feel 'any particular predilection for the career of a doctor. I was moved, rather', he says, 'by a sort of curiosity, which was, however, directed more towards human concerns than towards natural objects.'[1] Elsewhere he writes: 'I have no knowledge of having had any craving in my early childhood to help suffering humanity . . . In my youth I felt an overpowering need to understand something of the riddles of the world in which we live and perhaps even to contribute something to their solution.'[2] And in yet another passage in which he was discussing the sociological studies of his last years: 'My interest, after making a lifelong *détour* through the natural sciences, medicine, and psychotherapy, returned to the cultural problems which had fascinated me long before, when I was a youth scarcely old enough for thinking.'[3]

What immediately determined Freud's choice of a scientific career was, so he tells us, being present just when he was leaving school at a public reading of an extremely flowery essay on 'Nature', attributed (wrongly, it seems) to Goethe. But if it was to be science, practical considerations narrowed the choice to medicine. And it was as a medical student that Freud enrolled himself at the University in the autumn of 1873 at the age of seventeen. Even so, however, he was in no hurry to obtain a medical degree. For his first year or two he attended lectures on a variety of subjects, but gradually concentrated first on biology and then on physiology. His very first piece of research was in his third year at the University, when he was deputed by the Professor of Comparative Anatomy to investigate a detail in the anatomy of the eel, which involved the dissection of some

1. [*An Autobiographical Study* (1925d), near the opening of the work.]
2. ['Postscript to *The Question of Lay Analysis*' (1927a).]
3. ['Postscript (1935) to *An Autobiographical Study*' (1935a).]

four hundred specimens. Soon afterwards he entered the Physiological Laboratory under Brücke, and worked there happily for six years. It was no doubt from him that he acquired the main outlines of his attitude to physical science in general. During these years Freud worked chiefly on the anatomy of the central nervous system and was already beginning to produce publications. But it was becoming obvious that no livelihood which would be sufficient to meet the needs of the large family at home was to be picked up from these laboratory studies. So at last, in 1881, he decided to take his medical degree, and a year later, most unwillingly, gave up his position under Brücke and began work in the Vienna General Hospital.

What finally determined this change in his life was something more urgent than family considerations: in June 1882 he became engaged to be married, and thenceforward all his efforts were directed towards making marriage possible. His fiancée, Martha Bernays, came of a well-known Jewish family in Hamburg, and though for the moment she was living in Vienna she was very soon obliged to return to her remote North-German home. During the four years that followed, it was only for brief visits that he could have glimpses of her, and the two lovers had to content themselves with an almost daily interchange of letters. Freud now set himself to establishing a position and a reputation in the medical world. He worked in various departments of the hospital, but soon came to concentrate on neuroanatomy and neuropathology. During this period, too, he published the first inquiry into the possible medical uses of cocaine; and it was this that suggested to Koller the drug's employment as a local anaesthetic. He soon formed two immediate plans: one of these was to obtain an appointment as *Privatdozent*, a post not unlike that of a university lecturer in England, the other was to gain a travelling bursary which would enable him to spend some time in Paris, where the reigning figure was the great Charcot. Both of these aims, if they were realized, would, he felt, bring him real advantages, and in 1885, after a hard struggle, he achieved them both.

The months which Freud spent under Charcot at the Salpêtrière (the famous Paris hospital for nervous diseases) brought another change in the course of his life and this time a revolutionary one. So far his work had been concerned entirely with physical science and he was still carrying out histological studies on the brain while he was in Paris. Charcot's interests were at that period concentrated mainly on hysteria and hypnotism. In the world from which Freud came these subjects were regarded as barely respectable, but he became absorbed in them, and, though Charcot himself looked at them purely as branches of neuropathology, for Freud they meant the first beginnings of the investigation of the mind.

On his return to Vienna in the spring of 1886 Freud set up in private practice as a consultant in nervous diseases, and his long-delayed marriage followed soon afterwards. He did not, however, at once abandon all his neuropathological work: for several more years he studied in particular the cerebral palsies of children, on which he became a leading authority. At this period, too, he produced an important monograph on aphasia. But he was becoming more and more engaged in the treatment of the neuroses. After experimenting in vain with electrotherapy, he turned to hypnotic suggestion, and in 1888 visited Nancy to learn the technique used with such apparent success there by Liébeault and Bernheim. This still proved unsatisfactory and he was driven to yet another line of approach. He knew that a friend of his, Dr Josef Breuer, a Vienna consultant considerably his senior, had some ten years earlier cured a girl suffering from hysteria by a quite new procedure. He now persuaded Breuer to take up the method once more, and he himself applied it to several fresh cases with promising results. The method was based on the assumption that hysteria was the product of a psychical trauma which had been forgotten by the patient; and the treatment consisted in inducing her in a hypnotic state to recall the forgotten trauma to the accompaniment of appropriate emotions. Before very long Freud began to make changes both in the procedure and in the underlying theory; this led eventually to a breach with Breuer, and to the ultimate development by Freud of the whole system of ideas to which he soon gave the name of psychoanalysis.

From this moment onwards – from 1895, perhaps – to the very end of his life, the whole of Freud's intellectual existence revolved around this development, its far-reaching implications, and its theoretical and practical repercussions. It would, of course, be impossible to give in a few sentences any consecutive account of Freud's discoveries and ideas, but an attempt will be made presently to indicate in a disconnected fashion some of the main changes he has brought about in our habits of thought. Meanwhile we may continue to follow the course of his external life.

His domestic existence in Vienna was essentially devoid of episode: his home and his consulting rooms were in the same house from 1891 till his departure for London forty-seven years later. His happy marriage and his growing family – three sons and three daughters – provided a solid counterweight to the difficulties which, to begin with at least, surrounded his professional career. It was not only the nature of his discoveries that created prejudice against him in medical circles; just as great, perhaps, was the effect of the intense anti-semitic feeling which dominated the official world of Vienna: his appointment to a university professorship was constantly held back by political influence.

One particular feature of these early years calls for mention on account of its consequences. This was Freud's friendship with Wilhelm Fliess, a brilliant but unbalanced Berlin physician, who specialized in the ear and throat, but whose wider interests extended over human biology and the effects of periodic phenomena in vital processes. For fifteen years, from 1887 to 1902, Freud corresponded with him regularly, reported the development of his ideas, forwarded him long drafts outlining his future writings, and, most important of all, sent him an essay of some forty thousand words which has been given the name of a 'Project for a Scientific Psychology'. This essay was composed in 1895, at what might be described as the watershed of Freud's career, when he was reluctantly moving from physiology to psychology; it is an attempt to state the facts of psychology in purely neurological terms. This paper and all the rest of Freud's communications to Fliess have, by a lucky chance, survived: they throw a fascinating light on the development of Freud's ideas and show how much of the later findings of psychoanalysis were already present in his mind at this early stage.

Apart from his relations with Fliess, Freud had little outside support to begin with. He gradually gathered a few pupils round him in Vienna, but it was only after some ten years, in about 1906, that a change was inaugurated by the adhesion of a number of Swiss psychiatrists to his views. Chief among these were Bleuler, the head of the Zurich mental hospital, and his assistant Jung. This proved to be the beginning of the first spread of psychoanalysis. An international meeting of psychoanalysts gathered at Salzburg in 1908, and in 1909 Freud and Jung were invited to give a number of lectures in the United States. Freud's writings began to be translated into many languages, and groups of practising analysts sprang up all over the world. But the progress of psychoanalysis was not without its set-backs: the currents which its subject-matter stirred up in the mind ran too deep for its easy acceptance. In 1911 one of Freud's prominent Viennese supporters. Alfred Adler, broke away from him, and two or three years later Jung's differences from Freud led to their separation. Almost immediately after this came the First World War and an interruption of the international spread of psychoanalysis. Soon afterwards, too, came the gravest personal tragedies – the death of a daughter and of a favourite grandchild, and the onset of the malignant illness which was to pursue him relentlessly for the last sixteen years of his life. None of these troubles, however, brought any interruption to the development of Freud's observations and inferences. The structure of his ideas continued to expand and to find ever wider applications – particularly in the sociological field. By now he had become generally recognized as a figure of world celebrity, and no honour pleased him more than his election in 1936, the year of his eightieth birthday, as a Corresponding Member of the Royal Society. It was no doubt this fame, supported by the efforts of influential admirers, including, it is said, President Roosevelt, that protected him from the worst excesses of the National Socialists when Hitler invaded Austria in 1938, though they seized and destroyed his publications. Freud's departure from Vienna was nevertheless essential, and in June of that year, accompanied by some of his family, he made the journey to London, and it was there, a year later, on 23 September 1939, that he died.

It has become a journalistic cliché to speak of Freud as one of the revolutionary founders of modern thought and to couple his name with that of Einstein. Most people would however find it almost as hard to summarize the changes introduced by the one as by the other.

Freud's discoveries may be grouped under three headings – an instrument of research, the findings produced by the instrument, and the theoretical hypotheses inferred from the findings – though the three groups were of course mutually interrelated. Behind all of Freud's work, however, we should posit his belief in the universal validity of the law of determinism. As regards physical phenomena this belief was perhaps derived from his experience in Brücke's laboratory and so, ultimately, from the school of Helmholtz; but Freud extended the belief uncompromisingly to the field of mental phenomena, and here he may have been influenced by his teacher, the psychiatrist Meynert, and indirectly by the philosophy of Herbart.

First and foremost, Freud was the discoverer of the first instrument for the scientific examination of the human mind. Creative writers of genius had had fragmentary insight into mental processes, but no systematic method of investigation existed before Freud. It was only gradually that he perfected the instrument, since it was only gradually that the difficulties in the way of such an investigation became apparent. The forgotten trauma in Breuer's explanation of hysteria provided the earliest problem and perhaps the most fundamental of all, for it showed conclusively that there were active parts of the mind not immediately open to inspection either by an on-looker or by the subject himself. These parts of the mind were described by Freud, without regard for metaphysical or ter-minological disputes, as the unconscious. Their existence was equally demonstrated by the fact of post-hypnotic suggestion, where a person in a fully waking state performs an action which had been suggested to him some time earlier, though he had totally forgotten the suggestion itself. No examination of the mind could thus be considered complete unless it included this unconscious part of it in its scope. How was this to be accomplished? The obvious answer seemed to be: by means of hypnotic suggestion; and this was the instrument used by Breuer and, to begin with, by Freud. But it soon turned out to be an imperfect one, acting irregularly and uncertainly and sometimes not at all. Little by little, accordingly, Freud aban-doned the use of suggestion and replaced it by an entirely fresh instrument, which was later known as 'free association'. He adopted the unheard-of plan of simply asking the person whose mind he was investigating to say whatever came into his head. This crucial decision led at once to the most startling results; even in this primitive form Freud's instrument produced fresh insight. For, though things went along swimmingly for a while, sooner or later the flow of associations dried up: the subject would not or could not think of anything more to say. There thus came to light the fact of 'resistance', of a force, separate from the subject's conscious will, which was refusing to collaborate with the investigation. Here was one basis for a very fundamental piece of theory, for a hypothesis of the mind as something dynamic, as consisting in a number of mental forces, some conscious and some unconscious, operating now in harmony now in opposition with one another.

Though these phenomena eventually turned out to be of universal occurrence, they were first observed and studied in neurotic patients, and the earlier years of Freud's work were largely concerned with discovering means by which the 'resistance' of these patients could be overcome and what lay behind it could be brought to light. The solution was only made possible by an extraordinary piece of self-observation on Freud's part – what we should now describe as his self-analysis. We are fortunate in having a contemporary first-hand description of this event in his letters to Fliess which have already been mentioned. This analysis enabled him to discover the nature of the unconscious processes at work in the mind and to understand why there is such a strong resistance to their becoming conscious; it enabled him to devise techniques for overcoming or evading the resistance in his patients; and, most important of all, it enabled him to realize the very great difference between the mode of functioning of these unconscious processes and that of our familiar conscious ones. A word may be said on each of these three points, for in fact they constitute the core of Freud's contributions to our knowledge of the mind.

The unconscious contents of the mind were found to consist wholly in the activity of conative trends – desires or wishes – which derive their energy directly from the primary physical instincts. They function quite regardless of any consideration other than that of obtaining immediate satisfaction, and are thus liable to be out of step with those more conscious elements in the mind which are concerned with adaptation to reality and the avoidance of external dangers. Since, moreover, these primitive trends are to a great extent of a sexual or of a destructive nature, they are bound to come in conflict with the more social and civilized mental forces. Investigations along this path were what led Freud to his discoveries of the long-disguised secrets of the sexual life of children and of the Oedipus complex.

In the second place, his self-analysis led him to an inquiry into the nature of dreams. These turned out to be, like neurotic symptoms, the product of a conflict and a compromise between the primary unconscious impulses and the secondary conscious ones. By analysing them into their elements it was therefore possible to infer their hidden unconscious contents; and, since dreams are common phenomena of almost universal occurrence, their interpretation turned out to be one of the most useful technical contrivances for penetrating the resistances of neurotic patients.

Finally, the painstaking examination of dreams enabled Freud to classify the remarkable differences between what he termed the primary and secondary processes of thought, between events in the unconscious and conscious regions of the mind. In the unconscious, it was found, there is no sort of organization or coordination: each separate impulse seeks satisfaction independently of all the rest; they proceed uninfluenced by one another; contradictions are completely inoperative, and the most opposite impulses flourish side by side. So, too, in the unconscious, associations of ideas proceed along lines without any regard to logic: similarities are treated as identities, negatives are equated with positives. Again, the objects to which the conative trends are attached in the unconscious are extraordinarily changeable – one may be replaced by another along a whole chain of associations that have no rational basis. Freud perceived that the intrusion into conscious thinking of mechanisms that belong properly to the primary process accounts for the oddity not only of dreams but of many other normal and pathological mental events.

It is not much of an exaggeration to say that all the later part of Freud's work lay in an immense extension and elaboration of these early ideas. They were applied to an elucidation of the mechanisms not only of the psychoneuroses and psychoses but also of such normal processes as slips of the tongue, making jokes, artistic creation, political institutions, and religions; they played a part in throwing fresh light on many applied sciences – archaeology, anthropology, criminology, education; they also served to account for the effectiveness of psychoanalytic therapy. Lastly, too, Freud erected on the basis of these elementary observations a theoretical superstructure, what he named a 'metapsychology', of more general concepts. These, however, fascinating as many people will find them, he always insisted were in the nature of provisional hypotheses. Quite late in his life, indeed, influenced by the ambiguity of the term 'unconscious' and its many conflicting uses, he proposed a new structural account of the mind in which the uncoordinated instinctual trends were called the 'id', the organized realistic part the 'ego', and the critical and moralizing function the 'super-ego' – a new account which has certainly made for a clarification of many issues.

This, then, will have given the reader an outline of the external events of Freud's life and some notion of the scope of his discoveries. Is it legitimate to ask for more? to try to penetrate a little further and to inquire what sort of person Freud was? Possibly not. But human curiosity about great men is insatiable, and if it is not gratified with true accounts it will inevitably clutch at mythological ones. In two of Freud's early books (*The Interpretation of Dreams* and *The Psychopathology of Everyday Life*) the presentation of his thesis had forced on him the necessity of bringing up an unusual amount of personal material. Nevertheless, or perhaps for that very reason, he intensely objected to any intrusion into his private life, and he was correspondingly the subject of a wealth of myths. According to the first and most naïve rumours, for instance, he was an abandoned profligate, devoted to the corruption of public morals. Later fantasies have tended in the opposite direction: he has been represented as a harsh moralist, a ruthless disciplinarian, an autocrat, egocentric and unsmiling, and an essentially unhappy man. To anyone who was acquainted with him, even slightly, both these pictures must seem equally preposterous. The second of them was no doubt partly derived from a knowledge of his physical sufferings during his last years; but partly too it may have been due to the unfortunate impression produced by some of his most widespread portraits. He disliked being photographed, at least by professional photographers, and his features on occasion expressed the fact; artists too seem always to have been overwhelmed by the necessity for representing the inventor of psychoanalysis as a ferocious and terrifying figure. Fortunately, however, alternative versions exist of a more amiable and truer kind – snapshots, for instance, taken on a holiday or with his children, such as will be found in his eldest son's memoir of his father (*Glory Reflected*, by Martin Freud [1957]). In many ways, indeed, this delightful and amusing book serves to redress the balance from more official biographies, invaluable as they are, and reveals something of Freud as he was in ordinary life. Some of these portraits show us that in his earlier days he had well-filled features, but in later life, at any rate after the First World War and even before his illness, this was no longer so, and his features, as well as his whole figure (which was of medium height), were chiefly remarkable for the impression they gave of tense energy and alert observation. He was serious but kindly and considerate in his more formal manners, but in other circumstances could be an entertaining talker with a pleasantly ironical sense of humour. It was easy to discover his devoted fondness for his family and to recognize a man who would inspire affection. He had many miscellaneous interests – he was fond of travelling abroad, of country holidays, of mountain walks – and there were other, more engrossing subjects, art, archaeology, literature. Freud was a very well read man in many languages, not only in German. He read English and French fluently, besides having a fair knowledge of Spanish and Italian. It must be remembered, too, that though the later phases of his education were chiefly scientific (it is true that at the University he studied philosophy for a short time) at school he had learnt the classics and never lost his affection for them. We happen to have a letter written by him at the age of seventeen to a school friend[1]. In it

1. [Emil Fluss. The letter is included in the volume of Freud's correspondence (1960a).]

he describes his varying success in the different papers of his school-leaving examination: in Latin a passage from Virgil, and in Greek thirty-three lines from, of all things, *Oedipus Rex*.

In short, we might regard Freud as what in England we should consider the best kind of product of a Victorian up-bringing. His tastes in literature and art would obviously differ from ours, his views on ethics, though decidedly liberal, would not belong to the post-Freudian age. But we should see in him a man who lived a life of full emotion and of much suffering without embitterment. Complete honesty and directness were qualities that stood out in him, and so too did his intellectual readiness to take in and consider any fact, however new or extraordinary, that was presented to him. It was perhaps an inevitable corollary and extension of these qualities, combined with a general benevolence which a surface misanthropy failed to disguise, that led to some features of a surprising kind. In spite of his subtlety of mind he was essentially unsophisti-cated, and there were sometimes unexpected lapses in his critical faculty – a failure, for instance, to perceive an untrust-worthy authority in some subject that was off his own beat such as Egyptology or philology, and, strangest of all in someone whose powers of perception had to be experienced to be believed, an occasional blindness to defects in his acquaint-ances. But though it may flatter our vanity to declare that Freud was a human being of a kind like our own, that satisfaction can easily be carried too far. There must in fact have been something very extraordinary in the man who was first able to recognize a whole field of mental facts which had hitherto been excluded from normal consciousness, the man who first interpreted dreams, who first accepted the facts of infantile sexuality, who first made the distinction between the primary and secondary processes of thinking – the man who first made the unconscious mind real to us.

JAMES STRACHEY

[Those in search of further information will find it in the three-volume biography of Freud by Ernest Jones, an abridged version of which was published in Pelican in 1964 (reissued 1974), in the important volume of Freud's letters edited by his son and daughter-in-law, Ernst and Lucie Freud (1960a), in several further volumes of his correspondence, with Wilhelm Fliess (1950a), Karl Abraham (1965a), C. G. Jung (1974a), Oskar Pfister (1963a), Lou Andreas-Salomé (1966a), Edoardo Weiss (1970a) and Arnold Zweig (1968a), and above all in the many volumes of Freud's own works.]

CHRONOLOGICAL TABLE

This table traces very roughly some of the main turning-points in Freud's intellectual development and opinions. A few of the chief events in his external life are also included in it.

1856. 6 May. Birth at Freiberg in Moravia.

1860. Family settles in Vienna.

1865. Enters Gymnasium (secondary school).

1873. Enters Vienna University as medical student.

1876–82. Works under Brücke at the Institute of Physiology in Vienna.

1877. First publications: papers on anatomy and physiology.

1881. Graduates as Doctor of Medicine.

1882. Engagement to Martha Bernays.

1882–5. Works in Vienna General Hospital, concentrating on cerebral anatomy: numerous publications.

1884–7. Researches into the clinical uses of cocaine.

1885. Appointed *Privatdozent* (University Lecturer) in Neuropathology.

1885 (October)–1886 (February). Studies under Charcot at the Salpêtrière (hospital for nervous diseases) in Paris. Interest first turns to hysteria and hypnosis.

1886. Marriage to Martha Bernays. Sets up private practice in nervous diseases in Vienna.

1886–93. Continues work on neurology, especially on the cerebral palsies of children at the Kassowitz Institute in Vienna, with numerous publications. Gradual shift of interest from neurology to psychopathology.

1887. Birth of eldest child (Mathilde).

1887–1902. Friendship and correspondence with Wilhelm Fliess in Berlin. Freud's letters to him during this period, published posthumously in 1950, throw much light on the development of his views.

1887. Begins the use of hypnotic suggestion in his practice.

c. 1888. Begins to follow Breuer in using hypnosis for cathartic treatment of hysteria. Gradually drops hypnosis and substitutes free association.

1889. Visits Bernheim at Nancy to study his suggestion technique.

1889. Birth of eldest son (Martin).

1891. Monograph on Aphasia.

Birth of second son (Oliver).

1892. Birth of youngest son (Ernst).

1893. Publication of Breuer and Freud 'Preliminary Communication': exposition of trauma theory of hysteria and of cathartic treatment.

Birth of second daughter (Sophie).

1893–8. Researches and short papers on hysteria, obsessions, and anxiety.

1895. Jointly with Breuer, *Studies on Hysteria*: case histories and description by Freud of his technique, including first account of transference.

1893–6. Gradual divergence of views between Freud and Breuer. Freud introduces concepts of defence and repression and of neurosis being a result of a conflict between the ego and the libido.

1895. *Project for a Scientific Psychology*: included in Freud's letters to Fliess and first published in 1950. An abortive attempt to state psychology in neurological terms; but foreshadows much of Freud's later theories.

Birth of youngest child (Anna).

1896. Introduces the term 'psychoanalysis'.

Death of father (aged 80).

1897. Freud's self-analysis, leading to the abandonment of the trauma theory and the recognition of infantile sexuality and the Oedipus complex.

1900. *The Interpretation of Dreams*, with final chapter giving first full account of Freud's dynamic view of mental processes, of the unconscious, and of the dominance of the 'pleasure principle'.

1901. *The Psychopathology of Everyday Life*. This, together with the book on dreams, made it plain that Freud's theories applied not only to pathological states but also to normal mental life.

1902. Appointed Professor Extraordinarius.

1905. *Three Essays on the Theory of Sexuality*: tracing for the first time the course of development of the sexual instinct in human beings from infancy to maturity.

c. 1906. Jung becomes an adherent of psychoanalysis.

1908. First international meeting of psychoanalysts (at Salzburg).

1909. Freud and Jung invited to the USA to lecture.

Case history of the first analysis of a child (Little Hans, aged five): confirming inferences previously made from adult analyses, especially as to infantile sexuality and the Oedipus and castration complexes.

c. 1910. First emergence of the theory of 'narcissism'.

1911–15. Papers on the technique of psychoanalysis.

1911. Secession of Adler.

Application of psychoanalytic theories to a psychotic case: the autobiography of Dr Schreber.

1912–13. *Totem and Taboo*: application of psychoanalysis to anthropological material.

1914. Secession of Jung.

'On the History of the Psycho-Analytic Movement'. Includes a polemical section on Adler and Jung.

Writes his last major case history, of the 'Wolf Man' (not published till 1918).

1915. Writes a series of twelve 'metapsychological' papers on basic theoretical questions, of which only five have survived.

1915–17. *Introductory Lectures*: giving an extensive general account of the state of Freud's views up to the time of the First World War.

1919. Application of the theory of narcissism to the war neuroses.

1920. Death of second daughter.

Beyond the Pleasure Principle: the first explicit introduction of the concept of the 'compulsion to repeat' and of the theory of the 'death instinct'.

1921. *Group Psychology*. Beginnings of a systematic analytic study of the ego.

1923. *The Ego and the Id*. Largely revised account of the structure and functioning of the mind with the division into an id, an ego, and a super-ego.

1923. First onset of cancer.

1925. Revised views on the sexual development of women.

1926. *Inhibitions, Symptoms, and Anxiety*. Revised views on the problem of anxiety.

1927. *The Future of an Illusion*. A discussion of religion: the first of a number of sociological works to which Freud devoted most of his remaining years.

1930. *Civilization and its Discontents.* This includes Freud's first extensive study of the destructive instinct (regarded as a manifestation of the 'death instinct').

Freud awarded the Goethe Prize by the City of Frankfurt.

Death of mother (aged 95).

1933. Hitler seizes power in Germany: Freud's books publicly burned in Berlin.

1934–8. *Moses and Monotheism*: the last of Freud's works to appear during his lifetime.

1936. Eightieth birthday. Election as Corresponding Member of Royal Society.

1938. Hitler's invasion of Austria. Freud leaves Vienna for London. *An Outline of Psycho-Analysis.* A final, unfinished, but profound exposition of psychoanalysis.

1939. 23 September. Death in London.

JAMES STRACHEY

FRAGMENT OF AN ANALYSIS OF A CASE OF HYSTERIA ('DORA')
(1905 [1901])

EDITOR'S INTRODUCTION

BRUCHSTÜCK EINER HYSTERIE-ANALYSE

(A) German Editions:

(1901   Jan. 24. Completion of first draft under title 'Traum und Hysterie' ['Dreams and Hysteria'].)

1905   *Mschr. Psychiat. Neurol.*, **18** (4 and 5), Oct. and Nov., 285–310 and 408–67.

1909   *S.K.S.N.*, **2**, 1–110. (1912, 2nd ed.; 1921, 3rd ed.)

1924   *Gesammelte Schriften*, **8**, 3–126. (Revised ed.)

1932   *Vier Krankengeschichten*, 5–141.

1942   *Gesammelte Werke*, **5**, 163–286.

(B) English Translations:

'Fragment of an Analysis of a Case of Hysteria'

1925   *Collected Papers*, **3**, 13–146. (Tr. Alix and James Strachey.)

1953   *Standard Edition*, **7**, 1–122.

The present edition is a corrected reprint of the *Standard Edition* translation, with some editorial changes. A few changes and additions (including footnotes dated '1923') were made in the 1924 German edition.

Though this case history was not published until October and November, 1905, the greater part of it was written in January, 1901, while Freud was simultaneously engaged on the final stages of his *Psychopathology of Everyday Life* (1901*b*). His letters to Wilhelm Fliess (Freud, 1950*a*) contain a quantity of contemporary evidence on the subject.

On October 14, 1900 (Letter 139), Freud tells Fliess that he has recently begun work with a new patient, 'an eighteen-year-old girl'. This girl was evidently 'Dora', and, as we know from the case history itself (p. 42 *n*. below), her treatment came to an end some three months later, on December 31. Freud wrote out the case history during the following weeks. On January 25 (Letter 140) he writes: '"Dreams and Hysteria" was completed yesterday . . .' (This, as we are told in Freud's preface, p. 39 below, was the original title of the present paper.) He continues: 'It is a fragment of an analysis of a case of hysteria, in which the explanations are grouped round two dreams. So that it is in fact a continuation of the dream book.' (*The Interpretation of Dreams*, 1900*a*.) 'It further contains solutions of hysterical symptoms and considerations on the sexual-organic basis of the whole condition. Anyhow, it is the most subtle thing I have yet written and will produce an even more horrifying effect than usual. One does one's duty, however, and what one writes is not for the passing day. The work has already been accepted by Ziehen.' The latter was joint editor, with Wernicke, of the *Monatsschrift für Psychiatrie und Neurologie*, in which the paper ultimately appeared. A few days later, on January 30 (Letter 141), Freud continues: 'I hope you will not be disappointed by "Dreams and Hysteria". Its main concern is still with psychology – an estimation of the importance of dreams and an account of some of the peculiarities of unconscious thinking. There are only glimpses of the organic side – the erotogenic zones and bisexuality. But it [the organic side] is definitely mentioned and recognized and the way is paved for an exhaustive discussion of it another time. The case is a hysteria with *tussis nervosa* and aphonia, which can be traced back to the characteristics of a thumb-sucker; and the principal part in the conflicting mental processes is played by the opposition between an attraction towards men and one towards women,' These extracts show how this paper forms a link between *The*

Interpretation of Dreams and the *Three Essays on the Theory of Sexuality* (1905*d*). It looks back to the one and forward to the other.

Freud had finished writing the paper early in 1901 and clearly intended at that stage to publish it straight away. On June 9, in an unpublished letter to Fliess, he reported that '"Dreams and Hysteria" has been sent off and will meet the gaze of an astonished public in the autumn'. Yet, for reasons which are not entirely known to us he in fact deferred publication for another four years. We learn from Ernest Jones (1955, 286) that the work was sent first (before Ziehen had actually set eyes on it) to the *Journal für Psychologie und Neurologie*, whose editor, Brodmann, returned it, apparently on the grounds that it was a breach of medical discretion. This point of view may well have had some influence on Freud, but it seems probable that a concern to prevent his patient from suffering any injury – however remote the likelihood – was a more important factor than was any respect for conventional medical behaviour. Freud's own attitude to this problem is very clearly expressed in his 'Prefatory Remarks' (p. 35–8 f.).

We have no means of deciding the extent to which Freud revised the paper before its ultimate publication in 1905. All the internal evidence suggests, however, that he changed it very little. The last section of the 'Postscript' (pp. 162–4) was certainly added, as well as some passages at least in the 'Prefatory Remarks' and certain of the footnotes. But apart from these small additions it is fair to regard the paper as representing Freud's technical methods and theoretical views at the period immediately after the publication of *The Interpretation of Dreams*. It may seem surprising that his theory of sexuality had reached such a point of development so many years before the appearance of the *Three Essays* (1905*d*), which were actually published almost simultaneously with this paper. But the footnote on p. 85 explicitly vouches for the fact. Moreover, readers of the Fliess correspondence will be aware that much of this theory was in existence at an even earlier date.

It is curious that in his later writings Freud more than once assigns his treatment of 'Dora' to the wrong year – to 1899 instead of 1900. The mistake is also repeated twice in the foot-note which he added to the case history in 1923 (p. 42 *n.*). There can be no question that the autumn of 1900 was the correct date, since, quite apart from the external evidence quoted above, the date is absolutely fixed by the '1902' given at the end of the paper itself (p. 164).

This chronological summary, based on the data given in the case history, may make it easier for the reader to follow the events in the narrative:

1882	Dora born.
1888 (*Aet.* 6)	Father ill with T.B. Family move to B—.
1889 (*Aet.* 7)	Bed-wetting.
1890 (*Aet.* 8)	Dyspnoea.
1892 (*Aet.* 10)	Father's detached retina.
1894 (*Aet.* 12)	Father's confusional attack. His visit to Freud. Migraine and *tussis nervosa*.
1896 (*Aet.* 14)	Scene of the kiss.
1898 (*Aet.* 16)	(Early summer:) Dora's first visit to Freud. (End of June:) Scene by the lake. (Winter:) Death of Aunt. Dora in Vienna.
1899 (*Aet.* 17)	(March:) Appendicitis. (Autumn:) Family leave B— and move to factory town.
1900 (*Aet.* 18)	Family move to Vienna. Suicide threat. (October to December:) Treatment with Freud.
1901	(January:) Case history written.
1902	(April:) Dora's last visit to Freud.
1905	Case history published.

PREFATORY REMARKS

In 1895 and 1896[1] I put forward certain views upon the pathogenesis of hysterical symptoms and upon the mental processes occurring in hysteria. Since that time several years have passed. In now proposing, therefore, to substantiate those views by giving a detailed report of the history of a case and its treatment, I cannot avoid making a few introductory remarks, for the purpose partly of justifying from various standpoints the step I am taking, and partly of diminishing the expectations to which it will give rise.

No doubt it was awkward that I was obliged to publish the results of my enquiries without there being any possibility of other workers in the field testing and checking them, particularly as those results were of a surprising and by no means gratifying character. But it will be scarcely less awkward now that I am beginning to bring forward some of the material upon which my conclusions were based and make it accessible to the judgement of the world. I shall not escape blame by this means. Only, whereas before I was accused of giving *no* information about my patients, now I shall be accused of giving information about my patients which ought not to be given. I can only hope that in both cases the critics will be the same, and that they will merely have shifted the pretext for their reproaches; if so, I can resign in advance any possibility of ever removing their objections.

Even if I ignore the ill-will of narrow-minded critics such as these, the presentation of my case histories remains a problem which is hard for me to solve. The difficulties are partly of a technical kind, but are partly due to the nature of the circumstances themselves. If it is true that the causes of hysterical

1. [E.g. in *Studies on Hysteria* (Breuer and Freud, 1895) and 'The Aetiology of Hysteria' (Freud, 1896c).]

disorders are to be found in the intimacies of the patients' psychosexual life, and that hysterical symptoms are the expression of their most secret and repressed wishes, then the complete elucidation of a case of hysteria is bound to involve the revelation of those intimacies and the betrayal of those secrets. It is certain that the patients would never have spoken if it had occurred to them that their admissions might possibly be put to scientific uses; and it is equally certain that to ask them themselves for leave to publish their case would be quite unavailing. In such circumstances persons of delicacy, as well as those who were merely timid, would give first place to the duty of medical discretion and would declare with regret that the matter was one upon which they could offer science no enlightenment. But in my opinion the physician has taken upon himself duties not only towards the individual patient but towards science as well; and his duties towards science mean ultimately nothing else than his duties towards the many other patients who are suffering or will some day suffer from the same disorder. Thus it becomes the physician's duty to publish what he believes he knows of the causes and structure of hysteria, and it becomes a disgraceful piece of cowardice on his part to neglect doing so, as long as he can avoid causing direct personal injury to the single patient concerned. I think I have taken every precaution to prevent my patient from suffering any such injury. I have picked out a person the scenes of whose life were laid not in Vienna but in a remote provincial town, and whose personal circumstances must therefore be practically unknown in Vienna. I have from the very beginning kept the fact of her being under my treatment such a careful secret that only one other physician – and one in whose discretion I have complete confidence[1] – can be aware that the girl was a patient of mine. I have waited for four whole years since the end of the treatment and have postponed publication till hearing that a change has taken place in the patient's life of such a character as allows me to suppose that her own interest in the occurrences and

1. [No doubt Fliess. See pp. 31–2 above.]

psychological events which are to be related here may now have grown faint. Needless to say, I have allowed no name to stand which could put a non-medical reader upon the scent; and the publication of the case in a purely scientific and technical periodical should, further, afford a guarantee against unauthorized readers of this sort. I naturally cannot prevent the patient herself from being pained if her own case history should accidentally fall into her hands. But she will learn nothing from it that she does not already know; and she may ask herself who besides her could discover from it that she is the subject of this paper.

I am aware that – in this city, at least – there are many physicians who (revolting though it may seem) choose to read a case history of this kind not as a contribution to the psychopathology of the neuroses, but as a *roman à clef* designed for their private delectation. I can assure readers of this species that every case history which I may have occasion to publish in the future will be secured against their perspicacity by similar guarantees of secrecy, even though this resolution is bound to put quite extraordinary restrictions upon my choice of material.

Now in this case history – the only one which I have hitherto succeeded in forcing through the limitations imposed by medical discretion and unfavourable circumstances – sexual questions will be discussed with all possible frankness, the organs and functions of sexual life will be called by their proper names, and the pure-minded reader can convince himself from my description that I have not hesitated to converse upon such subjects in such language even with a young woman. Am I, then, to defend myself upon this score as well? I will simply claim for myself the rights of the gynaecologist – or rather, much more modest ones – and add that it would be the mark of a singular and perverse prurience to suppose that conversations of this kind are a good means of exciting or of gratifying sexual desires. For the rest, I feel inclined to express my opinion on this subject in a few borrowed words:

'It is deplorable to have to make room for protestations and declarations of this sort in a scientific work; but let no one reproach me on this account but rather accuse the spirit of the age, owing to which we have reached a state of things in which no serious book can any longer be sure of survival.' (Schmidt, 1902, Preface.)

I will now describe the way in which I have overcome the *technical* difficulties of drawing up the report of this case history. The difficulties are very considerable when the physician has to conduct six or eight psychotherapeutic treatments of the sort in a day, and cannot make notes during the actual session with the patient for fear of shaking the patient's confidence and of disturbing his own view of the material under observation. Indeed, I have not yet succeeded in solving the problem of how to record for publication the history of a treatment of long duration. As regards the present case, two circumstances have come to my assistance. In the first place the treatment did not last for more than three months; and in the second place the material which elucidated the case was grouped around two dreams (one related in the middle of the treatment and one at the end). The wording of these dreams was recorded immediately after the session, and they thus afforded a secure point of attachment for the chain of interpretations and recollections which proceeded from them. The case history itself was only committed to writing from memory after the treatment was at an end, but while my recollection of the case was still fresh and was heightened by my interest in its publication.[1] Thus the record is not absolutely – phonographically – exact, but it can claim to possess a high degree of trustworthiness. Nothing of any importance has been altered in it except in some places the order in which the explanations are given; and this has been done for the sake of presenting the case in a more connected form.

I next proceed to mention more particularly what is to be found in this paper and what is not to be found in it. The title of

1. [Freud had intended to publish it immediately after writing it. (See p. 33.)]

the work was originally 'Dreams and Hysteria', for it seemed
to me peculiarly well-adapted for showing how dream-
interpretation is woven into the history of a treatment and how
it can become the means of filling in amnesias and elucidating
symptoms. It was not without good reasons that in the year
1900 I gave precedence to a laborious and exhaustive study of
dreams (*The Interpretation of Dreams*) over the publications upon
the psychology of the neuroses which I had in view. And incidentally I was able to judge from its reception with what an
inadequate degree of comprehension such efforts are met by
other specialists at the present time. In this instance there was no
validity in the objection that the material upon which I had
based my assertions had been withheld and that it was therefore
impossible to become convinced of their truth by testing and
checking them. For every one can submit his own dreams to
analytic examination, and the technique of interpreting dreams
may be easily learnt from the instructions and examples which
I have given. I must once more insist, just as I did at that time,[1]
that a thorough investigation of the problems of dreams is
an indispensable prerequisite for any comprehension of the
mental processes in hysteria and the other psychoneuroses, and
that no one who wishes to shirk that preparatory labour has the
smallest prospect of advancing even a few steps into this region
of knowledge. Since, therefore, this case history presupposes a
knowledge of the interpretation of dreams, it will seem highly
unsatisfactory to any reader to whom this presupposition does
not apply. Such a reader will find only bewilderment in these
pages instead of the enlightenment he is in search of, and he will
certainly be inclined to project the cause of his bewilderment
on to the author and to pronounce his views fantastic. But in
reality this bewildering character attaches to the phenomena of
the neurosis itself; its presence there is only concealed by the
physician's familiarity with the facts, and it comes to light
again with every attempt at explaining them. It could only be

1. [Preface to the first edition of *The Interpretation of Dreams*, P.F.L.,
4, 44.]

completely banished if we could succeed in tracing back every single element of a neurosis to factors with which we were already familiar. But everything tends to show that, on the contrary, we shall be driven by the study of neuroses to assume the existence of many new things which will later on gradually become the subject of more certain knowledge. What is new has always aroused bewilderment and resistance.

Nevertheless, it would be wrong to suppose that dreams and their interpretation occupy such a prominent position in all psychoanalyses as they do in this example.

While the case history before us seems particularly favoured as regards the utilization of dreams, in other respects it has turned out poorer than I could have wished. But its short-comings are connected with the very circumstances which have made its publication possible. As I have already said, I should not have known how to deal with the material involved in the history of a treatment which had lasted, perhaps, for a whole year. The present history, which covers only three months, could be recollected and reviewed; but its results remain incomplete in more than one respect. The treatment was not carried through to its appointed end, but was broken off at the patient's own wish when it had reached a certain point. At that time some of the problems of the case had not even been attacked and others had only been imperfectly elucidated; whereas, if the work had been continued, we should no doubt have obtained the fullest possible enlightenment upon every particular of the case. In the following pages, therefore, I can present only a fragment of an analysis.

Readers who are familiar with the technique of analysis as it was expounded in the *Studies on Hysteria* [Breuer and Freud, 1895] will perhaps be surprised that it should not have been possible in three months to find a complete solution at least for those of the symptoms which were taken in hand. This will become intelligible when I explain that since the date of the *Studies* psychoanalytic technique has been completely revolutionized. At that time the work of analysis started out from the symptoms, and aimed at clearing them up one after the other. Since then I have abandoned that technique, because I found it totally inadequate for dealing with the finer structure of a neurosis. I now let the patient himself choose the subject of the day's work, and in that way I start out from whatever surface his unconscious happens to be presenting to his notice at the moment. But on this plan everything that has to do with the clearing-up of a particular symptom emerges piecemeal, woven into various contexts, and distributed over widely separated periods of time. In spite of this apparent disadvantage, the new technique is far superior to the old, and indeed there can be no doubt that it is the only possible one.

In face of the incompleteness of my analytic results, I had no choice but to follow the example of those discoverers whose good fortune it is to bring to the light of day after their long burial the priceless though mutilated relics of antiquity. I have restored what is missing, taking the best models known to me from other analyses; but, like a conscientious archaeologist, I have not omitted to mention in each case where the authentic parts end and my constructions begin.

There is another kind of incompleteness which I myself have intentionally introduced. I have as a rule not reproduced the process of interpretation to which the patient's associations and communications had to be subjected, but only the results of that process. Apart from the dreams, therefore, the technique of the analytic work has been revealed in only a very few places. My object in this case history was to demonstrate the intimate structure of a neurotic disorder and the determination of its symptoms; and it would have led to nothing but hopeless confusion if I had tried to complete the other task at the same time. Before the technical rules, most of which have been arrived at empirically, could be properly laid down, it would be necessary to collect material from the histories of a large number of treatments. Nevertheless, the degree of shortening produced by the omission of the technique is not to be exaggerated in this particular case. Precisely that portion of the technical work which is the most difficult never came into question with the patient; for the factor of 'transference', which is considered at the end of the case history [p. 157 ff.], did not come up for discussion during the short treatment.

For a third kind of incompleteness in this report neither the patient nor the author is responsible. It is, on the contrary, obvious that a single case history, even if it were complete and open to no doubt, cannot provide an answer to *all* the questions arising out of the problem of hysteria. It cannot give an insight into all the types of this disorder, into all the forms of internal structure of the neurosis, into all the possible kinds of relation between the mental and the somatic which are to be found in hysteria. It is not fair to expect from a single case more than it can offer. And any one who has hitherto been unwilling to believe that a psychosexual aetiology holds good generally and without exception for hysteria is scarcely likely to be convinced of the fact by taking stock of a single case history. He would do better to suspend his judgement until his own work has earned him the right to a conviction.[1]

1. [*Footnote added* 1923:] The treatment described in this paper was broken off on December 31, 1899. [This should be '1900'. See p. 33 f]. My account of it was written during the two weeks immediately following, but was not published until 1905. It is not to be expected that after more than twenty years of uninterrupted work I should see nothing to alter in my view of such a case and in my presentment of it; but it would obviously be absurd to bring the case history 'up to date' by means of emendations and additions. In all essentials, therefore, I have left it as it was, and in the text I have merely corrected a few oversights and inaccuracies to which my excellent English translators, Mr and Mrs James Strachey, have directed my attention. Such critical remarks as I have thought it permissible to add I have incorporated in these additional notes: so that the reader will be justified in assuming that I still hold to the opinions expressed in the text unless he finds them contradicted in the footnotes. The problem of medical discretion which I have discussed in this preface does not touch the remaining case histories contained in this volume [see below]; for three of them were published with the express assent of the patients (or rather, as regards Little Hans, with that of his father), while in the fourth case (that of Schreber) the subject of the analysis was not actually a person but a book produced

by him. In Dora's case the secret was kept until this year. I had long
been out of touch with her, but a short while ago I heard that she had
recently fallen ill again from other causes, and had confided to her
physician that she had been analysed by me when she was a girl. This
disclosure made it easy for my well-informed colleague to recognize her
as the Dora of 1899. [This, again, should be '1900'.] No fair judge of
analytic therapy will make it a reproach that the three months' treatment she received at that time effected no more than the relief of her
current conflict and was unable to give her protection against subsequent illnesses.

[This footnote first appeared in the eighth volume of Freud's *Gesammelte Schriften* (1924), and, in English in the third volume of his *Collected
Papers* (1925). Each of these volumes contained his five longer case
histories – that is, besides the present one, the cases (referred to in this
footnote) of Little Hans (1909*b*), the 'Rat Man' (1909*d*), Schreber
(1911*c*), and the 'Wolf Man' (1918*b*). – On the subject of Dora's later
history, see the paper by Felix Deutsch (1957).]

I

THE CLINICAL PICTURE

IN my *Interpretation of Dreams*, published in 1900, I showed that dreams in general can be interpreted, and that after the work of interpretation has been completed they can be replaced by perfectly correctly constructed thoughts which can be assigned a recognizable position in the chain of mental events. I wish to give an example in the following pages of the only practical application of which the art of interpreting dreams seems to admit. I have already mentioned in my book[1] how it was that I came upon the problem of dreams. The problem crossed my path as I was endeavouring to cure psychoneuroses by means of a particular psychotherapeutic method. For, among their other mental experiences, my patients told me their dreams, and these dreams seemed to call for insertion in the long thread of connections which spun itself out between a symptom of the disease and a pathogenic idea. At that time I learnt how to translate the language of dreams into the forms of expression of our own thought-language, which can be understood without further help. And I may add that this knowledge is essential for the psychoanalyst; for the dream is one of the roads along which consciousness can be reached by the psychical material which, on account of the opposition aroused by its content, has been cut off from consciousness and repressed, and has thus become pathogenic. The dream, in short, is one of the *détours by which repression can be evaded*; it is one of the principal means employed by what is known as the indirect method of representation in the mind. The following fragment from the history of the treatment of a hysterical girl is intended to show the way in which the interpretation of dreams plays a part in the work of analysis. It will at the same time give me a first opportunity of publishing at sufficient length to prevent further misunder-

1. *The Interpretation of Dreams*, Chapter II [*P.F.L.*, 4, 174 ff.].

standing some of my views upon the psychical processes of hysteria and upon its organic determinants. I need no longer apologize on the score of length, since it is now agreed that the exacting demands which hysteria makes upon physician and investigator can be met only by the most sympathetic spirit of inquiry and not by an attitude of superiority and contempt. For,

> Nicht Kunst und Wissenschaft allein,
> Geduld will bei dem Werke sein![1]

If I were to begin by giving a full and consistent case history, it would place the reader in a very different situation from that of the medical observer. The reports of the patient's relatives – in the present case I was given one by the eighteen-year-old girl's father – usually afford a very indistinct picture of the course of the illness. I begin the treatment, indeed, by asking the patient to give me the whole story of his life and illness, but even so the information I receive is never enough to let me see my way about the case. This first account may be compared to an un-navigable river whose stream is at one moment choked by masses of rock and at another divided and lost among shallows and sandbanks. I cannot help wondering how it is that the authorities can produce such smooth and precise histories in cases of hysteria. As a matter of fact the patients are incapable of giving such reports about themselves. They can, indeed, give the physician plenty of coherent information about this or that period of their lives; but it is sure to be followed by another period as to which their communications run dry, leaving gaps unfilled, and riddles unanswered; and then again will come yet another period which will remain totally obscure and unilluminated by even a single piece of serviceable informa-tion. The connections – even the ostensible ones – are for the most part incoherent, and the sequence of different events is

1. [Not Art and Science serve, alone;
Patience must in the work be shown.
Goethe, *Faust*, Part I (Scene 6).
(Bayard Taylor's translation.)]

uncertain. Even during the course of their story patients will repeatedly correct a particular or a date, and then perhaps, after wavering for some time, return to their first version. The patients' inability to give an ordered history of their life in so far as it coincides with the history of their illness is not merely characteristic of the neurosis.[1] It also possesses great theoretical significance. For this inability has the following grounds. In the first place, patients consciously and intentionally keep back part of what they ought to tell – things that are perfectly well known to them – because they have not got over their feelings of timidity and shame (or discretion, where what they say concerns other people); this is the share taken by *conscious* disingenuousness. In the second place, part of the anamnestic knowledge, which the patients have at their disposal at other times, disappears while they are actually telling their story, but without their making any deliberate reservations: the share taken by *unconscious* disingenuousness. In the third place, there are invariably true amnesias – gaps in the memory into which not only old recollections but even quite recent ones have fallen – and paramnesias, formed secondarily so as to fill in those gaps.[2] When the events themselves have been kept in mind, the purpose underlying the amnesias can be fulfilled just as surely by destroying a connection, and a connection is most surely broken

1. Another physician once sent his sister to me for psychotherapeutic treatment, telling me that she had for years been treated without success for hysteria (pains and defective gait). The short account which he gave me seemed quite consistent with the diagnosis. In my first hour with the patient I got her to tell me her history herself. When the story came out perfectly clearly and connectedly in spite of the remarkable events it dealt with, I told myself that the case could not be one of hysteria, and immediately instituted a careful physical examination. This led to the diagnosis of a not very advanced stage of tabes, which was later on treated with Hg injections (Ol. cinereum) by Professor Lang with markedly beneficial results.

2. Amnesias and paramnesias stand in a complementary relation to each other. When there are large gaps in the memory there will be few mistakes in it. And conversely, paramnesias can at a first glance completely conceal the presence of amnesias.

by altering the chronological order of events. The latter always proves to be the most vulnerable element in the store of memory and the one which is most easily subject to repression. Again, we meet with many recollections that are in what might be described as the first stage of repression, and these we find surrounded with doubts. At a later period the doubts would be replaced by a loss or a falsification of memory.[1]

That this state of affairs should exist in regard to the memories relating to the history of the illness is *a necessary correlate of the symptoms and one which is theoretically requisite.* In the further course of the treatment the patient supplies the facts which, though he had known them all along, had been kept back by him or had not occurred to his mind. The paramnesias prove untenable, and the gaps in his memory are filled in. It is only towards the end of the treatment that we have before us an intelligible, consistent, and unbroken case history. Whereas the practical aim of the treatment is to remove all possible symptoms and to replace them by conscious thoughts, we may regard it as a second and theoretical aim to repair all the damages to the patient's memory. These two aims are coincident. When one is reached, so is the other; and the same path leads to them both.

It follows from the nature of the facts which form the material of psychoanalysis that we are obliged to pay as much attention in our case histories to the purely human and social circumstances of our patients as to the somatic data and the symptoms of the disorder. Above all, our interest will be directed towards their family circumstances – and not only, as

---

1. If a patient exhibits doubts in the course of his narrative, an empirical rule teaches us to disregard such expressions of his judgement entirely. If the narrative wavers between two versions, we should incline to regard the first one as correct and the second as a product of repression. [Cf. a discussion of doubt in connection with dreams in *The Interpretation of Dreams,* 1900a (Chapter VII, Section A; *P.F.L.,* 4, 660 ff.). For the very different mechanism of doubt in obsessional neurosis, see the case history of the 'Rat Man', 1909d (Part II, Section C; *P.F.L.,* 9, 116 ff.).]

will be seen later, for the purpose of enquiring into their heredity.

The family circle of the eighteen-year-old girl who is the subject of this paper included, besides herself, her two parents and a brother who was one and a half years her senior. Her father was the dominating figure in this circle, owing to his intelligence and his character as much as to the circumstances of his life. It was those circumstances which provided the framework for the history of the patient's childhood and illness. At the time at which I began the girl's treatment her father was in his late forties, a man of rather unusual activity and talents, a large manufacturer in very comfortable circumstances. His daughter was most tenderly attached to him, and for that reason her critical powers, which developed early, took all the more offence at many of his actions and peculiarities.

Her affection for him was still further increased by the many severe illnesses which he had been through since her sixth year. At that time he had fallen ill with tuberculosis and the family had consequently moved to a small town in a good climate, situated in one of our southern provinces. There his lung trouble rapidly improved; but, on account of the precautions which were still considered necessary, both parents and children continued for the next ten years or so to reside chiefly in this spot, which I shall call B—. When her father's health was good, he used at times to be away, on visits to his factories. During the hottest part of the summer the family used to move to a health-resort in the hills.

When the girl was about ten years old, her father had to go through a course of treatment in a darkened room on account of a detached retina. As a result of this misfortune his vision was permanently impaired. His gravest illness occurred some two years later. It took the form of a confusional attack, followed by symptoms of paralysis and slight mental disturbances. A friend of his (who plays a part in the story with which we shall be concerned later on [see p. 60, *n.* 2]) persuaded him, while his condition had scarcely improved, to travel to Vienna with his physician and come to me for advice. I hesitated for some time as to whether I ought not to regard the case as one of tabo-paralysis, but I finally decided upon a diagnosis of a diffuse vascular affection; and since the patient admitted having had a specific infection before his marriage, I prescribed an energetic course of anti-luetic treatment, as a result of which all the remaining disturbances passed off. It is no doubt owing to this fortunate intervention of mine that four years later he brought his daughter, who had meanwhile grown unmistakably neurotic, and introduced her to me, and that after another two years he handed her over to me for psychotherapeutic treatment.

I had in the meantime also made the acquaintance in Vienna of a sister of his, who was a little older than himself. She gave clear evidence of a severe form of psychoneurosis without any characteristically hysterical symptoms. After a life which had been weighed down by an unhappy marriage, she died of a marasmus which made rapid advances and the symptoms of which were, as a matter of fact, never fully cleared up. An elder brother of the girl's father, whom I once happened to meet, was a hypochondriacal bachelor.

The sympathies of the girl herself, who, as I have said, became my patient at the age of eighteen, had always been with the father's side of the family, and ever since she had fallen ill she had taken as her model the aunt who has just been mentioned. There could be no doubt, too, that it was from her father's family that she had derived not only her natural gifts and her intellectual precocity but also the predisposition to her illness. I never made her mother's acquaintance. From the accounts given me by the girl and her father I was led to imagine her as an uncultivated woman and above all as a foolish one, who had concentrated all her interests upon domestic affairs, especially since her husband's illness and the estrangement to which it led. She presented the picture, in fact, of what might be called the 'housewife's psychosis'. She had no understanding of her children's more active interests, and was occupied all day long in cleaning the house with its furniture and utensils and in keeping them clean – to such an extent as to make it almost impossible to use or enjoy them. This condition, traces of which are to be found often enough in normal house-wives, inevitably reminds one of forms of obsessional washing and other kinds of obsessional cleanliness. But such women (and this applied to the patient's mother) are entirely without insight into their illness, so that one essential characteristic of an 'obsessional neurosis' is lacking. The relations between the girl and her mother had been unfriendly for years. The daughter looked down on her mother and used to criticize her mercilessly, and she had withdrawn completely from her influence.[1]

1. I do not, it is true, adopt the position that heredity is the only aetiological factor in hysteria. But, on the other hand – and I say this with particular reference to some of my earlier publications, e.g. 'Heredity and the Aetiology of the Neuroses' (1896a), in which I combated that view – I do not wish to give an impression of underestimating the importance of heredity in the aetiology of hysteria or of asserting that it can be dispensed with. In the case of the present patient the information I have given about her father and his brother and sister indicates a sufficiently heavy taint; and, indeed, if the view is taken that pathological conditions such as her mother's must also imply a heredi-tary predisposition, the patient's heredity may be regarded as a con-vergent one. To my mind, however, there is another factor which is of more significance in the girl's hereditary or, properly speaking, con-stitutional predisposition. I have mentioned that her father had contrac-ted syphilis before his marriage. Now a *strikingly high* percentage of the patients whom I have treated psychoanalytically come of fathers who have suffered from tabes or general paralysis. In consequence of the novelty of my therapeutic method, I see only the *severest* cases, which have already been under treatment for years without any success. In accordance with the Erb-Fournier theory, tabes or general paralysis in the male parent may be regarded as evidence of an earlier luetic infec-tion; and indeed I was able to obtain direct confirmation of such an infection in a number of cases. In the most recent discussion on the offspring of syphilitic parents (Thirteenth International Medical Con-gress, held in Paris, August 2nd to 9th, 1900: papers by Finger, Tarnow-sky, Jullien, etc.), I find no mention of the conclusion to which I have

During the girl's earlier years, her only brother (her elder by a year and a half) had been the model which her ambitions had striven to follow. But in the last few years the relations between the brother and sister had grown more distant. The young man used to try so far as he could to keep out of the family disputes; but when he was obliged to take sides he would support his mother. So that the usual sexual attraction had drawn together the father and daughter on the one side and the mother and son on the other.

The patient, to whom I shall in future give the name of 'Dora',[1] had even at the age of eight begun to develop neurotic symptoms. She became subject at that time to chronic dyspnoea with occasional accesses in which the symptom was very much aggravated. The first onset occurred after a short expedition in the mountains and was accordingly put down to over-exertion. In the course of six months, during which she was made to rest and was carefully looked after, this condition gradually passed off. The family doctor seems to have had not a moment's hesitation in diagnosing the disorder as purely nervous and in excluding any organic cause for the dyspnoea; but he evidently considered this diagnosis compatible with the aetiology of over-exertion.[2]

The little girl went through the usual infectious diseases of childhood without suffering any lasting damage. As she herself told me – and her words were intended to convey a deeper meaning [see p. 119 n.] – her brother was as a rule the first to start the illness and used to have it very slightly, and she would then follow suit with a severe form of it. When she was about twelve she began to suffer from unilateral headaches in the

---

been driven by my experience as a neuro-pathologist – namely, that syphilis in the male parent is a very relevant factor in the aetiology of the neuropathic constitution of children.

1. [The determinants of Freud's choice of this pseudonym were discussed by him in Chapter XII, Example A (1), of his *Psychopathology of Everyday Life* (1901b) P.F.L., **5**, 301–2.]

2. The probable precipitating cause of this first illness will be discussed later on [p. 117].

nature of a migraine, and from attacks of nervous coughing. At first these two symptoms always appeared together, but they became separated later on and ran different courses. The migraine grew rarer, and by the time she was sixteen she had quite got over it. But attacks of *tussis nervosa*, which had no doubt been started by a common catarrh, continued to occur over the whole period. When, at the age of eighteen, she came to me for treatment, she was again coughing in a characteristic manner. The number of these attacks could not be determined; but they lasted from three to five weeks, and on one occasion for several months. The most troublesome symptom during the first half of an attack of this kind, at all events in the last few years, used to be a complete loss of voice. The diagnosis that this was once more a nervous complaint had been established long since; but the various methods of treatment which are usual, including hydrotherapy and the local application of electricity, had produced no result. It was in such circumstances as these that the child had developed into a mature young woman of very independent judgement, who had grown accustomed to laugh at the efforts of doctors, and in the end to renounce their help entirely. Moreover, she had always been against calling in medical advice, though she had no personal objection to her family doctor. Every proposal to consult a new physician aroused her resistance, and it was only her father's authority which induced her to come to me at all.

I first saw her when she was sixteen, in the early summer. She was suffering from a cough and from hoarseness, and even at that time I proposed giving her psychological treatment. My proposal was not adopted, since the attack in question, like the others, passed off spontaneously, though it had lasted unusually long. During the next winter she came and stayed in Vienna with her uncle and his daughters after the death of the aunt of whom she had been so fond. There she fell ill of a feverish disorder which was diagnosed at the time as appendicitis.[1] In the following autumn, since her father's health seemed

1. On this point see the analysis of the second dream [p. 141].

to justify the step, the family left the health-resort of B— for good and all. They first moved to the town where her father's factory was situated, and then, scarcely a year later, settled permanently in Vienna.

Dora was by that time in the first bloom of youth – a girl of intelligent and engaging looks. But she was a source of heavy trials for her parents. Low spirits and an alteration in her character had now become the main features of her illness. She was clearly satisfied neither with herself nor with her family; her attitude towards her father was unfriendly, and she was on very bad terms with her mother, who was bent upon drawing her into taking a share in the work of the house. She tried to avoid social intercourse, and employed herself – so far as she was allowed to by the fatigue and lack of concentration of which she complained – with attending lectures for women and with carrying on more or less serious studies. One day her parents were thrown into a state of great alarm by finding on the girl's writing-desk, or inside it, a letter in which she took leave of them because, as she said, she could no longer endure her life.[1] Her father, indeed, being a man of some perspicacity, guessed that the girl had no serious suicidal intentions. But he was none the less very much shaken; and when one day, after a slight passage of words between him and his daughter, she had a first attack of loss of consciousness[2] – an event which was subsequently covered by an amnesia – it was determined, in spite

1. As I have already explained, the treatment of the case, and consequently my insight into the complex of events composing it, remained fragmentary. There are therefore many questions to which I have no solution to offer, or in which I can only rely upon hints and conjectures. This affair of the letter came up in the course of one of our sessions [p. 137], and the girl showed signs of astonishment. 'How on earth', she asked, 'did they find the letter? It was shut up in my desk.' But since she knew that her parents had read this draft of a farewell letter, I conclude that she had herself arranged for it to fall into their hands.

2. The attack was, I believe, accompanied by convulsions and delirious states. But since this event was not reached by the analysis either, I have no trustworthy recollections on the subject to fall back upon.

of her reluctance, that she should come to me for treatment.

No doubt this case history, as I have so far outlined it, does not upon the whole seem worth recording. It is merely a case of '*petite hystérie*' with the commonest of all somatic and mental symptoms: dyspnoea, *tussis nervosa*, aphonia, and possibly migraines, together with depression, hysterical unsociability, and a *taedium vitae* which was probably not entirely genuine. More interesting cases of hysteria have no doubt been published, and they have very often been more carefully described; for nothing will be found in the following pages on the subject of stigmata of cutaneous sensibility, limitation of the visual field, or similar matters. I may venture to remark, however, that all such collections of the strange and wonderful phenomena of hysteria have but slightly advanced our knowledge of a disease which still remains as great a puzzle as ever. What is wanted is precisely an elucidation of the *commonest* cases and of their most frequent and typical symptoms. I should have been very well satisfied if the circumstances had allowed me to give a complete elucidation of this case of *petite hystérie*. And my experiences with other patients leave me in no doubt that my analytic method would have enabled me to do so.

In 1896, shortly after the appearance of my *Studies on Hysteria* (written in conjunction with Dr J. Breuer, 1895), I asked an eminent fellow-specialist for his opinion on the psychological theory of hysteria put forward in that work. He bluntly replied that he considered it an unjustifiable generalization of conclusions which might hold good for a few cases. Since then I have seen an abundance of cases of hysteria, and I have been occupied with each case for a number of days, weeks, or years. In not a single one of them have I failed to discover the psychological determinants which were postulated in the *Studies*, namely, a psychical trauma, a conflict of affects, and – an additional factor which I brought forward in later publications – a disturbance in the sphere of sexuality. It is of course not to be expected that the patient will come to meet the physician half-way with material which has become pathogenic for the very reason of its efforts to lie concealed; nor must the inquirer rest content with the first 'No' that crosses his path.[1]

In Dora's case, thanks to her father's shrewdness which I have remarked upon more than once already, there was no need for me to look about for the points of contact between the circumstances of the patient's life and her illness, at all events in its most recent form. Her father told me that he and his family while they were at B— had formed an intimate friendship with a married couple who had been settled there for several years. Frau K. had nursed him during his long illness, and had in that way, he said, earned a title to his undying gratitude. Herr K. had always been most kind to Dora. He had gone for walks with her when he was there, and had made her small presents; but no one had thought any harm of that. Dora had taken the greatest care of the K.'s two little children, and been almost a mother to them. When Dora and her father had come to see me two years before in the summer, they had been just on their

1. Here is an instance of this. Another physician in Vienna, whose conviction of the unimportance of sexual factors in hysteria has probably been very much strengthened by such experiences as this, was consulted in the case of a fourteen-year-old girl who suffered from dangerous hysterical vomiting. He made up his mind to ask her the painful question whether by any chance she had ever had a love-affair with a man. 'No!' answered the child, no doubt with well-affected astonishment; and then repeated to her mother in her irreverent way: 'Only fancy! the old stupid asked me if I was in love!' She afterwards came to me for treatment, and proved – though not during our very first conversation – to have been a masturbator for many years, with a considerable leucorrhoeal discharge (which had a close bearing on her vomiting). She had finally broken herself of the habit, but was tormented in her abstinence by the most acute sense of guilt, so that she looked upon every misfortune that befell her family as a divine punishment for her transgression. Besides this, she was under the influence of the romance of an unmarried aunt, whose pregnancy (a second determinant for her vomiting) was supposed to have been happily hidden from her. The girl was looked upon as a 'mere child', but she turned out to be initiated into all the essentials of sexual relations.

way to stop with Herr and Frau K. who were spending the summer on one of our lakes in the Alps. Dora was to have spent several weeks at the K.'s, while her father had intended to return home after a few days. During that time Herr K. had been staying there as well. As her father was preparing for his departure the girl had suddenly declared with the greatest determination that she was going with him, and she had in fact put her decision into effect. It was not until some days later that she had thrown any light upon her strange behaviour. She had then told her mother – intending that what she said should be passed on to her father – that Herr K. had had the audacity to make her a proposal while they were on a walk after a trip upon the lake. Herr K. had been called to account by her father and uncle on the next occasion of their meeting, but he had denied in the most emphatic terms having on his side made any advances which could have been open to such a construction. He had then proceeded to throw suspicion upon the girl, saying that he had heard from Frau K. that she took no interest in anything but sexual matters, and that she used to read Mantegazza's *Physiology of Love* and books of that sort in their house on the lake. It was most likely, he had added, that she had been over-excited by such reading and had merely 'fancied' the whole scene she had described.

'I have no doubt', continued her father, 'that this incident is responsible for Dora's depression and irritability and suicidal ideas. She keeps pressing me to break off relations with Herr K. and more particularly with Frau K., whom she used positively to worship formerly. But that I cannot do. For, to begin with, I myself believe that Dora's tale of the man's immoral suggestions is a phantasy that has forced its way into her mind; and besides, I am bound to Frau K. by ties of honourable friendship and I do not wish to cause her pain. The poor woman is most unhappy with her husband, of whom, by the by, I have no very high opinion. She herself has suffered a great deal with her nerves, and I am her only support. With my state of health I need scarcely assure you that there is nothing wrong in our relations. We are just two poor wretches who give one another what comfort we can by an exchange of friendly sympathy. You know already that I get nothing out of my own wife. But Dora, who inherits my obstinacy, cannot be moved from her hatred of the K.s. She had her last attack after a conversation in which she had again pressed me to break with them. Please try and bring her to reason.'

Her father's words did not always quite tally with this pronouncement; for on other occasions he tried to put the chief blame for Dora's impossible behaviour on her mother – whose peculiarities made the house unbearable for every one. But I had resolved from the first to suspend my judgement of the true state of affairs till I had heard the other side as well.

The experience with Herr K. – his making love to her and the insult to her honour which was involved – seems to provide in Dora's case the psychical trauma which Breuer and I declared long ago[1] to be the indispensable prerequisite for the production of a hysterical disorder. But this new case also presents all the difficulties which have since led me to go beyond that theory,[2] besides an additional difficulty of a special kind. For,

1. [In their 'Preliminary Communication' (see Freud, 1893a).]

2. I have gone beyond that theory, but I have not abandoned it; that is to say, I do not today consider the theory incorrect, but incomplete. All that I have abandoned is the emphasis laid upon the so-called 'hypnoid state', which was supposed to be occasioned in the patient by the trauma, and to be the foundation for all the psychologically abnormal events which followed. If, where a piece of joint work is in question, it is legitimate to make a subsequent division of property, I should like to take this opportunity of stating that the hypothesis of 'hypnoid states' – which many reviewers were inclined to regard as the central portion of our work – sprang entirely from the initiative of Breuer. I regard the use of such a term as superfluous and misleading, because it interrupts the continuity of the problem as to the nature of the psychological process accompanying the formation of hysterical symptoms. – ['Hypnoid states' were referred to in the 'Preliminary Communication', but they were discussed at greater length by Breuer in his contribution to *Studies on Hysteria* (1895), Chapter III, Section 4,

as so often happens in histories of cases of hysteria, the trauma that we know of as having occurred in the patient's past life is insufficient to explain or to determine the *particular character* of the symptoms; we should understand just as much or just as little of the whole business if the result of the trauma had been symptoms quite other than *tussis nervosa*, aphonia, depression, and *taedium vitae*. But there is the further consideration that some of these symptoms (the cough and the loss of voice) had been produced by the patient years before the time of the trauma, and that their earliest appearances belong to her childhood, since they occurred in her eighth year. If, therefore, the trauma theory is not to be abandoned, we must go back to her childhood and look about there for any influences or impressions which might have had an effect analogous to that of a trauma. Moreover, it deserves to be remarked that in the investigation even of cases in which the first symptoms had not already set in in childhood I have been driven to trace back the patients' life history to their earliest years.[1]

When the first difficulties of the treatment had been overcome, Dora told me of an earlier episode with Herr K., which was even better calculated to act as a sexual trauma. She was fourteen years old at the time. Herr K. had made an arrangement with her and his wife that they should meet him one afternoon at his place of business in the principal square of B— so as to have a view of a church festival. He persuaded his wife, however, to stay at home, and sent away his clerks, so that he was alone when the girl arrived. When the time for the procession approached, he asked the girl to wait for him at the door which opened on to the staircase leading to the upper storey, while he pulled down the outside shutters. He then came back and, instead of going out by the open door, suddenly

P.F.L., **3**, 292 ff. Freud enters into his theoretical disagreements with Breuer in more detail in the first section of his 'History of the Psycho-Analytic Movement' (1914*d*).]

1. Cf. my paper on 'The Aetiology of Hysteria' (1896*c*).

clasped the girl to him and pressed a kiss upon her lips. This was surely just the situation to call up a distinct feeling of sexual excitement in a girl of fourteen who had never before been approached. But Dora had at that moment a violent feeling of disgust, tore herself free from the man, and hurried past him to the staircase and from there to the street door. She nevertheless continued to meet Herr K. Neither of them ever mentioned the little scene; and according to her account Dora kept it a secret till her confession during the treatment. For some time afterwards, however, she avoided being alone with Herr K. The K.s had just made plans for an expedition which was to last for some days and on which Dora was to have accompanied them. After the scene of the kiss she refused to join the party, without giving any reason.

In this scene – second in order of mention, but first in order of time – the behaviour of this child of fourteen was already entirely and completely hysterical. I should without question consider a person hysterical in whom an occasion for sexual excitement elicited feelings that were preponderantly or exclusively unpleasurable; and I should do so whether or no the person were capable of producing somatic symptoms. The elucidation of the mechanism of this *reversal of affect* is one of the most important and at the same time one of the most difficult problems in the psychology of the neuroses. In my own judgement I am still some way from having achieved this end; and I may add that within the limits of the present paper I shall be able to bring forward only a part of such knowledge on the subject as I do possess.[1]

1. [This is one of the problems which recurs constantly throughout Freud's writings. He touches upon it, for instance, in considering anxiety-dreams in Chapter VII, Section D, of the *Interpretation of Dreams*, 1900a, *P.F.L.*, 4, 738, in his paper on 'Repression' (1915d), *P.F.L.*, 11, 145f., in *Beyond the Pleasure Principle* (1920g), ibid., 11, 279, and again in *Inhibitions, Symptoms and Anxiety* (1926d), ibid., 10, 242–3, where a fresh solution is proposed.]

In order to particularize Dora's case it is not enough merely to draw attention to the reversal of affect; there has also been a *displacement* of sensation. Instead of the genital sensation which would certainly have been felt by a healthy girl in such circumstances,[1] Dora was overcome by the unpleasurable feeling which is proper to the tract of mucous membrane at the entrance to the alimentary canal – that is by disgust. The stimulation of her lips by the kiss was no doubt of importance in localizing the feeling at that particular place; but I think I can also recognize another factor in operation.[2]

The disgust which Dora felt on that occasion did not become a permanent symptom, and even at the time of the treatment it was only, as it were, potentially present. She was a poor eater and confessed to some disinclination for food. On the other hand, the scene had left another consequence behind it in the shape of a sensory hallucination which occurred from time to time and even made its appearance while she was telling me her story. She declared that she could still feel upon the upper part of her body the pressure of Herr K.'s embrace. In accordance with certain rules of symptom-formation which I have come to know, and at the same time taking into account certain other of the patient's peculiarities, which were otherwise inexplicable, – such as her unwillingness to walk past any man whom she saw engaged in eager or affectionate conversation with a lady, – I have formed in my own mind the following reconstruction of the scene. I believe that during the man's passionate embrace she felt not merely his kiss upon her lips but also the pressure of his erect member against her body. This perception was revolting to her; it was dismissed from her memory, repressed, and replaced by the innocent sensation of

1. Our appreciation of these circumstances will be facilitated when more light has been thrown upon them. [Cf. pp. 121–2.]

2. The causes of Dora's disgust at the kiss were certainly not adventitious, for in that case she could not have failed to remember and mention them. I happen to know Herr K., for he was the same person who had visited me with the patient's father [p. 48f.], and he was still quite young and of prepossessing appearance.

pressure upon her thorax, which in turn derived an excessive intensity from its repressed source. Once more, therefore, we find a displacement from the lower part of the body to the upper.[1] On the other hand, the compulsive piece of behaviour which I have mentioned was formed as though it were derived from the undistorted recollection of the scene: she did not like walking past any man who she thought was in a state of sexual excitement, because she wanted to avoid seeing for a second time the somatic sign which accompanies it. *physical*

It is worth remarking that we have here three symptoms – the disgust, the sensation of pressure on the upper part of the body, and the avoidance of men engaged in affectionate conversation – all of them derived from a single experience, and that it is only by taking into account the interrelation of these three phenomena that we can understand the way in which the formation of the symptoms came about. The disgust is the symptom of repression in the erotogenic oral zone,[2] which, as we shall hear [p. 85], had been over-indulged in Dora's infancy by the habit of sensual sucking. The pressure of the erect member probably led to an analogous change in the corresponding female organ, the clitoris; and the excitation of this second erotogenic zone was referred by a process of displacement to the simultaneous pressure against the thorax and became fixed there. Her avoidance of men who might possibly be in a state of sexual excitement follows the mechanism of a

1. The occurrence of displacements of this kind has not been assumed for the purpose of this single explanation; the assumption has proved indispensable for the explanation of a large class of symptoms. [Cf. below, p. 120, *n*.]. Since treating Dora I have come across another instance of an embrace (this time without a kiss) causing a fright. It was a case of a young woman who had previously been devotedly fond of the man she was engaged to, but had suddenly begun to feel a coldness towards him, accompanied by severe depression, and on that account came to me for treatment. There was no difficulty in tracing the fright back to an erection on the man's part, which she had perceived but had dismissed from her consciousness.

2. [See below, p. 86.]

phobia, its purpose being to safeguard her against any revival of the repressed perception.

In order to show that such a supplement to the story was possible, I questioned the patient very cautiously as to whether she knew anything of the physical signs of excitement in a man's body. Her answer, as touching the present, was 'Yes', but, as touching the time of the episode, 'I think not'. From the very beginning I took the greatest pains with this patient not to introduce her to any fresh facts in the region of sexual knowledge; and I did this, not from any conscientious motives, but because I was anxious to subject my assumptions to a rigorous test in this case. Accordingly, I did not call a thing by its name until her allusions to it had become so unambiguous that there seemed very slight risk in translating them into direct speech. Her answer was always prompt and frank: she knew about it already. But the question of *where* her knowledge came from was a riddle which her memories were unable to solve. She had forgotten the source of all her information on this subject.[1]

If I may suppose that the scene of the kiss took place in this way, I can arrive at the following derivation for the feelings of disgust.[2] Such feelings seem originally to be a reaction to the smell (and afterwards also to the sight) of excrement. But the genitals can act as a reminder of the excretory functions; and this applies especially to the male member, for that organ performs the function of micturition as well as the sexual function. Indeed, the function of micturition is the earlier known of the two, and the *only* one known during the pre-sexual period. Thus it happens that disgust becomes one of the means of affective expression in the sphere of sexual life. The Early

1. See the second dream [p. 139. – Cf. also pp. 68 *n.*, 97f. and 162 *n.*].

2. Here, as in all similar cases, the reader must be prepared to be met not by one but by several causes – by *overdetermination*. [Freud had mentioned this characteristic of hysterical symptoms in Section III of his chapter on the psychotherapy of hysteria in Breuer and Freud's *Studies on Hysteria*, 1895. It was also discussed by Breuer (with an acknowledgement to Freud) in Section III of his theoretical contribution to the same work. Cf. *P.F.L.*, **3**, 289–90 and 373–6.]

Christian Father's '*inter urinas et faeces nascimur*' clings to sexual life and cannot be detached from it in spite of every effort at idealization. I should like, however, expressly to emphasize my opinion that the problem is not solved by the mere pointing out of this path of association. The fact that this association *can* be called up does not show that it actually *will* be called up. And indeed in normal circumstances it will not be. A knowledge of the paths does not render less necessary a knowledge of the forces which travel along them.[1]

I did not find it easy, however, to direct the patient's attention to her relations with Herr K. She declared that she had done with him. The uppermost layer of all her associations during the sessions, and everything of which she was easily conscious and of which she remembered having been conscious the day before, was always connected with her father. It was quite true that she could not forgive her father for continuing his relations with Herr K. and more particularly with Frau K. But she viewed those relations in a very different light from that in which her father wished them to appear. In her mind there was no doubt that what bound her father to this young and beautiful woman was a common love-affair. Nothing that could help to confirm this view had escaped her perception, which in this connection was pitilessly sharp; *here there were no gaps to be found in her memory*. Their acquaintance with the K.s

1. All these discussions contain much that is typical and valid for hysteria in general. The subject of erection solves some of the most interesting hysterical symptoms. The attention that women pay to the outlines of men's genitals as seen through their clothing becomes, when it has been repressed, a source of the very frequent cases of avoiding company and of dreading society. – It is scarcely possible to exaggerate the pathogenic significance of the comprehensive tie uniting the sexual and the excremental, a tie which is at the basis of a very large number of hysterical phobias. [This topic recurs very frequently in Freud's writings. It appears, for instance, as early as 1897 in Draft K in the Fliess correspondence (Freud, 1950a), and in *Civilization and its Discontents* (1930a), *P.F.L.*, **12**, 296n.]

had begun before her father's serious illness; but it had not become intimate until the young woman had officially taken on the position of nurse during that illness, while Dora's mother had kept away from the sick-room. During the first summer holidays after his recovery things had happened which must have opened every one's eyes to the true character of this 'friendship'. The two families had taken a suite of rooms in common at the hotel. One day Frau K. had announced that she could not keep the bedroom which she had up till then shared with one of her children. A few days later Dora's father had given up his bedroom, and they had both moved into new rooms – the end rooms, which were only separated by the passage, while the rooms they had given up had not offered any such security against interruption. Later on, whenever she had reproached her father about Frau K., he had been in the habit of saying that he could not understand her hostility and that, on the contrary, his children had every reason for being grateful to Frau K. Her mother, whom she had asked for an explanation of this mysterious remark, had told her that her father had been so unhappy at that time that he had made up his mind to go into the wood and kill himself, and that Frau K., suspecting as much, had gone after him and had persuaded him by her entreaties to preserve his life for the sake of his family. Of course, Dora went on, she herself did not believe this story; no doubt the two of them had been seen together in the wood, and her father had thereupon invented this fairy tale of his suicide so as to account for their rendezvous.[1]

When they had returned to B—, her father had visited Frau K. every day at definite hours, while her husband was at his business. Everybody had talked about it and had questioned her about it pointedly. Herr K. himself had often complained bitterly to her mother, though he had spared her herself any allusions to the subject – which she seemed to attribute to

1. This is the point of connection with her own pretence at suicide [p. 53], which may thus be regarded as the expression of a longing for a love of the same kind.

delicacy of feeling on his part. When they had all gone for walks together, her father and Frau K. had always known how to manage things so as to be alone with each other. There could be no doubt that she had taken money from him, for she spent more than she could possibly have afforded out of her own purse or her husband's. Dora added that her father had begun to make handsome presents to Frau K., and in order to make these less conspicuous had at the same time become especially liberal towards her mother and herself. And, while previously Frau K. had been an invalid and had even been obliged to spend months in a sanatorium for nervous disorders because she had been unable to walk, she had now become a healthy and lively woman.

Even after they had left B— [for the manufacturing town], these relations, already of many years' standing, had been continued. From time to time her father used to declare that he could not endure the rawness of the climate, and that he must do something for himself; he would begin to cough and complain, until suddenly he would start off to B—, and from there write the most cheerful letters home. All these illnesses had only been pretexts for seeing his friend again. Then one day it had been decided that they were to move to Vienna and Dora began to suspect a hidden connection. And sure enough, they had scarcely been three weeks in Vienna when she heard that the K.s had moved there as well. They were in Vienna, so she told me, at that very moment, and she frequently met her father with Frau K. in the street. She also met Herr K. very often, and he always used to turn round and look after her; and once when he had met her out by herself he had followed her for a long way, so as to make sure where she was going and whether she might not have a rendezvous.

On one occasion during the course of the treatment her father again felt worse, and went off to B— for several weeks; and the sharp-sighted Dora had soon unearthed the fact that Frau K. had started off to the same place on a visit to her relatives there. It was at this time that Dora's criticisms of her father were the most frequent: he was insincere, he had a strain of falseness in his character, he only thought of his own enjoyment, and he had a gift for seeing things in the light which suited him best.

I could not in general dispute Dora's characterization of her father; and there was one particular respect in which it was easy to see that her reproaches were justified. When she was feeling embittered she used to be overcome by the idea that she had been handed over to Herr K. as the price of his tolerating the relations between her father and his wife; and her rage at her father's making such a use of her was visible behind her affection for him. At other times she was quite well aware that she had been guilty of exaggeration in talking like this. The two men had of course never made a formal agreement in which she was treated as an object for barter; her father in particular would have been horrified at any such suggestion. But he was one of those men who know how to evade a dilemma by falsifying their judgement upon one of the conflicting alternatives. If it had been pointed out to him that there might be danger for a growing girl in the constant and unsupervised companionship of a man who had no satisfaction from his own wife, he would have been certain to answer that he could rely upon his daughter, that a man like K. could never be dangerous to her, and that his friend was himself incapable of such intentions, or that Dora was still a child and was treated as a child by K. But as a matter of fact things were in a position in which each of the two men avoided drawing any conclusions from the other's behaviour which would have been awkward for his own plans. It was possible for Herr K. to send Dora flowers every day for a whole year while he was in the neighbourhood, to take every opportunity of giving her valuable presents, and to spend all his spare time in her company, without her parents noticing anything in his behaviour that was characteristic of love-making.

When a patient brings forward a sound and incontestable train of argument during psychoanalytic treatment, the physician is liable to feel a moment's embarrassment, and the patient may take advantage of it by asking: 'This is all perfectly correct and true, isn't it? What do you want to change in it, now that I've told it you?' But it soon becomes evident that the patient is using thoughts of this kind, which the analysis cannot attack, for the purpose of cloaking others which are anxious to escape from criticism and from consciousness. A string of reproaches against other people leads one to suspect the existence of a string of self-reproaches with the same content. All that need be done is to turn back each particular reproach on to the speaker himself. There is something undeniably automatic about this method of defending oneself against a self-reproach by making the same reproach against some one else. A model of it is to be found in the *tu quoque* arguments of children; if one of them is accused of being a liar, he will reply without an instant's hesitation: 'You're another.' A grown-up person who wanted to throw back abuse would look for some really exposed spot in his antagonist and would not lay the chief stress upon the same content being repeated. In paranoia the projection of a reproach on to another person without any alteration in its content and therefore without any consideration for reality becomes manifest as the process of forming delusions.

Dora's reproaches against her father had a 'lining' or 'backing' of self-reproaches of this kind with a corresponding content in every case, as I shall show in detail. She was right in thinking that her father did not wish to look too closely into Herr K.'s behaviour to his daughter, for fear of being disturbed in his own love-affair with Frau K. But Dora herself had done precisely the same thing. She had made herself an accomplice in the affair, and had dismissed from her mind every sign which tended to show its true character. It was not until after her adventure by the lake [p. 56] that her eyes were opened and that she began to apply such a severe standard to her father. During all the previous years she had given every possible assistance to her father's relations with Frau K. She would never go to see her if she thought her father was there; but, knowing that in that case the children would have been sent out, she would turn her steps in a direction where she would be sure to meet them, and would go for a walk with them. There had been some one in the house who had been anxious at an early stage to open her eyes to the nature of her father's relations with Frau K., and to induce her to take sides against her. This was her last governess, an unmarried woman, no longer young, who was well-read and of advanced views.[1] The teacher and her pupil were for a while upon excellent terms, until suddenly Dora became hostile to her and insisted on her dismissal. So long as the governess had any influence she used it for stirring up feeling against Frau K. She explained to Dora's mother that it was incompatible with her dignity to tolerate such an intimacy between her husband and another woman; and she drew Dora's attention to all the obvious features of their relations. But her efforts were vain. Dora remained devoted to Frau K. and would hear of nothing that might make her think ill of her relations with her father. On the other hand she very easily fathomed the motives by which her governess was actuated. She might be blind in one direction, but she was sharp-sighted enough in the other. She saw that the governess was in love with her father. When he was there, she seemed to be quite another person: at such times she could be amusing and obliging. While the family were living in the manufacturing town and Frau K. was not on the horizon, her hostility was directed against Dora's mother, who was then her more immediate rival. Up to this point Dora bore her no ill-will. She did not become angry until she observed that she herself was a subject of complete indifference to the governess, whose pretended affection for her was really meant for her father. While her

1. This governess used to read every sort of book on sexual life and similar subjects, and talked to the girl about them, at the same time asking her quite frankly not to mention their conversations to her parents, as one could never tell what line they might take about them. For some time I looked upon this woman as the source of all Dora's secret knowledge, and perhaps I was not entirely wrong in this. [See, however, the footnote on p. 162.]

father was away from the manufacturing town the governess had no time to spare for her, would not go for walks with her, and took no interest in her studies. No sooner had her father returned from B— than she was once more ready with every sort of service and assistance. Thereupon Dora dropped her.

The poor woman had thrown a most unwelcome light on a part of Dora's own behaviour. What the governess had from time to time been to Dora, Dora had been to Herr K.'s children. She had been a mother to them, she had taught them, she had gone for walks with them, she had offered them a complete substitute for the slight interest which their own mother showed in them. Herr K. and his wife had often talked of getting a divorce; but it never took place, because Herr K., who was an affectionate father, would not give up either of the two children. A common interest in the children had from the first been a bond between Herr K. and Dora. Her preoccupation with his children was evidently a cloak for something else that Dora was anxious to hide from herself and from other people.

The same inference was to be drawn both from her behaviour towards the children, regarded in the light of the governess's behaviour towards herself, and from her silent acquiescence in her father's relations with Frau K. - namely, that she had all these years been in love with Herr K. When I informed her of this conclusion she did not assent to it. It is true that she at once told me that other people besides (one of her cousins, for instance - a girl who had stopped with them for some time at B—) had said to her: 'Why you're simply wild about that man!' But she herself could not be got to recollect any feelings of the kind. Later on, when the quantity of material that had come up had made it difficult for her to persist in her denial, she admitted that she might have been in love with Herr K. at B—, but declared that since the scene by the lake it had all been over.[1] In any case it was quite certain that the reproaches which she made against her father of having been deaf to the most imperative calls of duty and of having seen things in the light

1. Compare the second dream.

which was most convenient from the point of view of his own passions – these reproaches recoiled on her own head.[1]

Her other reproach against her father was that his ill-health was only a pretext and that he exploited it for his own purposes. This reproach, too, concealed a whole section of her own secret history. One day she complained of a professedly new symptom, which consisted of piercing gastric pains. 'Whom are you copying now?' I asked her, and found I had hit the mark. The day before she had visited her cousins, the daughters of the aunt who had died. The younger one had become engaged, and this had given occasion to the elder one for falling ill with gastric pains, and she was to be sent off to Semmering.[2] Dora thought it was all just envy on the part of the elder sister; she always got ill when she wanted something, and what she wanted now was to be away from home so as not to have to look on at her sister's happiness.[3] But Dora's own gastric pains proclaimed the fact that she identified herself with her cousin, who, according to her, was a malingerer. Her grounds for this identification were either that she too envied the luckier girl her love, or that she saw her own story reflected in that of the elder sister, who had recently had a love-affair which had ended unhappily.[4] But she had also learned from observing Frau K. what useful things illnesses could become. Herr K. spent part of the year in travelling. Whenever he came back, he used to find his wife in bad health, although, as Dora knew, she had been quite well only the day before. Dora realized that the presence of the husband had the effect of making his wife ill, and that she was glad to

1. The question then arises: If Dora loved Herr K., what was the reason for her refusing him in the scene by the lake? Or at any rate, why did her refusal take such a brutal form, as though she were embittered against him? And how could a girl who was in love feel insulted by a proposal which was made in a manner neither tactless nor offensive?

2. [A fashionable health resort in the mountains, about fifty miles south of Vienna.]

3. An event of everyday occurrence between sisters.

4. I shall discuss later on what further conclusion I drew from these gastric pains [p. 115].

be ill so as to be able to escape the conjugal duties which she so much detested. At this point in the discussion Dora suddenly brought in an allusion to her own alternations between good and bad health during the first years of her girlhood at B—; and I was thus driven to suspect that her states of health were to be regarded as depending upon something else, in the same way as Frau K.'s. (It is a rule of psychoanalytic technique that an internal connection which is still undisclosed will announce its presence by means of a contiguity – a temporal proximity – of associations; just as in writing, if 'a' and 'b' are put side by side, it means that the syllable 'ab' is to be formed out of them.) Dora had had a very large number of attacks of coughing accompanied by loss of voice. Could it be that the presence or absence of the man she loved had had an influence upon the appearance and disappearance of the symptoms of her illness? If this were so, it must be possible to discover some coincidence or other which would betray the fact. I asked her what the average length of these attacks had been. 'From three to six weeks, perhaps.' How long had Herr K.'s absences lasted? 'Three to six weeks, too', she was obliged to admit. Her illness was therefore a demonstration of her love for K., just as his wife's was a demonstration of her *dislike*. It was only necessary to suppose that her behaviour had been the opposite of Frau K.'s and that she had been ill when he was absent and well when he had come back. And this really seemed to have been so, at least during the first period of the attacks. Later on it no doubt became necessary to obscure the coincidence between her attacks of illness and the absence of the man she secretly loved, lest its regularity should betray her secret. The length of the attacks would then remain as a trace of their original significance.

I remembered that long before, while I was working at Charcot's clinic [1885–6], I had seen and heard how in cases of hysterical mutism writing operated vicariously in the place of speech. Such patients were able to write more fluently, quicker, and better than others did or than they themselves had done previously. The same thing had happened with Dora. In the first days of her attacks of aphonia 'writing had always come specially easy to her'. No psychological elucidation was really required for this peculiarity, which was the expression of a physiological substitutive function enforced by necessity; it was noticeable, however, that such an elucidation was easily to be found. Herr K. used to write to her at length while he was travelling and to send her picture post-cards. It used to happen that she alone was informed as to the date of his return, and that his arrival took his wife by surprise. Moreover, that a person will correspond with an absent friend whom he cannot talk to is scarcely less obvious than that if he has lost his voice he will try to make himself understood in writing. Dora's aphonia, then, allowed of the following symbolic interpretation. When the man she loved was away she gave up speaking; speech had lost its value since she could not speak to *him*. On the other hand, writing gained in importance, as being the only means of communication with him in his absence.

Am I now going on to assert that in every instance in which there are periodical attacks of aphonia we are to diagnose the existence of a loved person who is at times away from the patient? Nothing could be further from my intention. The determination of Dora's symptoms is far too specific for it to be possible to expect a frequent recurrence of the same accidental aetiology. But, if so, what is the value of our elucidation of the aphonia in the present case? Have we not merely allowed ourselves to become the victims of a *jeu d'esprit*? I think not. In this connection we must recall the question which has so often been raised, whether the symptoms of hysteria are of psychical or of somatic origin, or whether, if the former is granted, they are necessarily *all* of them psychically determined. Like so many other questions to which we find investigators returning again and again without success, this question is not adequately framed. The alternatives stated in it do not cover the real essence of the matter. As far as I can see, every hysterical symptom involves the participation of *both* sides. It cannot occur without the presence of a certain degree of *somatic compliance*[1] offered by some normal or pathological process in or connected with one of the bodily organs. And it cannot occur more than once – and the capacity for repeating itself is one of the characteristics of a hysterical symptom – unless it has a psychical significance, a *meaning*. The hysterical symptom does not carry this meaning with it, but the meaning is lent to it, soldered to it, as it were; and in every instance the meaning can be a different one, according to the nature of the suppressed thoughts which are struggling for expression. However, there are a number of factors at work which tend to make less arbitrary the relations between the unconscious thoughts and the somatic processes that are at their disposal as a means of expression, and which tend to make those relations approximate to a few typical forms. For therapeutic purposes the most important determinants are those given by the fortuitous psychical material; the clearing-up of the symptoms is achieved by looking for their psychical significance. When everything that can be got rid of by psychoanalysis has been cleared away, we are in a position to form all kinds of conjectures, which probably meet the facts, as regards the somatic basis of the symptoms – a basis which is as a rule constitutional and organic. Thus in Dora's case we shall not content ourselves with a psychoanalytic interpretation of her attacks of coughing and aphonia; but we shall also indicate the organic factor which was the source of the 'somatic compliance' that enabled her to express her love for a man who was periodically absent. And if the connection between the symptomatic expression and the unconscious mental content should strike us as being in this case a clever *tour de force*, we shall be relieved to hear that it succeeds in creating the same impression in every other case and in every other instance.

1. [This seems to be Freud's earliest use of the term, which scarcely reappears in later works. (See the last words of his paper on psychogenic disturbances of vision, (1910i), *P.F.L.*, **10**, 114).]

I am prepared to be told at this point that there is no very great advantage in having been taught by psychoanalysis that the clue to the problem of hysteria is to be found not in 'a peculiar instability of the molecules of the nerves' or in a liability to 'hypnoid states' – but in a 'somatic compliance'. But in reply to the objection I may remark that this new view has not only to some extent pushed the problem further back, but has also to some extent diminished it. We have no longer to deal with the *whole* problem, but only with the portion of it involving that particular characteristic of hysteria *which differentiates it* from other psychoneuroses. The mental events in all psychoneuroses proceed for a considerable distance along the same lines before any question arises of the 'somatic compliance' which may afford the unconscious mental processes a physical outlet. When this factor is not forthcoming, something other than a hysterical symptom will arise out of the total situation; yet it will still be something of an allied nature, a phobia, perhaps, or an obsession – in short, a psychical symptom.

I now return to the reproach of 'malingering' which Dora brought against her father. It soon became evident that this reproach corresponded to self-reproaches not only concerning her earlier states of ill-health but also concerning the present time. At such points the physician is usually faced by the task of guessing and filling in what the analysis offers him in the shape only of hints and allusions. I was obliged to point out to the patient that her present ill-health was just as much actuated by motives and was just as tendentious as had been Frau K.'s illness, which she had understood so well. There could be no doubt, I said, that she had an aim in view which she hoped to gain by her illness. That aim could be none other than to detach her father from Frau K. She had been unable to achieve this by prayers or arguments; perhaps she hoped to succeed by frightening her father (there was her farewell letter), or by awakening his pity (there were her fainting-fits) [p. 53], or if all this was in vain, at least she would be taking her revenge on him. She knew very well, I went on, how much he was attached to her, and that tears used to come into his eyes whenever he was asked after his daughter's health. I felt quite convinced that she would recover at once if only her father were to tell her that he had sacrificed Frau K. for the sake of her health. But, I added, I hoped he would not let himself be persuaded to do this, for then she would have learned what a powerful weapon she had in her hands, and she would certainly not hesitate on every future occasion to make use once more of her potentialities for illness. Yet if her father refused to give way to her, I was quite sure she would not let herself be deprived of her illness so easily.

I will pass over the details which showed how entirely correct all of this was, and I will instead add a few general remarks upon the part played in hysteria by the *motives of illness*. A *motive* for being ill is sharply to be distinguished as a concept from a *potentiality* for illness – from the material out of which symptoms are formed. The motives have no share in the formation of symptoms, and indeed are not present at the beginning of the illness. They only appear secondarily to it; but it is not until they have appeared that the disease is fully constituted.[1]

1. [*Footnote added* 1923:] This is not quite right. The statement that the motives of illness are not present at the beginning of the illness, but only appear secondarily to it, cannot be maintained. In the very next paragraph motives for being ill are mentioned which were in existence before the outbreak of illness, and were partly responsible for that outbreak. I subsequently found a better way of meeting the facts, by introducing a distinction between the *primary and secondary gain from illness*. The motive for being ill is, of course, invariably the intention of securing some gain. What follows in the later sentences of this paragraph applies to the secondary gain. But in every neurotic illness a primary gain has also to be recognized. In the first place, falling ill involves a saving of psychical effort; it emerges as being economically the most convenient solution where there is a mental conflict (we speak of a 'flight into illness'), even though in most cases the ineffectiveness of such an escape becomes manifest at a later stage. This element in the

Their presence can be reckoned upon in every case in which there is real suffering and which is of fairly long standing. A symptom comes into the patient's mental life at first as an unwelcome guest; it has everything against it; and that is why it may vanish so easily, apparently of its own accord, under the influence of time. To begin with there is no use to which it can be put in the domestic economy of the mind; but very often it succeeds in finding one secondarily. Some psychical current or other finds it convenient to make use of it, and in that way the symptom manages to obtain a *secondary function* and remains, as it were, anchored fast in the patient's mental life. And so it happens that any one who tries to make him well is to his astonishment brought up against a powerful resistance, which teaches him that the patient's intention of getting rid of his complaint is not so entirely and completely serious as it seemed.[1] Let us imagine a workman, a bricklayer, let us say, who has fallen off a house and been crippled, and now earns his livelihood by begging at the street-corner. Let us then suppose that a miracle-worker comes along and promises him to make his crooked leg straight and capable of walking. It would be unwise, I think, to look forward to seeing an expression of peculiar

---

primary gain may be described as the *internal* or psychological one, and it is, so to say, a constant one. But beyond this, external factors (such as in the instance given [in the following paragraph in the text] of the situation of a woman subjugated by her husband) may contribute motives for falling ill; and these will constitute the *external* element in the primary gain. [The distinction between the primary and secondary gain from illness was fully discussed by Freud in Lecture 24 of his *Introductory Lectures* (1916–17), *P.F.L.*, **1**, 429–33, though it had been indicated earlier, in his paper on hysterical attacks (1909*a*, Section B), where the term 'flight into illness' was also used. At a much later date he returned to the topic once more (in *Inhibitions, Symptoms and Anxiety*, 1926*d*, particularly in Chapter III). The present account of the matter is, however, probably his clearest. – Cf. also below, p. 272.]

1. A man of letters, who incidentally is also a physician – Arthur Schnitzler – has expressed this piece of knowledge very correctly in his [play] *Paracelsus*.

bliss upon the man's features. No doubt at the time of the accident he felt he was extremely unlucky, when he realized that he would never be able to do any more work and would have to starve or live upon charity. But since then the very thing which in the first instance threw him out of employment has become his source of income: he lives by his disablement. If that is taken from him he may become totally helpless. He has in the meantime forgotten his trade and lost his habits of industry; he has grown accustomed to idleness, and perhaps to drink as well.

The motives for being ill often begin to be active even in childhood. A little girl in her greed for love does not enjoy having to share the affection of her parents with her brothers and sisters; and she notices that the whole of their affection is lavished on her once more whenever she arouses their anxiety by falling ill. She has now discovered a means of enticing out her parents' love, and will make use of that means as soon as she has the necessary psychical material at her disposal for producing an illness. When such a child has grown up to be a woman she may find all the demands she used to make in her childhood countered owing to her marriage with an inconsiderate husband, who may subjugate her will, mercilessly exploit her capacity for work, and lavish neither his affection nor his money upon her. In that case ill-health will be her one weapon for maintaining her position. It will procure her the care she longs for; it will force her husband to make pecuniary sacrifices for her and to show her consideration, as he would never have done while she was well; and it will compel him to treat her with solicitude if she recovers, for otherwise a relapse will threaten. Her state of ill-health will have every appearance of being objective and involuntary – the very doctor who treats her will bear witness to the fact; and for that reason she will not need to feel any conscious self-reproaches at making such successful use of a means which she had found effective in her years of childhood.

And yet illnesses of this kind *are* the result of intention. They are as a rule levelled at a particular person, and consequently vanish with that person's departure. The crudest and most commonplace views on the character of hysterical disorders – such as are to be heard from uneducated relatives or nurses – are in a certain sense right. It is true that the paralysed and bedridden woman would spring to her feet if a fire were to break out in her room, and that the spoiled wife would forget all her sufferings if her child were to fall dangerously ill or if some catastrophe were to threaten the family circumstances. People who speak of the patients in this way are right except upon a single point: they overlook the psychological distinction between what is conscious and what is unconscious. This may be permissible where children are concerned, but with adults it is no longer possible. That is why all these asseverations that it is 'only a question of willing' and all the encouragements and abuse that are addressed to the patient are of no avail. An attempt must first be made by the roundabout methods of analysis to convince the patient herself of the existence in her of an intention to be ill.

It is in combating the motives of illness that the weak point in every kind of therapeutic treatment of hysteria lies. This is quite generally true, and it applies equally to psychoanalysis. Destiny has an easier time of it in this respect: it need not concern itself either with the patient's constitution or with his pathogenic material; it has only to take away a motive for being ill, and the patient is temporarily or perhaps even permanently freed from his illness. How many fewer miraculous cures and spontaneous disappearances of symptoms should we physicians have to register in cases of hysteria, if we were more often given a sight of the human interests which the patient keeps hidden from us! In one case, some stated period of time has elapsed; in a second, consideration for some other person has ceased to operate; in a third, the situation has been fundamentally changed by some external event – and the whole disorder, which up till then had shown the greatest obstinacy, vanishes at a single blow, apparently of its own accord, but really because it has been deprived of its most powerful motive, one of the uses to which it has been put in the patient's life.

Motives that support the patient in being ill are probably to be found in all fully developed cases. But there are some in which the motives are purely internal – such as desire for self-punishment, that is, penitence and remorse. It will be found much easier to solve the therapeutic problem in such cases than in those in which the illness is related to the attainment of some external aim.[1] In Dora's case that aim was clearly to touch her father's heart and to detach him from Frau K.

None of her father's actions seemed to have embittered her so much as his readiness to consider the scene by the lake as a product of her imagination. She was almost beside herself at the idea of its being supposed that she had merely fancied something on that occasion. For a long time I was in perplexity as to what the self-reproach could be which lay behind her passionate repudiation of this explanation of the episode. It was justifiable to suspect that there was something concealed, for a reproach which misses the mark gives no lasting offence. On the other hand, I came to the conclusion that Dora's story must correspond to the facts in every respect. No sooner had she grasped Herr K.'s intention than, without letting him finish what he had to say, she had given him a slap in the face and hurried away. Her behaviour must have seemed as incomprehensible to the man after she had left him as to us, for he must long before have gathered from innumerable small signs that he was secure of the girl's affections. In our discussion of Dora's second dream we shall come upon the solution of this riddle as well as upon the self-reproach which we have hitherto failed to discover [p. 147 ff.].

As she kept on repeating her complaints against her father

1. [Later, however, Freud took a very different view of the therapeutic difficulties in cases of *unconscious* desire for self-punishment. See, e.g., Chapter V of *The Ego and the Id* (1923b), *P.F.L.*, **11**, 390f.]

with a wearisome monotony, and as at the same time her cough continued, I was led to think that this symptom might have some meaning in connection with her father. And apart from this, the explanation of the symptom which I had hitherto obtained was far from fulfilling the requirements which I am accustomed to make of such explanations. According to a rule which I had found confirmed over and over again by experience, though I had not yet ventured to erect it into a general principle, a symptom signifies the representation – the realization – of a phantasy with a sexual content, that is to say, it signifies a sexual situation. It would be better to say that at least *one* of the meanings of a symptom is the representation of a sexual phantasy, but that no such limitation is imposed upon the content of its other meanings. Any one who takes up psychoanalytic work will quickly discover that a symptom has more than one meaning and serves to represent several unconscious mental processes simultaneously. And I should like to add that in my estimation a single unconscious mental process or phantasy will scarcely ever suffice for the production of a symptom.

An opportunity very soon occurred for interpreting Dora's nervous cough in this way by means of an imagined sexual situation. She had once again been insisting that Frau K. only loved her father because he was '*ein vermögender Mann*' ['a man of means']. Certain details of the way in which she expressed herself (which I pass over here, like most other purely technical parts of the analysis) led me to see that behind this phrase its opposite lay concealed, namely, that her father was '*ein unvermögender Mann*' ['a man without means']. This could only be meant in a sexual sense – that her father, as a man, was without means, was impotent.[1] Dora confirmed this interpretation from her conscious knowledge; whereupon I pointed out the contradiction she was involved in if on the one hand she continued to insist that her father's relation with Frau K. was a common

---

1. ['*Unvermögend*' means literally 'unable', and is commonly used in the sense of both 'not rich' and 'impotent'.]

love-affair, and on the other hand maintained that her father was impotent, or in other words incapable of carrying on an affair of such a kind. Her answer showed that she had no need to admit the contradiction. She knew very well, she said, that there was more than one way of obtaining sexual gratification. (The source of this piece of knowledge, however, was once more untraceable.) I questioned her further, whether she referred to the use of organs other than the genitals for the purpose of sexual intercourse, and she replied in the affirmative. I could then go on to say that in that case she must be thinking of precisely those parts of the body which in her case were in a state of irritation, – the throat and the oral cavity. To be sure, she would not hear of going so far as this in recognizing her own thoughts; and indeed, if the occurrence of the symptom was to be made possible at all, it was essential that she should not be completely clear on the subject. But the conclusion was inevitable that with her spasmodic cough, which, as is usual, was referred for its exciting stimulus to a tickling in her throat, she pictured to herself a scene of sexual gratification *per os* between the two people whose love-affair occupied her mind so incessantly. A very short time after she had tacitly accepted this explanation her cough vanished – which fitted in very well with my view; but I do not wish to lay too much stress upon this development, since her cough had so often before disappeared spontaneously.

This short piece of the analysis may perhaps have excited in the medical reader – apart from the scepticism to which he is entitled – feelings of astonishment and horror; and I am prepared at this point to look into these two reactions so as to discover whether they are justifiable. The astonishment is probably caused by my daring to talk about such delicate and unpleasant subjects to a young girl – or, for that matter, to any woman who is sexually active. The horror is aroused, no doubt, by the possibility that an inexperienced girl could know about practices of such a kind and could occupy her imagination with

them. I would advise recourse to moderation and reasonable-
ness upon both points. There is no cause for indignation either
in the one case or in the other. It is possible for a man to talk to
girls and women upon sexual matters of every kind without
doing them harm and without bringing suspicion upon himself, so long as, in the first place, he adopts a particular way of
doing it, and, in the second place, can make them feel convinced that it is unavoidable. A gynaecologist, after all, under
the same conditions, does not hesitate to make them submit to
uncovering every possible part of their body. The best way of
speaking about such things is to be dry and direct; and that is
at the same time the method furthest removed from the prurience with which the same subjects are handled in 'society', and
to which girls and women alike are so thoroughly accustomed.
I call bodily organs and processes by their technical names, and I
tell these to the patient if they – the names, I mean – happen to
be unknown to her. *J'appelle un chat un chat.* I have certainly
heard of some people – doctors and laymen – who are scandal-
ized by a therapeutic method in which conversations of this
sort occur, and who appear to envy either me or my patients
the titillation which, according to their notions, such a method
must afford. But I am too well acquainted with the respectability of these gentry to excite myself over them. I shall avoid
the temptation of writing a satire upon them. But there is one
thing that I will mention: often, after I have for some time
treated a patient who had not at first found it easy to be open
about sexual matters, I have had the satisfaction of hearing her
exclaim: 'Why, after all, your treatment is far more respectable
than Mr X's conversation!'

No one can undertake the treatment of a case of hysteria until
he is convinced of the impossibility of avoiding the mention of
sexual subjects, or unless he is prepared to allow himself to be
convinced by experience. The right attitude is: '*pour faire une
omelette il faut casser des œufs.*' The patients themselves are easy to
convince; and there are only too many opportunities of doing
so in the course of the treatment. There is no necessity for feel-

ing any compunction at discussing the facts of normal or abnormal sexual life with them. With the exercise of a little caution all that is done is to translate into conscious ideas what was already known in the unconscious; and, after all, the whole effectiveness of the treatment is based upon our knowledge that the affect attached to an unconscious idea operates more strongly and, since it cannot be inhibited, more injuriously than the affect attached to a conscious one. There is never any danger of corrupting an inexperienced girl. For where there is no knowledge of sexual processes even in the unconscious, no hysterical symptom will arise; and where hysteria is found there can no longer be any question of 'innocence of mind' in the sense in which parents and educators use the phrase. With children of ten, of twelve, or of fourteen, with boys and girls alike, I have satisfied myself that the truth of this statement can invariably be relied upon.

As regards the second kind of emotional reaction, which is not directed against me this time, but against my patient – supposing that my view of her is correct – and which regards the perverse nature of her phantasies as horrible, I should like to say emphatically that a medical man has no business to indulge in such passionate condemnation. I may also remark in passing that it seems to me superfluous for a physician who is writing upon the aberrations of the sexual instincts to seize every opportunity of inserting into the text expressions of his personal repugnance at such revolting things. We are faced by a fact; and it is to be hoped that we shall grow accustomed to it, when we have put our own tastes on one side. We must learn to speak without indignation of what we call the sexual perversions – instances in which the sexual function has extended its limits in respect either to the part of the body concerned or to the sexual object chosen. The uncertainty in regard to the boundaries of what is to be called normal sexual life, when we take different races and different epochs into account, should in itself be enough to cool the zealot's ardour. We surely ought not to forget that the perversion which is the most repellent to us, the sensual love of a man for a man, was not only tolerated by a people so far our superiors in cultivation as were the Greeks, but was actually entrusted by them with important social functions. The sexual life of each one of us extends to a slight degree – now in this direction, now in that – beyond the narrow lines imposed as the standard of normality. The perversions are neither bestial nor degenerate in the emotional sense of the word. They are a development of germs all of which are contained in the undifferentiated sexual disposition of the child, and which, by being suppressed or by being diverted to higher, asexual aims – by being 'sublimated'[1] – are destined to provide the energy for a great number of our cultural achievements. When, therefore, any one has *become* a gross and manifest pervert, it would be more correct to say that he has *remained* one, for he exhibits a certain stage of *inhibited development*. All psychoneurotics are persons with strongly marked perverse tendencies, which have been repressed in the course of their development and have become unconscious. Consequently their unconscious *phantasies* show precisely the same content as the documentarily recorded *actions* of perverts – even though they have not read Krafft-Ebing's *Psychopathia Sexualis*, to which simple-minded people attribute such a large share of the responsibility for the production of perverse tendencies. Psychoneuroses are, so to speak, the *negative* of perversions. In neurotics their sexual constitution, under which the effects of heredity are included, operates in combination with any accidental influences in their life which may disturb the development of normal sexuality. A stream of water which meets with an obstacle in the river-bed is dammed up and flows back into old channels which had formerly seemed fated to run dry. The motive forces leading to the formation of hysterical symptoms draw their strength not only from

1. [Cf. the second of Freud's *Three Essays* (1905*d*), Section [1], *P.F.L.*, 7, 93–4.]

repressed *normal* sexuality but also from unconscious perverse activities.[1]

The less repellent of the so-called sexual perversions are very widely diffused among the whole population, as every one knows except medical writers upon the subject. Or, I should rather say, they know it too; only they take care to forget it at the moment when they take up their pens to write about it. So it is not to be wondered at that this hysterical girl of nearly nineteen, who had heard of the occurrence of such a method of sexual intercourse (sucking at the male organ), should have developed an unconscious phantasy of this sort and should have given it expression by an irritation in her throat and by coughing. Nor would it have been very extraordinary if she had arrived at such a phantasy even without having had any enlightenment from external sources – an occurrence which I have quite certainly observed in other patients. For in her case a noteworthy fact afforded the necessary somatic prerequisite for this independent creation of a phantasy which would coincide with the practices of perverts. She remembered very well that in her childhood she had been a thumb-sucker. Her father, too, recollected breaking her of the habit after it had persisted into her fourth or fifth year. Dora herself had a clear picture of a scene from her early childhood in which she was sitting on the floor in a corner sucking her left thumb and at the same time tugging with her right hand at the lobe of her brother's ear as he sat quietly beside her. Here we have an instance of the complete form of self-gratification by sucking, as it has also been described to me by other patients, who had subsequently become anaesthetic and hysterical.

One of these patients gave me a piece of information which

1. These remarks upon the sexual perversions had been written some years before the appearance of Bloch's excellent book (*Beiträge zur Ätiologie der Psychopathia sexualis*, 1902 and 1903). See also my *Three Essays on the Theory of Sexuality*, published this year [1905*d*, particularly the first essay, in which most of the points in the present paragraph are enlarged upon. For the following paragraph, see the third section of the second essay, *P.F.L.*, 7, 45ff. and 99ff.].

shed a clear light on the origin of this curious habit. This young woman had never broken herself of the habit of sucking. She retained a memory of her childhood, dating back, according to her, to the first half of her second year, in which she saw herself sucking at her nurse's breast and at the same time pulling rhythmically at the lobe of her nurse's ear. No one will feel inclined to dispute, I think, that the mucous membrane of the lips and mouth is to be regarded as a primary 'erotogenic zone',[1] since it preserves this earlier significance in the act of kissing, which is looked upon as normal. An intense activity of this erotogenic zone at an early age thus determines the subsequent presence of a somatic compliance on the part of the tract of mucous membrane which begins at the lips. Thus, at a time when the sexual object proper, that is, the male organ, has already become known, circumstances may arise which once more increase the excitation of the oral zone, whose erotogenic character has, as we have seen, been retained. It then needs very little creative power to substitute the sexual object of the moment (the penis) for the original object (the nipple) or for the finger which does duty for it, and to place the current sexual object in the situation in which satisfaction was originally obtained. So we see that this excessively repulsive and perverted phantasy of sucking at a penis has the most innocent origin. It is a new version of what may be described as a prehistoric impression of sucking at the mother's or nurse's breast – an impression which has usually been revived by contact with children who are being nursed. In most instances a cow's udder has aptly played the part of an image intermediate between a nipple and a penis.[2]

The interpretation we have just been discussing of Dora's throat symptoms may also give rise to a further remark. It may be asked how this sexual situation imagined by her can be

1. [Cf. the first of Freud's *Three Essays* (1905*d*), P.F.L., 7, 82ff.]
2. [See the confirmation of this detail in the case of 'Little Hans' (1909*b*), below, pp. 170–71.]

compatible with our other explanation of the symptoms. That explanation, it will be remembered, was to the effect that the coming and going of the symptoms reflected the presence and absence of the man she was in love with, and, as regards his wife's behaviour, expressed the following thought: 'If *I* were his wife, I should love him in quite a different way; I should be ill (from longing, let us say) when he was away, and well (from joy) when he was home again.' To this objection I must reply that my experience in the clearing-up of hysterical symptoms has shown that it is not necessary for the various meanings of symptoms to be compatible with one another, that is, to fit together into a connected whole. It is enough that the unity should be constituted by the subject-matter which has given rise to all the various phantasies. In the present case, moreover, compatibility even of the first kind is not out of the question. One of the two meanings is related more to the cough, and the other to the aphonia and the periodicity of the disorder. A closer analysis would probably have disclosed a far greater number of mental elements in relation to the details of the illness.

We have already learnt that it quite regularly happens that a single symptom corresponds to several meanings *simultaneously*. We may now add that it can express several meanings *in succession*. In the course of years a symptom can change its meaning or its chief meaning, or the leading role can pass from one meaning to another. It is as though there were a conservative trait in the character of neuroses which ensures that a symptom that has once been formed shall if possible be retained, even though the unconscious thought to which it gave expression has lost its meaning. Moreover, there is no difficulty in explaining this tendency towards the retention of a symptom upon a mechanical basis. The production of a symptom of this kind is so difficult, the translation of a purely psychical excitation into physical terms – the process which I have called 'conversion' – depends on the concurrence of so many favourable conditions, the somatic compliance necessary for conversion is so seldom forthcoming, that an impulsion towards the discharge of an unconscious excitation will so far as possible make use of any channel for discharge which may already be in existence. It appears to be far more difficult to create a fresh conversion than to form paths of association between a new thought which is in need of discharge and the old one which is no longer in need of it. The current flows along these paths from the new source of excitation to the old point of discharge – pouring into the symptom, in the words of the Gospel, like new wine into an old bottle. These remarks would make it seem that the somatic side of a hysterical symptom is the more stable of the two and the harder to replace, while the psychical side is a variable element for which a substitute can more easily be found. Yet we should not try to infer anything from this comparison as regards the relative importance of the two elements. From the point of view of mental therapeutics the mental side must always be the more significant.

Dora's incessant repetition of the same thoughts about her father's relations with Frau K. made it possible to derive still further important material from the analysis.

A train of thought such as this may be described as excessively intense, or better *reinforced*, or 'supervalent' ['*überwertig*'] in Wernicke's [1900, 140] sense. It shows its pathological character in spite of its apparently reasonable content, by the single peculiarity that no amount of conscious and voluntary effort of thought on the patient's part is able to dissipate or remove it. A normal train of thought, however intense it may be, can eventually be disposed of. Dora felt quite rightly that her thoughts about her father required to be judged in a special way. 'I can think of nothing else', she complained again and again. 'I know my brother says we children have no right to criticize this behaviour of Father's. He declares that we ought not to trouble ourselves about it, and ought even to be glad, perhaps, that he has found a woman he can love, since Mother understands him so little. I can quite see that, and I should like to think the same as my brother, but I can't. I can't forgive him for it.'[1]

Now what is one to do in the face of a supervalent thought like this, after one has heard what its conscious grounds are and listened to the ineffectual protests made against it? Reflection will suggest that *this excessively intense train of thought must owe its reinforcement to the unconscious.* It cannot be resolved by any effort of thought, either because it itself reaches with its root down into unconscious, repressed material, or because another unconscious thought lies concealed behind it. In the latter case, the concealed thought is usually the direct contrary of the supervalent one. Contrary thoughts are always closely connected with each other and are often paired off in such a way that *the one thought is excessively intensely conscious while its counterpart is repressed and unconscious.* This relation between the two thoughts is an effect of the process of repression. For repression is often achieved by means of an excessive reinforcement of the thought contrary to the one which is to be repressed. This process I call *reactive* reinforcement, and the thought which asserts itself with excessive intensity in consciousness and (in the same way as a prejudice) cannot be removed I call a *reactive thought.* The two thoughts then act towards each other much like the two needles of an astatic galvanometer. The reactive thought keeps the objectionable one under repression by means of a certain surplus of intensity; but for that reason it itself is 'damped' and proof against conscious efforts of thought. So that the way to deprive the excessively intense thought of its reinforcement is by bringing its repressed contrary into consciousness.

We must also be prepared to meet with instances in which the supervalence of a thought is due not to the presence of one only of these two causes but to a concurrence of both of them.

1. A supervalent thought of this kind is often the only symptom, beyond deep depression, of a pathological condition which is usually described as 'melancholia', but which can be cleared up by psychoanalysis like a hysteria.

Other complications, too, may arise, but they can easily be fitted into the general scheme.

Let us now apply our theory to the instance provided by Dora's case.[1] We will begin with the first hypothesis, namely, that her preoccupation with her father's relations to Frau K. owed its obsessive character to the fact that its root was unknown to her and lay in the unconscious. It is not difficult to divine the nature of that root from her circumstances and her conduct. Her behaviour obviously went far beyond what would have been appropriate to filial concern. She felt and acted more like a jealous wife – in a way which would have been comprehensible in her mother. By her ultimatum to her father ('either her or me'), by the scenes she used to make, by the suicidal intentions she allowed to transpire, – by all this she was clearly putting herself in her mother's place. If we have rightly guessed the nature of the imaginary sexual situation which underlay her cough, in that phantasy she must have been putting herself in Frau K.'s place. She was therefore identifying herself both with the woman her father had once loved and with the woman he loved now. The inference is obvious that her affection for her father was a much stronger one than she knew or than she would have cared to admit: in fact, that she was in love with him.

I have learnt to look upon unconscious love relations like this (which are marked by their abnormal consequences) – between a father and a daughter, or between a mother and a son – as a revival of germs of feeling in infancy. I have shown at length elsewhere[2] at what an early age sexual attraction makes itself

1. [Of the two possibilities – viz. that the supervalent thought may be due (a) to *direct* and (b) to *reactive* reinforcement from the unconscious – (a) is discussed in this and the next two paragraphs, while (b) is shown to be present in two forms – the first of which is considered in the three paragraphs that follow, and the second in the remainder of the section.]

2. In my *Interpretation of Dreams*, 1900a [Chapter V, Section D (β), P.F.L., 4, 358 ff.], and in the third of my *Three Essays*, 1905d [P.F.L., 7, 150 f.].

felt between parents and children, and I have explained that the legend of Oedipus is probably to be regarded as a poetical rendering of what is typical in these relations. Distinct traces are probably to be found in most people of an early partiality of this kind – on the part of a daughter for her father, or on the part of a son for his mother; but it must be assumed to be more intense from the very first in the case of those children whose constitution marks them down for a neurosis, who develop prematurely and have a craving for love. At this point certain other influences, which need not be discussed here, come into play, and lead to a fixation of this rudimentary feeling of love or to a reinforcement of it; so that it turns into something (either while the child is still young or not until it has reached the age of puberty) which must be put on a par with a sexual inclination and which, like the latter, has the forces of the libido at its command.[1] The external circumstances of our patient were by no means unfavourable to such an assumption. The nature of her disposition had always drawn her towards her father, and his numerous illnesses were bound to have increased her affection for him. In some of these illnesses he would allow no one but her to discharge the lighter duties of nursing. He had been so proud of the early growth of her intelligence that he had made her his confidante while she was still a child. It was really she and not her mother whom Frau K.'s appearance had driven out of more than one position.

When I told Dora that I could not avoid supposing that her affection for her father must at a very early moment have amounted to her being completely in love with him, she of course gave me her usual reply: 'I don't remember that.' But she immediately went on to tell me something analogous about a seven-year-old girl who was her cousin (on her mother's side) and in whom she often thought she saw a kind of reflection of her own childhood. This little girl had (not for the first time)

1. The decisive factor in this connection is no doubt the early appearance of true genital sensations, either spontaneously or as a result of seduction or masturbation. (See below [p. 115 f.].)

been the witness of a heated dispute between her parents, and, when Dora happened to come in on a visit soon afterwards, whispered in her ear: 'You can't think how I hate that person!' (pointing to her mother), 'and when she's dead I shall marry Daddy.' I am in the habit of regarding associations such as this, which bring forward something that agrees with the content of an assertion of mine, as a confirmation from the unconscious of what I have said. No other kind of 'Yes' can be extracted from the unconscious; there is no such thing at all as an unconscious 'No'.[1]

For years on end she had given no expression to this passion for her father. On the contrary, she had for a long time been on the closest terms with the woman who had supplanted her with her father, and she had actually, as we know from her self-reproaches, facilitated this woman's relations with her father. Her own love for her father had therefore been recently revived; and, if so, the question arises to what end this had happened. Clearly as a reactive symptom, so as to suppress something else – something, that is, that still exercised power in the unconscious. Considering how things stood, I could not help supposing in the first instance that what was suppressed was her love of Herr K. I could not avoid the assumption that she was still in love with him, but that, for unknown reasons, since the scene by the lake her love had aroused in her violent feelings of opposition, and that the girl had brought forward and re-inforced her old affection for her father in order to avoid any further necessity for paying conscious attention to the love which she had felt in the first years of her girlhood and which had now become distressing to her. In this way I gained an

1. [*Footnote added* 1923:] There is another very remarkable and entirely trustworthy form of confirmation from the unconscious, which I had not recognized at the time this was written: namely, an exclamation on the part of the patient of 'I didn't think that', or 'I didn't think of that'. This can be translated point-blank into: 'Yes, I was unconscious of that.' [See the longer discussion on this subject in Freud's paper on 'Negation' (1925h), *P.F.L.*, **11**, 437 ff.]

insight into a conflict which was well calculated to unhinge the girl's mind. On the one hand she was filled with regret at having rejected the man's proposal, and with longing for his company and all the little signs of his affection; while on the other hand these feelings of tenderness and longing were combated by powerful forces, amongst which her pride was one of the most obvious. Thus she had succeeded in persuading herself that she had done with Herr K. – that was the advantage she derived from this typical process of repression; and yet she was obliged to summon up her infantile affection for her father and to exaggerate it, in order to protect herself against the feelings of love which were constantly pressing forward into consciousness. The further fact that she was almost incessantly a prey to the most embittered jealousy seemed to admit of still another determination.[1]

My expectations were by no means disappointed when this explanation of mine was met by Dora with a most emphatic negative. The 'No' uttered by a patient after a repressed thought has been presented to his conscious perception for the first time does no more than register the existence of a repression and its severity; it acts, as it were, as a gauge of the repression's strength. If this 'No', instead of being regarded as the expression of an impartial judgement (of which, indeed, the patient is incapable), is ignored, and if work is continued, the first evidence soon begins to appear that in such a case 'No' signifies the desired 'Yes'. Dora admitted that she found it impossible to be as angry with Herr K. as he had deserved. She told me that one day she had met Herr K. in the street while she was walking with a cousin of hers who did not know him. The other girl had exclaimed all at once: 'Why, Dora, what's wrong with you? You've gone as white as a sheet!' She herself had felt nothing of this change of colour; but I explained to her that the expression of emotion and the play of features obey the unconscious rather than the conscious, and are a means of

1. We shall come upon this [in a moment].

betraying the former.[1] Another time Dora came to me in the worst of tempers after having been uniformly cheerful for several days. She could give no explanation of this. She felt so contrary today, she said; it was her uncle's birthday, and she could not bring herself to congratulate him, she did not know why. My powers of interpretation were at a low ebb that day; I let her go on talking, and she suddenly recollected that it was Herr K.'s birthday too – a fact which I did not fail to use against her. And it was then no longer hard to explain why the handsome presents she had had on her own birthday a few days before had given her no pleasure. One gift was missing, and that was Herr K.'s, the gift which had plainly once been the most prized of all.

Nevertheless Dora persisted in denying my contention for some time longer, until, towards the end of the analysis, the conclusive proof of its correctness came to light [pp. 149–50].

I must now turn to consider a further complication to which I should certainly give no space if I were a man of letters engaged upon the creation of a mental state like this for a short story, instead of being a medical man engaged upon its dissection. The element to which I must now allude can only serve to obscure and efface the outlines of the fine poetic conflict which we have been able to ascribe to Dora. This element would rightly fall a sacrifice to the censorship of a writer, for he, after all, simplifies and abstracts when he appears in the character of a psychologist. But in the world of reality, which I am trying to depict here, a complication of motives, an

1. Compare the lines:

> Ruhig mag ich Euch erscheinen,
> Ruhig gehen sehn.

> [Quiet can I watch thy coming,
> Quiet watch thee go.

The words (from Schiller's ballad 'Ritter Toggenburg') are addressed to a knight on his departure for the Crusades by his ostensibly indifferent but in fact devoted lady-love.]

accumulation and conjunction of mental activities – in a word, overdetermination – is the rule. For behind Dora's supervalent train of thought which was concerned with her father's relations with Frau K. there lay concealed a feeling of jealousy which had that lady as its *object* – a feeling, that is, which could only be based upon an affection on Dora's part for one of her own sex. It has long been known and often been pointed out that at the age of puberty boys and girls show clear signs, even in normal cases, of the existence of an affection for people of their own sex. A romantic and sentimental friendship with one of her schoolfriends, accompanied by vows, kisses, promises of eternal correspondence, and all the sensibility of jealousy, is the common precursor of a girl's first serious passion for a man. Thenceforward, in favourable circumstances, the homosexual current of feeling often runs completely dry. But if a girl is not happy in her love for a man, the current is often set flowing again by the libido in later years and is increased up to a greater or lesser degree of intensity. If this much can be established without difficulty of healthy persons, and if we take into account what has already been said [p. 84] about the fuller development in neurotics of the normal germs of perversion, we shall expect to find in these latter too a fairly strong homosexual predisposition. It must, indeed, be so; for I have never yet come through a single psychoanalysis of a man or a woman without having to take into account a very considerable current of homosexuality. When, in a hysterical woman or girl, the sexual libido which is directed towards men has been energetically suppressed, it will regularly be found that the libido which is directed towards women has become vicariously reinforced and even to some extent conscious.

I shall not in this place go any further into this important subject, which is especially indispensable to an understanding of hysteria in men, because Dora's analysis came to an end before it could throw any light on this side of her mental life. But I should like to recall the governess, whom I have already mentioned [p. 68 f.], and with whom Dora had at first enjoyed the closest interchange of thought, until she discovered that she was being admired and fondly treated not for her own sake but for her father's; whereupon she had obliged the governess to leave. She used also to dwell with noticeable frequency and a peculiar emphasis on the story of another estrangement which appeared inexplicable even to herself. She had always been on particularly good terms with the younger of her two cousins – the girl who had later on become engaged [p. 70] – and had shared all sorts of secrets with her. When, for the first time after Dora had broken off her stay by the lake, her father was going back to B—, she had naturally refused to go with him. This cousin had then been asked to travel with him instead, and she had accepted the invitation. From that time forward Dora had felt a coldness towards her, and she herself was surprised to find how indifferent she had become, although, as she admitted, she had very little ground for complaint against her. These instances of sensitiveness led me to inquire what her relations with Frau K. had been up till the time of the breach. I then found that the young woman and the scarcely grown girl had lived for years on a footing of the closest intimacy. When Dora stayed with the K.s she used to share a bedroom with Frau K., and the husband used to be quartered elsewhere. She had been the wife's confidante and adviser in all the difficulties of her married life. There was nothing they had not talked about. Medea had been quite content that Creusa should make friends with her two children; and she certainly did nothing to interfere with the relations between the girl and the children's father. How Dora managed to fall in love with the man about whom her beloved friend had so many bad things to say is an interesting psychological problem. We shall not be far from solving it when we realize that thoughts in the unconscious live very comfortably side by side, and even contraries get on together without disputes – a state of things which persists often enough even in the conscious.

When Dora talked about Frau K., she used to praise her 'adorable white body' in accents more appropriate to a lover than to a defeated rival. Another time she told me, more in sorrow than in anger, that she was convinced the presents her father had brought her had been chosen by Frau K., for she recognized her taste. Another time, again, she pointed out that, evidently through the agency of Frau K., she had been given a present of some jewellery which was exactly like some that she had seen in Frau K.'s possession and had wished for aloud at the time. Indeed, I can say in general that I never heard her speak a harsh or angry word against the lady, although from the point of view of her supervalent thought she should have regarded her as the prime author of her misfortunes. She seemed to behave inconsequently; but her apparent inconsequence was precisely the manifestation of a complicating current of feeling. For how had this woman to whom Dora was so enthusiastically devoted behaved to her? After Dora had brought forward her accusation against Herr K., and her father had written to him and had asked for an explanation, Herr K. had replied in the first instance by protesting sentiments of the highest esteem for her and by proposing that he should come to the manufacturing town to clear up every misunderstanding. A few weeks later, when her father spoke to him at B—, there was no longer any question of esteem. On the contrary, Herr K. spoke of her with disparagement, and produced as his trump card the reflection that no girl who read such books and was interested in such things could have any title to a man's respect. Frau K., therefore, had betrayed her and had calumniated her; for it had only been with her that she had read Mantegazza and discussed forbidden topics. It was a repetition of what had happened with the governess: Frau K. had not loved her for her own sake but on account of her father. Frau K. had sacrificed her without a moment's hesitation so that her relations with her father might not be disturbed. This mortification touched her, perhaps, more nearly and had a greater pathogenic effect than the other one, which she tried to use as a screen for it, – the fact that she had been sacrificed by her father. Did not the obstinacy with which she retained the particular amnesia concerning the sources of her forbidden knowledge [p. 62] point directly to the great emotional importance for her of the accusation against her upon that score, and consequently to her betrayal by her friend?

I believe, therefore, that I am not mistaken in supposing that Dora's supervalent train of thought, which was concerned with her father's relations with Frau K., was designed not only for the purpose of suppressing her love for Herr K., which had once been conscious, but also to conceal her love for Frau K., which was in a deeper sense unconscious. The supervalent train of thought was directly contrary to the latter current of feeling. She told herself incessantly that her father had sacrificed her to this woman, and made noisy demonstrations to show that she grudged her the possession of her father; and in this way she concealed from herself the contrary fact, which was that she grudged her father Frau K.'s love, and had not forgiven the woman she loved for the disillusionment she had been caused by her betrayal. The jealous emotions of a woman were linked in the unconscious with a jealousy such as might have been felt by a man. These masculine or, more properly speaking, *gynaecophilic* currents of feeling are to be regarded as typical of the unconscious erotic life of hysterical girls.[1]

1. [See the footnote on p. 162.]

II

THE FIRST DREAM

JUST at a moment when there was a prospect that the material that was coming up for analysis would throw light upon an obscure point in Dora's childhood, she reported that a few nights earlier she had once again had a dream which she had already dreamt in exactly the same way on many previous occasions. A periodically recurrent dream was by its very nature particularly well calculated to arouse my curiosity; and in any case it was justifiable in the interests of the treatment to consider the way in which the dream worked into the analysis as a whole. I therefore determined to make an especially careful investigation of it.

Here is the dream as related by Dora: '*A house was on fire.*[1] *My father was standing beside my bed and woke me up. I dressed quickly. Mother wanted to stop and save her jewel-case; but Father said: "I refuse to let myself and my two children be burnt for the sake of your jewel-case." We hurried downstairs, and as soon as I was outside I woke up.*'

As the dream was a recurrent one, I naturally asked her when she had first dreamt it. She told me she did not know. But she remembered having had the dream three nights in succession at L— (the place on the lake where the scene with Herr K. had taken place), and it had now come back again a few nights earlier, here [in Vienna].[2] My expectations from the clearing-up of the dream were naturally heightened when I heard of its connection with the events at L—. But I wanted to discover first what had been the exciting cause of its recent recurrence, and I therefore asked Dora to take the dream bit by bit and tell

1. In answer to an inquiry Dora told me that there had never really been a fire at their house.

2. The content of the dream makes it possible to establish that it in fact occurred *for the first time* at L—.

me what occurred to her in connection with it. She had already had some training in dream interpretation from having previously analysed a few minor specimens.

'Something occurs to me,' she said, 'but it cannot belong to the dream, for it is quite recent, whereas I have certainly had the dream before.'

'That makes no difference,' I replied. 'Start away! It will simply turn out to be the most recent thing that fits in with the dream.'

'Very well, then. Father has been having a dispute with Mother in the last few days, because she locks the dining-room door at night. My brother's room, you see, has no separate entrance, but can only be reached through the dining-room. Father does not want my brother to be locked in like that at night. He says it will not do: something might happen in the night so that it might be necessary to leave the room.'

'And that made you think of the risk of fire?'

'Yes.'

'Now, I should like you to pay close attention to the exact words you used. We may have to come back to them. You said that "*something might happen in the night so that it might be necessary to leave the room*".'[1]

But Dora had now discovered the connecting link between the recent exciting cause of the dream and the original one, for she continued:

'When we arrived at L— that time, Father and I, he openly said he was afraid of fire. We arrived in a violent thunderstorm, and saw the small wooden house without any lightning-conductor. So his anxiety was quite natural.'

1. I laid stress on these words because they took me aback. They seemed to have an ambiguous ring about them. Are not certain physical needs referred to in the same words? Now, in a line of associations ambiguous words (or, as we may call them, 'switch-words') act like points at a junction. If the points are switched across from the position in which they appear to lie in the dream, then we find ourselves on another set of rails; and along this second track run the thoughts which we are in search of but which still lie concealed behind the dream.

What I now had to do was to establish the relation between the events at L— and the recurrent dreams which she had had there. I therefore said: 'Did you have the dream during your first nights at L— or during your last ones? in other words, before or after the scene in the wood by the lake of which we have heard so much?' (I must explain that I knew that the scene had not occurred on the very first day, and that she had remained at L— for a few days after it without giving any hint of the incident.)

Her first reply was that she did not know, but after a while she added: 'Yes. I think it was after the scene.'

So now I knew that the dream was a reaction to that experience. But why had it recurred there three times? I continued my questions: 'How long did you stop on at L— after the scene?'

'Four more nights. On the following day I went away with Father.'

'Now I am certain that the dream was an immediate effect of your experience with Herr K. It was at L— that you dreamed it for the first time, and not before. You have only introduced this uncertainty in your memory so as to obliterate the connection in your mind.[1] But the figures do not quite fit in to my satisfaction yet. If you stayed at L— for four nights longer, the dream might have occurred four times over. Perhaps this was so?'

She no longer disputed my contention; but instead of answering my question she proceeded:[2] 'In the afternoon after our trip on the lake, from which we (Herr K. and I) returned at midday, I had gone to lie down as usual on the sofa in the bedroom to have a short sleep. I suddenly awoke and saw Herr K. standing beside me . . .'

'In fact, just as you saw your father standing beside your bed in the dream?'

'Yes. I asked him sharply what it was he wanted there. By

1. Compare what was said on pp. 46–7 on the subject of doubt accompanying a recollection.

2. This was because a fresh piece of material had to emerge from her memory before the question I had put could be answered.

way of reply he said he was not going to be prevented from coming into his own bedroom when he wanted; besides, there was something he wanted to fetch. This episode put me on my guard, and I asked Frau K. whether there was not a key to the bedroom door. The next morning I locked myself in while I was dressing. That afternoon, when I wanted to lock myself in so as to lie down again on the sofa, the key was gone. I was convinced that Herr K. had removed it.'

'Then here we have the theme of locking or not locking a room which appeared in the first association to the dream and also happened to occur in the exciting cause of the recent recurrence of the dream.[1] I wonder whether the phrase "*I dressed quickly*" may not also belong to this context?'

'It was then that I made up my mind not to stop on with the K.s without Father. On the subsequent mornings I could not help feeling afraid that Herr K. would surprise me while I was dressing: *so I always dressed very quickly*. You see, Father lived at the hotel, and Frau K. used always to go out early so as to go on expeditions with him. But Herr K. did not annoy me again.'

'I understand. On the afternoon of the day after the scene in the wood you formed your intention of escaping from his persecution, and during the second, third, and fourth nights you had time to repeat that intention in your sleep. (You already knew on the second afternoon – before the dream, therefore – that you would not have the key on the following morning to lock yourself in with while you were dressing; and you could then form the design of dressing as quickly as possible.) But your dream recurred each night, for the very reason that it corresponded to an *intention*. An intention remains in existence until it has been carried out. You said to yourself, as it were: "I

1. I suspected, though I did not as yet say so to Dora, that she had seized upon this element on account of a symbolic meaning which it possessed. '*Zimmer*' ['room'] in dreams stands very frequently for '*Frauenzimmer*' [a slightly derogatory word for 'woman'; literally, 'women's apartments']. The question whether a woman is 'open' or 'shut' can naturally not be a matter of indifference. It is well known, too, what sort of 'key' effects the opening in such a case.

shall have no rest and I can get no quiet sleep until I am out of this house." In your account of the dream you turned it the other way and said: "*As soon as I was outside I woke up*".'

At this point I shall interrupt my report of the analysis in order to compare this small piece of dream-interpretation with the general statements I have made upon the mechanism of the formation of dreams. I argued in my book, *The Interpretation of Dreams* (1900a), that every dream is a wish which is represented as fulfilled, that the representation acts as a disguise if the wish is a repressed one, belonging to the unconscious, and that except in the case of children's dreams only an unconscious wish or one which reaches down into the unconscious has the force necessary for the formation of a dream. I fancy my theory would have been more certain of general acceptance if I had contented myself with maintaining that every dream had a meaning, which could be discovered by means of a certain process of interpretation; and that when the interpretation had been completed the dream could be replaced by thoughts which would fall into place at an easily recognizable point in the waking mental life of the dreamer. I might then have gone on to say that the meaning of a dream turned out to be of as many different sorts as the processes of waking thought; that in one case it would be a fulfilled wish, in another a realized fear, or again a reflection persisting on into sleep, or an intention (as in the instance of Dora's dream), or a piece of creative thought during sleep, and so on. Such a theory would no doubt have proved attractive from its very simplicity, and it might have been supported by a great many examples of dreams that had been satisfactorily interpreted, as for instance by the one which has been analysed in these pages.

But instead of this I formulated a generalization according to which the meaning of dreams is limited to a single form, to the representation of *wishes*, and by so doing I aroused a universal inclination to dissent. I must, however, observe that I did not consider it either my right or my duty to simplify a psychological process so as to make it more acceptable to my readers, when my researches had shown me that it presented a complication which could not be reduced to uniformity until the inquiry had been carried into another field. It is therefore of special importance to me to show that apparent exceptions – such as this dream of Dora's, which has shown itself in the first instance to be the continuation into sleep of an intention formed during the day – nevertheless lend fresh support to the rule which is in dispute. [See p. 122 ff.]

Much of the dream, however, still remained to be interpreted, and I proceeded with my questions: 'What is this about the jewel-case that your mother wanted to save?'

'Mother is very fond of jewellery and had had a lot given her by Father.'

'And you?'

'I used to be very fond of jewellery too, once; but I have not worn any since my illness. Once, four years ago' (a year before the dream), 'Father and Mother had a great dispute about a piece of jewellery. Mother wanted to be given a particular thing – pearl drops to wear in her ears. But Father does not like that kind of thing, and he brought her a bracelet instead of the drops. She was furious, and told him that as he had spent so much money on a present she did not like he had better just give it to someone else.'

'I dare say you thought to yourself you would accept it with pleasure.'

'I don't know.[1] I don't in the least know how Mother comes into the dream; she was not with us at L— at the time.'[2]

1. The regular formula with which she confessed to anything that had been repressed.

2. This remark gave evidence of a complete misunderstanding of the rules of dream-interpretation, though on other occasions Dora was perfectly familiar with them. This fact, coupled with the hesitancy and meagreness of her associations with the jewel-case, showed me that we were here dealing with material which had been very intensely repressed.

'I will explain that to you presently. Does nothing else occur to you in connection with the jewel-case? So far you have only talked about jewellery and have said nothing about a case.'

'Yes, Herr K. had made me a present of an expensive jewel-case a little time before.'

'Then a return-present would have been very appropriate. Perhaps you do not know that "jewel-case" ["*Schmuck-kästchen*"] is a favourite expression for the same thing that you alluded to not long ago by means of the reticule you were wearing[1] – for the female genitals, I mean.'

'I knew *you* would say that.'[2]

'That is to say, *you* knew that it *was* so. – The meaning of the dream is now becoming even clearer. You said to yourself: "This man is persecuting me; he wants to force his way into my room. My 'jewel-case' is in danger, and if anything happens it will be Father's fault." For that reason in the dream you chose a situation which expresses the opposite – a danger from which your father is *saving* you. In this part of the dream everything is turned into its opposite; you will soon discover why. As you say, the mystery turns upon your mother. You ask how she comes into the dream? She is, as you know, your former rival in your father's affections. In the incident of the bracelet, you would have been glad to accept what your mother had rejected. Now let us put "give" instead of "accept" and "withhold" instead of "reject". Then it means that you were ready to give your father what your mother withheld from him; and the thing in question was connected with jewellery.[3] Now bring your mind back to the jewel-case which Herr K. gave you. You have there the starting-point for a parallel line of thoughts, in which Herr K. is to be put in the place of your father just as he was in the matter of standing beside your bed. He gave you a

1. This reference to the reticule will be explained further on [p. 112 f].

2. A very common way of putting aside a piece of knowledge that emerges from the repressed.

3. We shall be able later on to interpret even the drops in a way which will fit in with the context [p. 128 ff.].

jewel-case; so you are to give him your jewel-case. That was why I spoke just now of a "return-present". In this line of thoughts your mother must be replaced by Frau K. (You will not deny that she, at any rate, was present at the time.) So you are ready to give Herr K. what his wife withholds from him. That is the thought which has had to be repressed with so much energy, and which has made it necessary for every one of its elements to be turned into its opposite. The dream confirms once more what I had already told you before you dreamt it – that you are summoning up your old love for your father in order to protect yourself against your love for Herr K. But what do all these efforts show? Not only that you are afraid of Herr K., but that you are still more afraid of yourself, and of the temptation you feel to yield to him. In short, these efforts prove once more how deeply you loved him.'[1]

Naturally Dora would not follow me in this part of the interpretation. I myself, however, had been able to arrive at a further step in the interpretation, which seemed to me indispensable both for the anamnesis of the case and for the theory of dreams. I promised to communicate this to Dora at the next session.

The fact was that I could not forget the hint which seemed to be conveyed by the ambiguous words already noticed – *that it might be necessary to leave the room; that an accident might happen in the night.* Added to this was the fact that the elucidation of the dream seemed to me incomplete so long as a particular requirement remained unsatisfied; for, though I do not wish to insist

---

1. I added: 'Moreover, the re-appearance of the dream in the last few days forces me to the conclusion that you consider that the same situation has arisen once again, and that you have decided to give up the treatment – to which, after all, it is only your father who makes you come.' The sequel showed how correct my guess had been. At this point my interpretation touches for a moment upon the subject of 'transference' – a theme which is of the highest practical and theoretical importance, but into which I shall not have much further opportunity of entering in the present paper. [See, however, p. 157 ff.]

that this requirement is a universal one, I have a predilection for discovering a means of satisfying it. A regularly formed dream stands, as it were, upon two legs, one of which is in contact with the main and current exciting cause, and the other with some momentous event in the years of childhood. The dream sets up a connection between those two factors – the event during childhood and the event of the present day – and it endeavours to re-shape the present on the model of the remote past. For the wish which creates the dream always springs from the period of childhood; and it is continually trying to summon childhood back into reality and to correct the present day by the measure of childhood. I believed that I could already clearly detect those elements of Dora's dream which could be pieced together into an allusion to an event in childhood.

I opened the discussion of the subject with a little experiment, which was, as usual, successful. There happened to be a large match-stand on the table. I asked Dora to look round and see whether she noticed anything special on the table, something that was not there as a rule. She noticed nothing. I then asked her if she knew why children were forbidden to play with matches.

'Yes; on account of the risk of fire. My uncle's children are very fond of playing with matches.'

'Not only on that account. They are warned not to "play with fire", and a particular belief is associated with the warning.'

She knew nothing about it. – 'Very well, then; the fear is that if they do they will wet their bed. The antithesis of "water" and "fire" must be at the bottom of this. Perhaps it is believed that they will dream of fire and then try and put it out with water. I cannot say exactly.[1] But I notice that the antithesis of water and fire has been extremely useful to you in the dream. Your mother wanted to save the jewel-case so that it should not be *burnt*; while in the dream-thoughts it is a question of the

1. [Freud returned to this question three or four times–cf. his paper on the acquisition of fire (1932a), *P.F.L.*, **13**, 227 ff.]

"jewel-case" not being *wetted*. But fire is not only used as the contrary of water, it also serves directly to represent love (as in the phrase "to be *consumed* with love"). So that from "fire" one set of rails runs by way of this symbolic meaning to thoughts of love; while the other set runs by way of the contrary "water", and, after sending off a branch line which provides another connection with "love" (for love also makes things wet), leads in a different direction. And what direction can that be? Think of the expressions you used: that *an accident might happen in the night*, and that *it might be necessary to leave the room*. Surely the allusion must be to a physical need? And if you transpose the accident into childhood what can it be but bedwetting? But what is usually done to prevent children from wetting their bed? Are they not woken up in the night out of their sleep, *exactly as your father woke you up in the dream*? This, then, must be the actual occurrence which enabled you to substitute your father for Herr K., who really woke you up out of your sleep. I am accordingly driven to conclude that you were addicted to bed-wetting up to a later age than is usual with children. The same must also have been true of your brother; for your father said: "*I refuse to let my two children* go to their destruction . . ." Your brother has no other sort of connection with the real situation at the K.'s; he had not gone with you to L—. And now, what have your recollections to say to this?'

'I know nothing about myself,' was her reply, 'but my brother used to wet his bed up till his sixth or seventh year; and it used sometimes to happen to him in the daytime too.'

I was on the point of remarking to her how much easier it is to remember things of that kind about one's brother than about oneself, when she continued the train of recollections which had been revived: 'Yes. I used to do it too, for some time, but not until my seventh or eighth year. It must have been serious, because I remember now that the doctor was called in. It lasted till a short time before my nervous asthma' [p. 51].

'And what did the doctor say to it?'

'He explained it as nervous weakness; it would soon pass off, he thought; and he prescribed a tonic.'[1]

The interpretation of the dream now seemed to me to be complete.[2] But Dora brought me an addendum to the dream on the very next day. She had forgotten to relate, she said, that each time after waking up she had smelt smoke. Smoke, of course, fitted in well with fire, but it also showed that the dream had a special relation to myself; for when she used to assert that there was nothing concealed behind this or that, I would often say by way of rejoinder: 'There can be no smoke without fire!' Dora objected, however, to such a purely personal interpretation, saying that Herr K. and her father were passionate smokers – as I am too, for the matter of that. She herself had smoked during her stay by the lake, and Herr K. had rolled a cigarette for her before he began his unlucky proposal. She thought, too, that she clearly remembered having noticed the smell of smoke on the three occasions of the dream's occurrence at L—, and not for the first time at its recent reappearance. As she would give me no further information, it was left to me to determine how this addendum was to be introduced into the texture of the dream-thoughts. One thing which I had to go upon was the fact that the smell of smoke had only come up as an addendum to the dream, and must therefore have had to overcome a particularly strong effort on the part of repression.[3] Accordingly it was probably related to the thoughts which were the most

1. This physician was the only one in whom she showed any confidence, because this episode showed her that he had not penetrated her secret. She felt afraid of any other doctor about whom she had not yet been able to form a judgement, and we can now see that the motive of her fear was the possibility that he might guess her secret.

2. The essence of the dream might perhaps be translated into words such as these: 'The temptation is so strong. Dear Father, protect me again as you used to in my childhood, and prevent my bed from being wetted!'

3. [See below, p. 140, n. 2.]

obscurely presented and the most successfully repressed in the dream, to the thoughts, that is, concerned with the temptation to show herself willing to yield to the man. If that were so, the addendum to the dream could scarcely mean anything else than the longing for a kiss, which, with a smoker, would necessarily smell of smoke. But a kiss had passed between Herr K. and Dora some two years further back [p. 58 f.], and it would certainly have been repeated more than once if she had given way to him. So the thoughts of temptation seemed in this way to have harked back to the earlier scene, and to have revived the memory of the kiss against whose seductive influence the little 'thumb-sucker' had defended herself at the time, by the feeling of disgust. Taking into consideration, finally, the indications which seemed to point to there having been a transference on to me – since I am a smoker too – I came to the conclusion that the idea had probably occurred to her one day during a session that she would like to have a kiss from me. This would have been the exciting cause which led her to repeat the warning dream and to form her intention of stopping the treatment. Everything fits together very satisfactorily upon this view; but owing to the characteristics of 'transference' its validity is not susceptible of definite proof. [Cf. p. 159 and n.]

I might at this point hesitate whether I should first consider the light thrown by this dream on the history of the case, or whether I should rather begin by dealing with the objection to my theory of dreams which may be based on it. I shall take the former course.

The significance of enuresis in the early history of neurotics is worth going into thoroughly. For the sake of clearness I will confine myself to remarking that Dora's case of bed-wetting was not the usual one. The disorder was not simply that the habit had persisted beyond what is considered the normal period, but, according to her explicit account, it had begun by disappearing and had then returned at a relatively late age – after her sixth year [p. 108]. Bed-wetting of this kind has, to the best of my knowledge, no more likely cause than masturbation, a habit whose importance in the aetiology of bed-wetting in general is still insufficiently appreciated. In my experience, the children concerned have themselves at one time been very well aware of this connection, and all its psychological consequences follow from it as though they had never forgotten it. Now, at the time when Dora reported the dream, we were engaged upon a line of enquiry which led straight towards an admission that she had masturbated in childhood. A short while before, she had raised the question of why it was that precisely she had fallen ill, and, before I could answer, had put the blame on her father. The justification for this was forthcoming not out of her unconscious thoughts but from her conscious knowledge. It turned out, to my astonishment, that the girl knew what the nature of her father's illness had been. After his return from consulting me [p. 49] she had overheard a conversation in which the name of the disease had been mentioned. At a still earlier period – at the time of the detached retina [p. 48] – an oculist who was called in must have hinted at a luetic aetiology; for the inquisitive and anxious girl overheard an old aunt of hers saying to her mother: 'He was ill before his marriage, you know', and adding something which she could not understand, but which she subsequently connected in her mind with improper subjects.

Her father, then, had fallen ill through leading a loose life, and she assumed that he had handed on his bad health to her by heredity. I was careful not to tell her that, as I have already mentioned (p. 50 n.), I too was of opinion that the offspring of luetics were very specially predisposed to severe neuro-psychoses. The line of thought in which she brought this accusation against her father was continued in her unconscious material. For several days on end she identified herself with her mother by means of slight symptoms and peculiarities of manner, which gave her an opportunity for some really remarkable achievements in the direction of intolerable behaviour. She then allowed it to transpire that she was thinking of a stay she had made at Franzensbad,[1] which she had visited with her mother – I forget in what year. Her mother was suffering from abdominal pains and from a discharge (a catarrh) which necessitated a cure at Franzensbad. It was Dora's view – and here again she was probably right – that this illness was due to her father, who had thus handed on his venereal disease to her mother. It was quite natural that in drawing this conclusion she should, like the majority of laymen, have confused gonorrhoea and syphilis, as well as what is contagious and what is hereditary. The persistence with which she held to this identification with her mother almost forced me to ask her whether she too was suffering from a venereal disease; and I then learnt that she was afflicted with a catarrh (leucorrhoea) whose beginning, she said, she could not remember.

I then understood that behind the train of thought in which she brought these open accusations against her father there lay concealed as usual a *self*-accusation. I met her half-way by assuring her that in my view the occurrence of leucorrhoea in young girls pointed primarily to masturbation, and I considered that all the other causes which were commonly assigned to that complaint were put in the background by masturbation.[2] I added that she was now on the way to finding an answer to her own question of why it was that precisely she had fallen ill – by confessing that she had masturbated, probably in childhood. Dora denied flatly that she could remember any such thing. But a few days later she did something which I could not help regarding as a further step towards the confession. For on that day she wore at her waist – a thing she never did on any other occasion before or after – a small reticule of a shape which had just come into fashion; and, as she lay on the sofa and talked, she kept playing with it – opening it, putting a finger into it, shutting it again, and so on. I looked on for some time, and

1. [The Bohemian Spa.]
2. [*Footnote added* 1923:] This is an extreme view which I should no longer maintain today.

then explained to her the nature of a 'symptomatic act'.[1] I give the name of symptomatic acts to those acts which people perform, as we say, automatically, unconsciously, without attending to them, or as if in a moment of distraction. They are actions to which people would like to deny any significance, and which, if questioned about them, they would explain as being indifferent and accidental. Closer observation, however, will show that these actions, about which consciousness knows nothing or wishes to know nothing, in fact give expression to unconscious thoughts and impulses, and are therefore most valuable and instructive as being manifestations of the unconscious which have been able to come to the surface. There are two sorts of conscious attitudes possible towards these symptomatic acts. If we can ascribe inconspicuous motives to them we recognize their existence; but if no such pretext can be found for conscious use we usually fail altogether to notice that we have performed them. Dora found no difficulty in producing a motive: 'Why should I not wear a reticule like this, as it is now the fashion to do?' But a justification of this kind does not dismiss the possibility of the action in question having an unconscious origin. Though on the other hand the existence of such an origin and the meaning attributed to the act cannot be conclusively established. We must content ourselves with recording the fact that such a meaning fits in quite extraordinarily well with the situation as a whole and with the programme laid down by the unconscious.

On some other occasion I will publish a collection of these symptomatic acts as they are to be observed in the healthy and in neurotics. They are sometimes very easy to interpret. Dora's reticule, which came apart at the top in the usual way, was nothing but a representation of the genitals, and her playing with it, her opening it and putting her finger in it, was an entirely unembarrassed yet unmistakable pantomimic announcement of what she would like to do with them – namely,

1. See my *Psychopathology of Everyday Life*, 1901*b* [Chapter IX, *P.F.L.*, 5, 247 ff.].

to masturbate. A very entertaining episode of a similar kind occurred to me a short time ago. In the middle of a session the patient – a lady who was no longer young – brought out a small ivory box, ostensibly in order to refresh herself with a sweet. She made some efforts to open it, and then handed it to me so that I might convince myself how hard it was to open. I expressed my suspicion that the box must mean something special, for this was the very first time I had seen it, although its owner had been coming to me for more than a year. To this the lady eagerly replied: 'I always have this box about me; I take it with me wherever I go.' She did not calm down until I had pointed out to her with a laugh how well her words were adapted to quite another meaning. The box – [in German] Dose, πύξις–, like the reticule and the jewel-case, was once again only a substitute for the shell of Venus, for the female genitals.

There is a great deal of symbolism of this kind in life, but as a rule we pass it by without heeding it. When I set myself the task of bringing to light what human beings keep hidden within them, not by the compelling power of hypnosis, but by observing what they say and what they show, I thought the task was a harder one than it really is. He that has eyes to see and ears to hear may convince himself that no mortal can keep a secret. If his lips are silent, he chatters with his finger-tips; betrayal oozes out of him at every pore. And thus the task of making conscious the most hidden recesses of the mind is one which it is quite possible to accomplish.

Dora's symptomatic act with the reticule did not immediately precede the dream. She started the sessions which brought us the narrative of the dream with another symptomatic act. As I came into the room in which she was waiting she hurriedly concealed a letter which she was reading. I naturally asked her whom the letter was from, and at first she refused to tell me. Something then came out which was a matter of complete indifference and had no relation to the treatment. It was a letter from her grandmother, in which she begged Dora to write to her more often. I believe that Dora only wanted to play 'secrets' with me, and to hint that she was on the point of allowing her secret to be torn from her by the doctor. I was then in a position to explain her antipathy to every new doctor. She was afraid lest he might arrive at the foundation of her illness, either by examining her and discovering her catarrh, or by questioning her and eliciting the fact of her addiction to bed-wetting – lest he might guess, in short, that she had masturbated. And afterwards she would speak very contemptuously of the doctor whose perspicacity she had evidently over-estimated beforehand. [Cf. p. 109, *n*. 1.]

The reproaches against her father for having made her ill, together with the self-reproach underlying them, the leucorrhoea, the playing with the reticule, the bed-wetting after her sixth year, the secret which she would not allow the doctors to tear from her – the circumstantial evidence of her having masturbated in childhood seems to me complete and without a flaw. In the present case I had begun to suspect the masturbation when she had told me of her cousin's gastric pains (p. 70), and had then identified herself with her by complaining for days together of similar painful sensations. It is well known that gastric pains occur especially often in those who masturbate. According to a personal communication made to me by Wilhelm Fliess, it is precisely gastralgias of this character which can be interrupted by an application of cocaine to the 'gastric spot' discovered by him in the nose, and which can be cured by the cauterization of the same spot.[1] In confirmation of my suspicion Dora gave me two facts from her conscious knowledge: she herself had frequently suffered from gastric pains, and she had good reasons for believing that her cousin was a masturbator. It is a very common thing for patients to recognize in other people a connection which, on account of their emotional resistances, they cannot perceive in themselves. And, indeed, Dora no longer denied my supposition, although she still

1. [Some account of this will be found in Section I of Kris's introduction to Freud's correspondence with Fliess (Freud, 1950*a*).]

remembered nothing. Even the date which she assigned to the bed-wetting, when she said that it lasted 'till a short time before the appearance of the nervous asthma' [p. 108], appears to me to be of clinical significance. Hysterical symptoms hardly ever appear so long as children are masturbating, but only afterwards, when a period of abstinence has set in;[1] they form a substitute for masturbatory satisfaction, the desire for which continues to persist in the unconscious until another and more normal kind of satisfaction appears – where that is still attainable. For upon whether it is still attainable or not depends the possibility of a hysteria being cured by marriage and normal sexual intercourse. But if the satisfaction afforded in marriage is again removed – as it may be owing to *coitus interruptus*, psychological estrangement, or other causes – then the libido flows back again into its old channel and manifests itself once more in hysterical symptoms.

I should like to be able to add some definite information as to when and under what particular influence Dora gave up masturbating; but owing to the incompleteness of the analysis I have only fragmentary material to present. We have heard that the bed-wetting lasted until shortly before she first fell ill with dyspnoea. Now the only light she was able to throw upon this first attack was that at the time of its occurrence her father was away from home for the first time since his health had improved. In this small recollection there must be a trace of an allusion to the aetiology of the dyspnoea. Dora's symptomatic acts and certain other signs gave me good reasons for supposing that the child, whose bedroom had been next door to her parents', had overheard her father in his wife's room at night and had heard him (for he was always short of breath) breathing hard while they had intercourse. Children, in such circumstances, divine something sexual in the uncanny sounds that

1. This is also true in principle of adults; but in their case a *relative* abstinence, a diminution in the amount of masturbation, is a sufficient cause, so that, if the libido is very strong, hysteria and masturbation may be simultaneously present.

reach their ears. Indeed, the movements expressive of sexual excitement lie within them ready to hand, as innate pieces of mechanism. I maintained years ago that the dyspnoea and palpitations that occur in hysteria and anxiety neurosis are only detached fragments of the act of copulation;[1] and in many cases, as in Dora's, I have been able to trace back the symptom of dyspnoea or nervous asthma to the same exciting cause – to the patient's having overheard sexual intercourse taking place between adults. The sympathetic excitement which may be supposed to have occurred in Dora on such an occasion may very easily have made the child's sexuality veer round and have replaced her inclination to masturbation by an inclination to anxiety. A little while later, when her father was away and the child, devotedly in love with him, was wishing him back, she must have reproduced in the form of an attack of asthma the impression she had received. She had preserved in her memory the event which had occasioned the first onset of the symptom, and we can conjecture from it the nature of the train of thought, charged with anxiety, which had accompanied the attack. The first attack had come on after she had over-exerted herself on an expedition in the mountains [p. 51], so that she had probably been really a little out of breath. To this was added the thought that her father was forbidden to climb mountains and was not allowed to over-exert himself, because he suffered from shortness of breath; then came the recollection of how much he had exerted himself with her mother that night, and the question whether it might not have done him harm; next came concern whether *she* might not have over-exerted herself in masturbating – an act which, like the other, led to a sexual orgasm accompanied by slight dyspnoea – and finally came a return of the dyspnoea in an intensified form as a symptom. Part of this material I was able to obtain directly from the

---

1. [In Section III of Freud's first paper on anxiety neurosis (1895*b*), *P.F.L.*, **10**, 59. Much later he put forward another explanation of the physical accompaniments of anxiety, in Chapter VIII of *Inhibitions, Symptoms and Anxiety* (1926*d*), ibid., **10**, 288–9.]

analysis, but the rest required supplementing. But the way in which the occurrence of masturbation in Dora's case was verified has already shown us that material belonging to a single subject can only be collected piece by piece at various times and in different connections.[1]

There now arise a whole series of questions of the greatest importance concerning the aetiology of hysteria: is Dora's case to be regarded as aetiologically typical? does it represent the only type of causation? and so on. Nevertheless, I am sure that I am taking the right course in postponing my answer to such questions until a considerable number of other cases have been similarly analysed and published. Moreover, I should have to

1. The proof of infantile masturbation in other cases is established in a precisely similar way. The evidence for it is mostly of a similar nature: indications of the presence of leucorrhoea, bed-wetting, hand-cere-monials (obsessional washing), and such things. It is always possible to discover with certainty from the nature of the symptoms of the case whether the habit was discovered by the person in charge of the child or not, or whether this sexual activity was brought to an end by long efforts on the child's part to break itself of the habit, or by a sudden change. In Dora's case the masturbation had remained undiscovered, and had come to an end at a single blow (cf. her secret, her fear of doctors, and the replacement by dyspnoea). The patients, it is true, invariably dispute the conclusiveness of circumstantial evidence such as this, and they do so even when they have retained a conscious recollec-tion of the catarrh or of their mother's warning (e.g. 'That makes people stupid; it's dangerous'). But some time later the memory, which has been so long repressed, of this piece of infantile sexual life emerges with certainty, and it does so in every instance. I am reminded of the case of a patient of mine suffering from obsessions, which were direct deriva-tives of infantile masturbation. Her peculiarities, such as self-prohibi-tions and self-punishments, the feeling that if she had done this she must not do that, the idea that she must not be interrupted, the introduction of pauses between one procedure (with her hands), and the next, her hand-washing, etc. – all of these turned out to be unaltered fragments of her nurse's efforts to break her of the habit. The only thing which had remained permanently in her memory were the words of warning: 'Ugh! That's dangerous!' Compare also in this connection my *Three Essays on the Theory of Sexuality*, 1905*d* [the section on 'Masturbatory Sexual Manifestations' in the second essay (*P.F.L.*, **7**, 102 ff.)].

begin by criticizing the way in which the questions are framed. Instead of answering 'Yes' or 'No' to the question whether the aetiology of this case is to be looked for in masturbation during childhood, I should first have to discuss the concept of aetiology as applied to the psychoneuroses. It would then become evident that the standpoint from which I should be able to answer the question would be very widely removed from the standpoint from which it was put. Let it suffice if we can reach the conviction that in this case the occurrence of masturbation in childhood is established, and that its occurrence cannot be an accidental element nor an immaterial one in the conformation of the clinical picture.[1]

A consideration of the significance of the leucorrhoea to which Dora admitted promises to give us a still better understanding of her symptoms. She had learnt to call her affection a 'catarrh' at the time when her mother had had to visit Franzensbad on account of a similar complaint [p. 112]; and the word 'catarrh' acted once again as a 'switch-word' [p. 100 n.], and enabled the whole set of thoughts upon her father's responsibility for her illness to manifest themselves in the symptom of the cough. The cough, which no doubt originated in the first instance from a slight actual catarrh, was, moreover, an

1. Dora's brother must have been concerned in some way with her having acquired the habit of masturbation; for in this connection she told me, with all the emphasis which betrays the presence of a 'screen memory', that her brother used regularly to pass on all his infectious illnesses to her, and that while he used to have them lightly she used, on the contrary, to have them severely [p. 51]. In the dream her brother as well as she was saved from 'destruction' [p. 99]; he, too, had been subject to bed-wetting, but had got over the habit before his sister [p. 108]. Her declaration that she had been able to keep abreast with her brother up to the time of her first illness, but that after that she had fallen behind him in her studies, was in a certain sense also a 'screen memory'. It was as though she had been a boy up till that moment, and had then become girlish for the first time. She had in truth been a wild creature; but after the 'asthma' she became quiet and well-behaved. That illness formed the boundary between two phases of her sexual life, of which the first was masculine in character, and the second feminine.

imitation of her father (whose lungs were affected), and could serve as an expression of her sympathy and concern for him. But besides this, it proclaimed aloud, as it were, something of which she may then have been still unconscious: 'I am my father's daughter. I have a catarrh, just as he has. He has made me ill, just as he has made Mother ill. It is from him that I have got my evil passions, which are punished by illness.'[1]

Let us next attempt to put together the various determinants that we have found for Dora's attacks of coughing and hoarseness. In the lowest stratum we must assume the presence of a real and organically determined irritation of the throat – which acted like the grain of sand around which an oyster forms its pearl. This irritation was susceptible to fixation, because it concerned a part of the body which in Dora had to a high degree retained its significance as an erotogenic zone. And the irritation was consequently well fitted to give expression to excited states of the libido. It was brought to fixation by what was probably its first psychical coating – her sympathetic imitation of her ill father – and by her subsequent self-reproaches on account of her 'catarrh'. The same group of symptoms, moreover, showed itself capable of representing her relations with Herr K.; it could express her regret at his absence and her wish to make him a better wife. After a part of her libido had once more turned towards her father, the symp-

1. This word ['catarrh'] played the same part with the fourteen-year-old girl whose case history I have compressed into a few lines on p. 55 n. I had established the child in a pension with an intelligent lady, who took charge of her for me. The lady reported that the little girl could not bear her to be in the room while she was going to bed, and that when she was in bed she had a marked cough, of which there was no trace in the daytime. When the girl was questioned about these symptoms, the only thing that occurred to her was that her grandmother coughed in the same way, and that she was said to have a catarrh. It was clear from this that the child herself had a catarrh, and that she did not want to be observed while she performed her evening ablutions. This catarrh, which, thanks to its name, had been *displaced from the lower to the upper part of her body* [see p. 61], exhibited a quite unusual degree of intensity.

tom obtained what was perhaps its last meaning; it came to represent sexual intercourse with her father by means of Dora's identifying herself with Frau K. I can guarantee that this series is by no means complete. Unfortunately, an incomplete analysis cannot enable us to follow the chronological sequence of the changes in a symptom's meaning, or to display clearly the succession and coexistence of its various meanings. It may legitimately be expected of a complete analysis that it should fulfil these demands.

I must now proceed to touch upon some further relations existing between Dora's genital catarrh and her hysterical symptoms. At a time when any psychological elucidation of hysteria was still very remote, I used to hear experienced fellow-doctors who were my seniors maintain that in the case of hysterical patients suffering from leucorrhoea any increase in the catarrh was regularly followed by an intensification of the hysterical troubles, and especially of loss of appetite and vomiting. No one was very clear about the nature of the connection, but I fancy the general inclination was towards the opinion held by gynaecologists. According to their hypothesis, as is well known, disorders of the genitals exercise upon the nervous functions a direct and far-reaching influence in the nature of an organic disturbance – though a therapeutic test of this theory is apt to leave one in the lurch. In the light of our present knowledge we cannot exclude the possibility of the existence of a direct organic influence of this sort; but it is at all events easier to indicate its psychical coating. The pride taken by women in the appearance of their genitals is quite a special feature of their vanity; and disorders of the genitals which they think calculated to inspire feelings of repugnance or even disgust have an incredible power of humiliating them, of lowering their self-esteem, and of making them irritable, sensitive, and distrustful. An abnormal secretion of the mucous membrane of the vagina is looked upon as a source of disgust.

It will be remembered that Dora had a lively feeling of disgust after being kissed by Herr K., and that we saw grounds for completing her story of the scene of the kiss by supposing that, while she was being embraced, she noticed the pressure of the man's erect member against her body [p. 60 ff.]. We now learn further that the same governess whom Dora cast off on account of her faithlessness had, from her own experience of life, propounded to Dora the view that all men were frivolous and untrustworthy. To Dora that must mean that all men were like her father. But she thought her father suffered from venereal disease – for had he not handed it on to her and her mother? She might therefore have imagined to herself that all men suffered from venereal disease, and naturally her conception of venereal disease was modelled on her one experience of it – a personal one at that. To suffer from venereal disease, therefore, meant for her to be afflicted with a disgusting discharge. So may we not have here a further motive for the disgust she felt at the moment of the embrace? Thus the disgust which was transferred on to the contact of the man would be a feeling which had been projected according to the primitive mechanism I have already mentioned (p. 67), and would be related ultimately to her own leucorrhoea.

I suspect that we are here concerned with unconscious processes of thought which are twined around a pre-existing structure of organic connections, much as festoons of flowers are twined around a wire; so that on another occasion one might find other lines of thought inserted between the same points of departure and termination. Yet a knowledge of the thought-connections which have been effective in the individual case is of a value which cannot be exaggerated for clearing up the symptoms. It is only because the analysis was prematurely broken off that we have been obliged in Dora's case to resort to framing conjectures and filling in deficiencies. Whatever I have brought forward for filling up the gaps is based upon other cases which have been more thoroughly analysed.

The dream from the analysis of which we have derived this

information corresponded, as we have seen, to an intention which Dora carried with her into her sleep. It was therefore repeated each night until the intention had been carried out; and it reappeared years later when an occasion arose for forming an analogous intention. The intention might have been consciously expressed in some such words as these: 'I must fly from this house, for I see that my virginity is threatened here; I shall go away with my father, and I shall take precautions not to be surprised while I am dressing in the morning.' These thoughts were clearly expressed in the dream; they formed part of a mental current which had achieved consciousness and a dominating position in waking life. Behind them can be discerned obscure traces of a train of thought which formed part of a contrary current and had consequently been suppressed. This other train of thought culminated in the temptation to yield to the man, out of gratitude for the love and tenderness he had shown her during the last few years, and it may perhaps have revived the memory of the only kiss she had so far had from him. But according to the theory which I developed in my *Interpretation of Dreams* such elements as these are not enough for the formation of a dream. On that theory a dream is not an intention represented as having been carried out, but a wish represented as having been fulfilled, and, moreover, in most cases a wish dating from childhood. It is our business now to discover whether this principle may not be contradicted by the present dream.

The dream does in fact contain infantile material, though it is impossible at a first glance to discover any connections between that material and Dora's intention of flying from Herr K.'s house and the temptation of his presence. Why should a recollection have emerged of her bed-wetting when she was a child and of the trouble her father used to take to teach the child clean habits? We may answer this by saying that it was only by the help of this train of thought that it was possible to suppress the other thoughts which were so intensely occupied with the temptation to yield or that it was possible to secure the dominance of the intention which had been formed of combating those other thoughts. The child decided to fly *with* her father; in reality she fled *to* her father because she was afraid of the man who was pursuing her; she summoned up an infantile affection for her father so that it might protect her against her present affection for a stranger. Her father was himself partly responsible for her present danger, for he had handed her over to this strange man in the interests of his own love-affair. And how much better it had been when that same father of hers had loved no one more than her, and had exerted all his strength to save her from the dangers that had then threatened her! The infantile, and now unconscious, wish to put her father in the strange man's place had the potency necessary for the formation of a dream. If there were a past situation similar to a present one, and differing from it only in being concerned with one instead of with the other of the two persons mentioned in the wish, that situation would become the main one in the dream. But there *had* been such a situation. Her father had once stood beside her bed, just as Herr K. had the day before, and had woken her up, with a kiss perhaps, as Herr K. may have meant to do. Thus her intention of flying from the house was not in itself capable of producing a dream; but it became so by being associated with another intention which was founded upon infantile wishes. The wish to replace Herr K. by her father provided the necessary motive power for the dream. Let me recall the interpretation I was led to adopt of Dora's reinforced train of thought about her father's relations with Frau K. My interpretation was that she had at that point summoned up an infantile affection for her father so as to be able to keep her repressed love for Herr K. in its state of repression [p. 92]. This same sudden revulsion in the patient's mental life was reflected in the dream.

I have made one or two observations in my *Interpretation of Dreams*[1] on the relation between the waking thoughts which are continued into sleep (the 'day's residues') and the uncon-

1. [Chapter VII, Section C (*P.F.L.*, 4, 713–14).]

scious wish which forms the dream. I will quote them here as they stand, for I have nothing to add to them, and the analysis of this dream of Dora's proves afresh that the facts are as I have supposed: 'I am ready to admit that there is a whole class of dreams the *instigation* to which arises principally or even exclusively from the residues of daytime life; and I think that even my wish that I might at long last become a Professor Extraordinarius[1] might have allowed me to sleep through the night in peace if my worry over my friend's health had not still persisted from the previous day. But the worry alone could not have made a dream. The *motive force* which the dream required had to be provided by a wish; it was the business of the worry to get hold of a wish to act as the motive force of the dream.

'The position may be explained by an analogy. A daytime thought may very well play the part of *entrepreneur* for a dream; but the *entrepreneur*, who, as people say, has the idea and the initiative to carry it out, can do nothing without capital; he needs a *capitalist* who can afford the outlay, and the capitalist who provides the psychical outlay for the dream is invariably and indisputably, whatever may be the thoughts of the previous day, *a wish from the unconscious*.'

Any one who has learnt to appreciate the delicacy of the fabric of structures such as dreams will not be surprised to find that Dora's wish that her father might take the place of the man who was her tempter called up in her memory not merely a casual collection of material from her childhood, but precisely such material as was most intimately bound up with the suppression of her temptation. For if Dora felt unable to yield to her love for the man, if in the end she repressed that love instead of surrendering to it, there was no factor upon which her decision depended more directly than upon her premature sexual enjoyment and its consequence – her bed-wetting, her

1. This is a reference to the analysis of a dream quoted in the book as an example [the dream of 'Otto looking ill', in Chapter V, Section D (*P.F.L.*, 4, 372 ff.).]

catarrh, and her disgust. An early history of this kind can afford a basis for two kinds of behaviour in response to the demands of love in maturity – which of the two will depend upon the summation of constitutional determinants in the subject. He will either exhibit an abandonment to sexuality which is entirely without resistances and borders upon perversity; or there will be a reaction – he will repudiate sexuality, and will at the same time fall ill of a neurosis. In the case of our present patient, her constitution and the high level of her intellectual and moral upbringing decided in favour of the latter course.

I should like, further, to draw special attention to the fact that the analysis of this dream has given us access to certain details of the pathogenically operative events which had otherwise been inaccessible to memory, or at all events to reproduction. The recollection of the bed-wetting in childhood had, as we have seen, already been repressed. And Dora had never mentioned the details of her persecution by Herr K.; they had never occurred to her mind.

I add a few remarks which may help towards the synthesis of this dream.[1] The dream-work began on the afternoon of the day after the scene in the wood, after Dora had noticed that she was no longer able to lock the door of her room [p. 102]. She then said to herself: 'I am threatened by a serious danger here,' and formed her intention of not stopping on in the house alone but of going off with her father. This intention became capable of forming a dream, because it succeeded in finding a continuation in the unconscious. What corresponded to it there was her summoning up her infantile love for her father as a protection against the present temptation. The change which thus took place in her became fixed and brought her into the

1. [The remainder of this section was printed as a footnote in editions earlier than 1924. On the subject of the 'synthesis' of dreams see *The Interpretation of Dreams*, Chapter VI, beginning of Section C (*P.F.L.*, 4, 420–21).]

attitude shown by her *supervalent* train of thought – jealousy of Frau K. on her father's account, as though she herself were in love with him. There was a conflict within her between a temptation to yield to the man's proposal and a composite force rebelling against that feeling. This latter force was made up of motives of respectability and good sense, of hostile feelings caused by the governess's disclosures (jealousy and wounded pride, as we shall see later [p. 146 f.]), and of a neurotic element, namely, the tendency to a repudiation of sexuality which was already present in her and was based on her childhood history. Her love for her father, which she summoned up to protect her against the temptation, had its origin in this same childhood history.

Her intention of flying to her father, which, as we have seen, reached down into the unconscious, was transformed by the dream into a situation which presented as fulfilled the wish that her father should save her from the danger. In this process it was necessary to put on one side a certain thought which stood in the way; for it was her father himself who had brought her into the danger. The hostile feeling against her father (her desire for revenge), which was here suppressed, was, as we shall discover, one of the motive forces of the second dream [p. 137 f.].

According to the necessary conditions of dream-formation the imagined situation must be chosen so as to reproduce a situation in infancy. A special triumph is achieved if a recent situation, perhaps even the very situation which is the exciting cause of the dream, can be transformed into an infantile one. This has actually been achieved in the present case, by a purely chance disposition of the material. Just as Herr K. had stood beside her sofa and woken her up, so her father had often done in her childhood. The whole trend of her thoughts could be most aptly symbolized by her substitution of her father for Herr K. in that situation.

But the reason for which her father used to wake her up long ago had been to prevent her from making her bed wet.

This 'wet' had a decisive influence on the further content of the dream; though it was represented in it only by a distant allusion and by its opposite.

The opposite of 'wet' and 'water' can easily be 'fire' and 'burning'. The chance that, when they arrived at the place [L—], her father had expressed his anxiety at the risk of fire [p. 100], helped to decide that the danger from which her father was to rescue her should be a fire. The situation chosen for the dream-picture was based upon this chance, and upon the opposition to 'wet': 'There was a fire. Her father was standing beside her bed to wake her.' Her father's chance utterance would, no doubt, not have obtained such an important position in the dream if it had not fitted in so excellently with the dominating current of feeling, which was determined to regard him at any cost as a protector and saviour. 'He foresaw the danger from the very moment of our arrival! He was in the right!' (In actual fact, it was he who had brought the girl into danger.)

In consequence of certain connections which can easily be made from it, the word 'wet' served in the dream-thoughts as a nodal point between several groups of ideas. 'Wet' was connected not only with the bed-wetting, but also with the group of ideas relating to sexual temptation which lay suppressed behind the content of the dream. Dora knew that there was a kind of getting wet involved in sexual intercourse, and that during the act of copulation the man presented the woman with something liquid *in the form of drops*. She also knew that the danger lay precisely in that, and that it was her business to protect her genitals from being moistened.

'Wet' and 'drops' at the same time opened the way to the other group of associations – the group relating to the disgusting catarrh, which in her later years had no doubt possessed the same mortifying significance for her as the bed-wetting had in her childhood. 'Wet' in this connection had the same meaning as 'dirtied'. Her genitals, which ought to have been kept clean, had been dirtied already by the catarrh – and this applied to her mother no less than to herself (p. 112). She seemed to understand that her mother's mania for cleanliness was a reaction against this dirtying.

The two groups of ideas met in this one thought: 'Mother got both things from her father: the sexual wetness and the dirtying discharge.' Dora's jealousy of her mother was inseparable from the group of thoughts relating to her infantile love for her father which she summoned up for her protection. But this material was not yet capable of representation. If, however, a recollection could be found which was equally closely connected with both the groups related to the word 'wet', but which avoided any offensiveness, then such a recollection would be able to take over the representation in the dream of the material in question.

A recollection of this sort was furnished by the episode of the 'drops' – the jewellery ['Schmuck'] that Dora's mother wanted to have [p. 104]. In appearance the connection between this reminiscence and the two groups of thoughts relating to sexual wetness and to being dirtied was a purely external and superficial one, of a verbal character. For 'drops' was used ambiguously as a 'switch-word' [p. 100 n.], while 'jewellery' ['Schmuck'] was taken as an equivalent to 'clean', and thus as a rather forced contrary of 'dirtied'.[1] But in reality the most substantial connections can be shown to have existed between the things denoted themselves. The recollection originated from the material connected with Dora's jealousy of her mother, which, though its roots were infantile, had persisted far beyond that period. By means of these two verbal bridges it was possible to transfer on to the single reminiscence of the 'jewel-drops' the whole of the significance attaching to the ideas of her

1. [The German word 'Schmuck' has a much wider meaning than the English 'jewellery', though that is the sense in which it occurs in the compound 'Schmuckkästchen', 'jewel-case'. As a substantive, 'Schmuck' denotes 'finery' of all kinds, not only personal adornments, but embellishments of objects and decorations in general. In an adjectival sense, it can mean 'smart', 'tidy', or 'neat'.]

parents' sexual intercourse, and of her mother's gonorrhoea
and tormenting passion for cleanliness.

But a still further displacement had to be effected before this
material appeared in the dream. Though 'drops' is nearer to
the original 'wet', it was the more distant 'jewellery' that
found a place in the dream. When, therefore, this element had
been inserted into the dream-situation which had already been
established, the account might have run: 'Mother wanted to
stop and save her jewellery.' But a subsequent influence now
made itself felt, and led to the further alteration of 'jewellery'
into 'jewel-case'. This influence came from elements in the
underlying group relating to the temptation offered by Herr K.
He had never given her jewellery, but he had given her a 'case'
for it [p. 105], which meant for her all the marks of preference
and all the tenderness for which she felt she ought now to have
been grateful. And the composite word thus formed, 'jewel-
case', had beyond this a special claim to be used as a representa-
tive element in the dream. Is not 'jewel-case' ['Schmuck-
kästchen'] a term commonly used to describe female genitals
that are immaculate and intact? And is it not, on the other hand,
an innocent word? Is it not, in short, admirably calculated
both to betray and to conceal the sexual thoughts that lie behind
the dream?

'Mother's jewel-case' was therefore introduced in two places
in the dream; and this element replaced all mention of Dora's
infantile jealousy, of the drops (that is, of the sexual wetness),
of being dirtied by the discharge, and, on the other hand, of her
present thoughts connected with the temptation – the thoughts
which were urging her to reciprocate the man's love, and which
depicted the sexual situation (alike desirable and menacing) that
lay before her. The element of 'jewel-case' was more than any
other a product of condensation and displacement, and a compromise between contrary mental currents. The multiplicity of
its origin – both from infantile and contemporary sources – is
no doubt pointed to by its double appearance in the content of
the dream.

The dream was a reaction to a fresh experience of an exciting nature; and this experience must inevitably have revived the memory of the only previous experience which was at all analogous to it. The latter was the scene of the kiss in Herr K.'s place of business, when she had been seized with disgust [p. 58 f.]. But this same scene was associatively accessible from other directions too, namely, from the group of thoughts relating to the catarrh (p. 120 f.), and from her present temptation. The scene therefore brought to the dream a contribution of its own which had to be made to fit in with the dream situation that had already been laid down: 'There was a fire' ... no doubt the kiss smelt of smoke; so she smelt smoke in the dream, and the smell persisted till after she was awake [p. 109].

By inadvertence, I unfortunately left a gap in the analysis of the dream. Dora's father was made to say, 'I refuse to let my two children go to their destruction ...' ('as a result of masturbation' should no doubt be added from the dream-thoughts). Such speeches in dreams are regularly constructed out of pieces of actual speeches which have either been made or heard.[1] I ought to have made enquiries as to the actual source of this speech. The results of my enquiry would no doubt have shown that the structure of the dream was still more complicated, but would at the same time have made it easier to penetrate.

Are we to suppose that when this dream occurred at L— it had precisely the same content as when it recurred during the treatment? It does not seem necessary to do so. Experience shows that people often assert that they have had the same dream, when as a matter of fact the separate appearances of the recurrent dream have differed from one another in numerous details and in other respects that were of no small importance. Thus one of my patients told me that she had had her favourite dream again the night before, and that it always recurred in the same form: she had dreamed of swimming in the blue sea, of

1. [Cf. *The Interpretation of Dreams*, Chapter VI, Section F; *P.F.L.*, 4, 545 ff.].

joyfully cleaving her way through the waves, and so on. On closer investigation it turned out that upon a common background now one detail and now another was brought out; on one occasion, even, she was swimming in a frozen sea and was surrounded by icebergs. This patient had other dreams, which turned out to be closely connected with the recurrent one, though even she made no attempt to claim that they were identical with it. Once, for instance, she was looking at a view of Heligoland (based on a photograph, but life-size) which showed the upper and lower parts of the island simultaneously; on the sea was a ship, in which were two people whom she had known in her youth, and so on.

What is certain is that in Dora's case the dream which occurred during the treatment had gained a new significance connected with the present time, though perhaps its manifest content had not changed. The dream-thoughts behind it included a reference to my treatment, and it corresponded to a renewal of the old intention of withdrawing from a danger. If her memory was not deceiving her when she declared that even at L— she had noticed the smoke after she woke up, it must be acknowledged that she had brought my proverb, 'There can be no smoke without fire' [p. 109], very ingeniously into the completed form of the dream, in which it seemed to serve as an overdetermination of the last element. It was undeniably a mere matter of chance that the most recent exciting cause – her mother's locking the dining-room door so that her brother was shut into his bedroom [p. 100] – had provided a connection with her persecution by Herr K. at L—, where her decision had been made when she found she could not lock her bedroom door. It is possible that her brother did not appear in the dream on the earlier occasions, so that the words 'my two children' did not form part of its content until after the occurrence of its latest exciting cause.

III

THE SECOND DREAM

A FEW weeks after the first dream the second occurred, and when it had been dealt with the analysis was broken off. It cannot be made as completely intelligible as the first, but it afforded a desirable confirmation of an assumption which had become necessary about the patient's mental state [p. 144 f.], it filled up a gap in her memory [p. 146], and it made it possible to obtain a deep insight into the origin of another of her symptoms [p. 142].

Dora described the dream as follows: '*I was walking about in a town which I did not know. I saw streets and squares which were strange to me.*[1] *Then I came into a house where I lived, went to my room, and found a letter from Mother lying there. She wrote saying that as I had left home without my parents' knowledge she had not wished to write to me to say that Father was ill. "Now he is dead and if you like*[2] *you can come." I then went to the station ["Bahnhof"] and asked about a hundred times: "Where is the station?" I always got the answer: "Five minutes." I then saw a thick wood before me which I went into and there I asked a man whom I met. He said to me: "Two and a half hours more."*[3] *He offered to accompany me. But I refused and went alone. I saw the station in front of me and could not reach it. At the same time I had the usual feeling of anxiety that one has in dreams when one cannot move forward. Then I was at home. I must have been travelling in the meantime, but I know nothing about that. I walked into the porter's lodge, and enquired for our flat. The maidservant opened the door to me and*

---

1. To this she subsequently made an important addendum: '*I saw a monument in one of the squares.*'

2. To this came the addendum: '*There was a question-mark after this word, thus: "like?".*'

3. In repeating the dream she said: '*Two hours.*'

replied that Mother and the others were already at the cemetery ["Friedhof"].'[1]

It was not without some difficulty that the interpretation of this dream proceeded. In consequence of the peculiar circumstances in which the analysis was broken off – circumstances connected with the content of the dream – the whole of it was not cleared up. And for this reason, too, I am not equally certain at every point of the order in which my conclusions were reached. I will begin by mentioning the subject-matter with which the current analysis was dealing at the time when the dream intervened. For some time Dora herself had been raising a number of questions about the connection between some of her actions and the motives which presumably underlay them. One of these questions was: 'Why did I say nothing about the scene by the lake for some days after it had happened?' Her second question was: 'Why did I then suddenly tell my parents about it?' Moreover, her having felt so deeply injured by Herr K.'s proposal seemed to me in general to need explanation, especially as I was beginning to realize that Herr K. himself had not regarded his proposal to Dora as a mere frivolous attempt at seduction. I looked upon her having told her parents of the episode as an action which she had taken when she was already under the influence of a morbid craving for revenge. A normal girl, I am inclined to think, will deal with a situation of this kind by herself.

I shall present the material produced during the analysis of this dream in the somewhat haphazard order in which it recurs to my mind.

She was wandering about alone in a strange town and saw streets and squares. Dora assured me that it was certainly not B—, which I had first hit upon, but a town in which she had never

1. In the next session Dora brought me two addenda to this: '*I saw myself particularly distinctly going up the stairs,*' and '*After she had answered I went to my room, but not the least sadly, and began reading a big book that lay on my writing-table.*'

been. It was natural to suggest that she might have seen some pictures or photographs and have taken the dream-pictures from them. After this remark of mine came the addendum about the monument in one of the squares and immediately afterwards her recognition of its source. At Christmas[1] she had been sent an album from a German health-resort, containing views of the town; and the very day before the dream she had looked this out to show it to some relatives who were stopping with them. It had been put in a box for keeping pictures in, and she could not lay her hands on it at once. She had therefore said to her mother: '*Where is the box?*'[2] One of the pictures was of a square with a monument in it. The present had been sent to her by a young engineer, with whom she had once had a passing acquaintance in the manufacturing town. The young man had accepted a post in Germany, so as to become sooner self-supporting; and he took every opportunity of reminding Dora of his existence. It was easy to guess that he intended to come forward as a suitor one day, when his position had improved. But that would take time, and it meant waiting.

The wandering about in a strange town was overdetermined. It led back to one of the exciting causes from the day before. A young cousin of Dora's had come to stay with them for the holidays, and Dora had had to show him round Vienna. This cause was, it is true, a matter of complete indifference to her. But her cousin's visit reminded her of her own first brief visit to Dresden. On that occasion she had been a stranger and had wandered about, not failing, of course, to visit the famous picture gallery. Another [male] cousin of hers, who was with them and knew Dresden, had wanted to act as a guide and take her round the gallery. *But she declined and went alone*, and stopped in front of the pictures that appealed to her. She remained *two*

---

1. [The dream occurred a few days after Christmas (see p. 146).]

2. In the dream she said: '*Where is the station?*' The resemblance between the two questions led me to make an inference which I shall go into presently [p. 136].

hours in front of the Sistine Madonna, rapt in silent admiration. When I asked her what had pleased her so much about the picture she could find no clear answer to make. At last she said: 'The Madonna.'

There could be no doubt that these associations really belonged to the material concerned in forming the dream. They included portions which reappeared in the dream unchanged ('she declined and went alone' and 'two hours'). I may remark at once that 'pictures' was a nodal point in the network of her dream-thoughts (the pictures in the album, the pictures at Dresden). I should also like to single out, with a view to subsequent investigation, the theme of the 'Madonna', of the virgin mother. But what was most evident was that in this first part of the dream she was identifying herself with a young man. This young man was wandering about in a strange place, he was striving to reach a goal, but he was being kept back, he needed patience and must wait. If in all this she had been thinking of the engineer, it would have been appropriate for the goal to have been the possession of a woman, of herself. But instead of this it was – a station. Nevertheless, the relation of the question in the dream to the question which had been put in real life allows us to substitute '*box*' for 'station'.[1] A box and a woman: the notions begin to agree better.

She asked quite a hundred times . . . This led to another exciting cause of the dream, and this time to one that was less indifferent. On the previous evening they had had company, and afterwards her father had asked her to fetch him the brandy: he could not get to sleep unless he had taken some brandy. She had asked her mother for the key of the sideboard; but the latter had been deep in conversation, and had not answered her, until Dora had exclaimed with the exaggeration of impatience: 'I've asked you *a hundred times* already where the key is.' As a matter

1. ['*Schachtel*', the word which was used for 'box' by Dora in her question, is a depreciatory term for 'woman'.]

of fact, she had of course only repeated the question about *five times*.[1]

'Where is the *key*?' seems to me to be the masculine counterpart to the question 'Where is the *box*?'[2] They are therefore questions referring to – the genitals.

Dora went on to say that during this same family gathering some one had toasted her father and had expressed the hope that he might continue to enjoy the best of health for many years to come, etc. At this a strange quiver passed over her father's tired face, and she had understood what thoughts he was having to keep down. Poor sick man! who could tell what span of life was still to be his?

This brings us to the *contents of the letter* in the dream. Her father was dead, and she had left home by her own choice. In connection with this letter I at once reminded Dora of the farewell letter which she had written to her parents or had at least composed for their benefit [p. 53]. This letter had been intended to give her father a fright, so that he should give up Frau K.; or at any rate to take revenge on him if he could not be induced to do that. We are here concerned with the subject of her death and of her father's death. (Cf. 'cemetery' later on in the dream.) Shall we be going astray if we suppose that the situation which formed the façade of the dream was a phantasy of revenge directed against her father? The feelings of pity for him which she remembered from the day before would be quite in keeping with this. According to the phantasy she had left home and gone among strangers, and her father's heart had broken with grief and with longing for her. Thus she would be revenged. She understood very clearly what it was that her father needed when he could not get to sleep without a drink of

1. In the dream the number five occurs in the mention of the period of 'five minutes'. In my book on the interpretation of dreams I have given several examples of the way in which numbers occurring in the dream-thoughts are treated by dreams. We frequently find them torn out of their true context and inserted into a new one. [See *The Interpretation of Dreams*, Section F of Chapter VI; *P.F.L.*, 4, 540 ff.]

2. See the first dream, p. 102.

brandy.[1] We will make a note of Dora's *craving for revenge* as a new element to be taken into account in any subsequent synthesis of her dream-thoughts.

But the contents of the letter must be capable of further determination. What was the source of the words 'if you like'? It was at this point that the addendum of there having been a question-mark after the word 'like' occurred to Dora, and she then recognized these words as a quotation out of the letter from Frau K. which had contained the invitation to L—, the place by the lake. In that letter there had been a question-mark placed, in a most unusual fashion, in the very middle of a sentence, after the intercalated words 'if you would like to come'.

So here we were back again at the scene by the lake [p. 56] and at the problems connected with it. I asked Dora to describe the scene to me in detail. At first she produced little that was new. Herr K.'s exordium had been somewhat serious; but she had not let him finish what he had to say. No sooner had she grasped the purport of his words than she had slapped him in the face and hurried away. I enquired what his actual words had been. Dora could only remember one of his pleas: 'You know I get nothing out of my wife.'[2] In order to avoid meeting him again she had wanted to get back to L— on foot, by walking round the lake, and *she had asked a man whom she met how far it was*. On his replying that it was *'Two and a half hours'*, she had given up her intention and had after all gone back to the boat, which left soon afterwards. Herr K. had been there too and had come up to her and begged her to forgive him and not to mention the incident. But she had made no reply. – Yes. The

---

1. There can be no doubt that sexual satisfaction is the best soporific, just as sleeplessness is almost always the consequence of lack of satisfaction. Her father could not sleep because he was debarred from sexual intercourse with the woman he loved. (Compare in this connection the phrase discussed just below: 'I get nothing out of my wife.') [Cf. also the words quoted from Dora's father on p. 57.]

2. These words will enable us to solve one of our problems [p. 147].

wood in the dream had been just like the wood by the shore of the lake, the wood in which the scene she had just described once more had taken place. But she had seen precisely the same thick wood the day before, in a picture at the Secessionist exhibition. In the background of the picture there were *nymphs*.[1]

At this point a certain suspicion of mine became a certainty. The use of *'Bahnhof'* ['station'; literally, 'railway-court'][2] and *'Friedhof'* ['cemetery'; literally, 'peace-court'] to represent the female genitals was striking enough in itself, but it also served to direct my awakened curiosity to the similarly formed *'Vorhof'* ['vestibulum'; literally, 'fore-court'] – an anatomical term for a particular region of the female genitals. This might have been no more than mistaken ingenuity. But now, with the addition of 'nymphs' visible in the background of a 'thick wood', no further doubts could be entertained. Here was a symbolic geography of sex! 'Nymphae',[3] as is known to physicians though not to laymen (and even by the former the term is not very commonly used), is the name given to the labia minora, which lie in the background of the 'thick wood' of the pubic hair. But any one who employed such technical names as 'vestibulum' and 'nymphae' must have derived his knowledge from books, and not from popular ones either, but from anatomical text-books or from an encyclopaedia – the common refuge of youth when it is devoured by sexual curiosity. If this interpretation were correct, therefore, there lay concealed behind the first situation in the dream a phantasy of defloration,

1. Here for the third time we come upon 'picture' (views of towns, the Dresden gallery), but in a much more significant connection. Because of what appears in the picture (the wood, the nymphs), the *'Bild'* ['picture'] is turned into a *'Weibsbild'* [literally, 'picture of a woman' – a somewhat derogatory expression for 'woman'].

2. Moreover, a 'station' is used for purposes of *'Verkehr'* ['traffic', 'intercourse', 'sexual intercourse']: this fact determines the psychical coating in a number of cases of railway phobia.

3. [In German the same word, *'Nymphen'*, represents both 'nymphs' and 'nymphae'.]

the phantasy of a man seeking to force an entrance into the female genitals.[1]

I informed Dora of the conclusions I had reached. The impression made upon her must have been forcible, for there immediately appeared a piece of the dream which had been forgotten: *she went calmly to her room, and began reading a big book that lay on her writing-table.*[2] The emphasis here was upon the two details 'calmly' and 'big' in connection with 'book'. I asked whether the book was in encyclopaedia *format*, and she said it was. Now children never read about forbidden subjects in an encyclopaedia *calmly*. They do it in fear and trembling, with an uneasy look over their shoulder to see if some one may not be coming. Parents are very much in the way while reading of this kind is going on. But this uncomfortable situation had been radically improved, thanks to the dream's power of fulfilling wishes. Dora's father was dead, and the others had already gone to the cemetery. She might calmly read whatever she

1. The phantasy of defloration formed the second component of the situation. The emphasis upon the difficulty of getting forward and the anxiety felt in the dream indicated the stress which the dreamer was so ready to lay upon her virginity – a point alluded to in another place by means of the Sistine Madonna. These sexual thoughts gave an unconscious ground-colouring to the wishes (which were perhaps merely kept secret) concerned with the suitor who was waiting for her in Germany. We have already [p. 137 f.] recognized the phantasy of revenge as the first component of the same situation in the dream. The two components do not coincide completely, but only in part. We shall subsequently come upon the traces of a third and still more important train of thought. [See p. 149, n. 1.]

2. On another occasion, instead of 'calmly' she said 'not the least sadly' (p. 134, *n.*) – I can quote this dream as fresh evidence for the correctness of an assertion made in my *Interpretation of Dreams* (Chapter VII, Section A; *P.F.L.*, 4, 664) [see also p. 109 above] to the effect that those pieces of a dream which are at first forgotten and are only subsequently remembered are invariably the most important from the point of view of understanding the dream. In the same place I went on to the conclusion that the forgetting of dreams must also be explained as an effect of endopsychic resistance. – [The first sentence of this footnote was added in 1924.]

chose. Did not this mean that one of her motives for revenge was a revolt against her parents' constraint? If her father was dead she could read or love as she pleased.

At first she would not remember ever having read anything in an encyclopaedia; but she then admitted that a recollection of an occasion of the kind did occur to her, though it was of an innocent enough nature. At the time when the aunt she was so fond of had been so seriously ill and it had already been settled that Dora was to go to Vienna, a *letter* had come from another uncle, to say that they could not go to Vienna, as a boy of his, a cousin of Dora's therefore, had fallen dangerously ill with appendicitis. Dora had thereupon looked up in the encyclopaedia to see what the symptoms of appendicitis were. From what she had then read she still recollected the characteristic localization of the abdominal pain.

I then remembered that shortly after her aunt's death Dora had had an attack of what had been alleged to be appendicitis [p. 52]. Up till then I had not ventured to count that illness among her hysterical productions. She told me that during the first few days she had had high fever and had felt the pain in her abdomen that she had read about in the encyclopaedia. She had been given cold fomentations but had not been able to bear them. On the second day her period had set in, accompanied by violent pains. (Since her health had been bad, the periods had been very irregular.) At that time she used to suffer continually from constipation.

It was not really possible to regard this state as a purely hysterical one. Although hysterical fever does undoubtedly occur, yet it seemed too arbitrary to put down the fever accompanying this questionable illness to hysteria instead of to some organic cause operative at the time. I was on the point of abandoning the track, when she herself helped me along it by producing her last addendum to the dream: *she saw herself particularly distinctly going up the stairs.*

I naturally required a special determinant for this. Dora objected that she would anyhow have had to go upstairs if she had wanted to get to her flat, which was on an upper floor. It was easy to brush aside this objection (which was probably not very seriously intended) by pointing out that if she had been able to travel in her dream from the unknown town to Vienna without making a railway journey she ought also to have been able to leave out a flight of stairs. She then proceeded to relate that after the appendicitis she had not been able to walk properly and had dragged her right foot. This state of things had continued for a long time, and on that account she had been particularly glad to avoid stairs. Even now her foot sometimes dragged. The doctors whom she had consulted at her father's desire had been very much astonished at this most unusual after-effect of an appendicitis, especially as the abdominal pains had not recurred and did not in any way accompany the dragging of the foot.[1]

Here, then, we have a true hysterical symptom. The fever may have been organically determined – perhaps by one of those very frequent attacks of influenza that are not localized in any particular part of the body. Nevertheless it was now established that the neurosis had seized upon this chance event and made use of it for an utterance of its own. Dora had therefore given herself an illness which she had read up about in the encyclopaedia, and she had punished herself for dipping into its pages. But she was forced to recognize that the punishment could not possibly apply to her reading the innocent article in question. It must have been inflicted as the result of a process of displacement, after another occasion of more guilty reading had become associated with this one; and the guilty occasion must

---

1. We must assume the existence of some somatic connection between the painful abdominal sensations known as 'ovarian neuralgia' and locomotor disturbances in the leg on the same side; and we must suppose that in Dora's case the somatic connection had been given an interpretation of a particularly specialized sort, that is to say, that it had been overlaid with and brought into the service of a particular psychological meaning. The reader is referred to my analogous remarks in connection with the analysis of Dora's symptom of coughing and with the relation between catarrh and loss of appetite [pp. 120–21 f.].

lie concealed in her memory behind the contemporaneous innocent one.[1] It might still be possible, perhaps, to discover the nature of the subjects she had read about on that other occasion.

What, then, was the meaning of this condition, of this attempted simulation of a perityphlitis? The remainder of the disorder, the dragging of one leg, was entirely out of keeping with perityphlitis. It must, no doubt, fit in better with the secret and possibly sexual meaning of the clinical picture; and if it were elucidated might in its turn throw light on the meaning which we were in search of. I looked about for a method of approaching the puzzle. Periods of time had been mentioned in the dream; and time is assuredly never a matter of indifference in any biological event. I therefore asked Dora when this attack of appendicitis had taken place; whether it had been before or after the scene by the lake. Every difficulty was resolved at a single blow by her prompt reply: 'Nine months later.' The period of time is sufficiently characteristic. Her supposed attack of appendicitis had thus enabled the patient with the modest means at her disposal (the pains and the menstrual flow) to realize a phantasy of *childbirth*.[2] Dora was naturally aware of the significance of this period of time, and could not dispute the probability of her having, on the occasion under discussion, read up in the encyclopaedia about pregnancy and childbirth. But what was all this about her dragging her leg? I could now hazard a guess. That is how people walk when they have twisted a foot. So she had made a 'false step': which was true indeed if she could give birth to a child nine months after the scene by the lake. But there was still another requirement upon the fulfilment of which I had to insist. I am convinced

1. This is quite a typical example of the way in which symptoms arise from exciting causes which appear to be entirely unconnected with sexuality.

2. I have already indicated [p. 80] that the majority of hysterical symptoms, when they have attained their full pitch of development, represent an imagined situation of sexual life – such as a scene of sexual intercourse, pregnancy, childbirth, confinement, etc.

that a symptom of this kind can only arise where it has an *infantile* prototype. All my experience hitherto has led me to hold firmly to the view that recollections derived from the impressions of later years do not possess sufficient force to enable them to establish themselves as symptoms. I scarcely dared hope that Dora would provide me with the material that I wanted from her childhood, for the fact is that I am not yet in a position to assert the general validity of this rule, much as I should like to be able to do so. But in this case there came an immediate confirmation of it. Yes, said Dora, once when she was a child she had twisted the same foot; she had slipped on one of the steps as she was going *downstairs* at B—. The foot – and it was actually the same one that she afterwards dragged – had swelled up and had to be bandaged and she had had to lie up for some weeks. This had been a short time before the attack of nervous asthma in her eighth year [p. 51].

The next thing to do was to turn to account our knowledge of the existence of this phantasy: 'If it is true that you were delivered of a child nine months after the scene by the lake, and that you are going about to this very day carrying the consequences of your false step with you, then it follows that in your unconscious you must have regretted the upshot of the scene. In your unconscious thoughts, that is to say, you have made an emendation in it. The assumption that underlies your phantasy of childbirth is that on that occasion something took place,[1] that on that occasion you experienced and went through everything that you were in fact obliged to pick up later on from the encyclopaedia. So you see that your love for Herr K. did not come to an end with the scene, but that (as I maintained) it has persisted down to the present day – though it is

---

1. The phantasy of defloration [p. 139 f.] is thus found to have an application to Herr K., and we begin to see why this part of the dream contained material taken from the scene by the lake – the refusal, two and a half hours, the wood, the invitation to L—.

true that you are unconscious of it.' – And Dora disputed the
fact no longer.[1]

1. I may here add a few supplementary interpretations to those that
have already been given: The '*Madonna*' was obviously Dora herself; in
the first place because of the 'adorer' who had sent her the pictures
[p. 135], in the second place because she had won Herr K.'s love chiefly
by the motherliness she had shown towards his children [p. 55], and
lastly because she had had a child though she was still a girl (this being a
direct allusion to the phantasy of childbirth). Moreover, the notion of
the 'Madonna' is a favourite counter-idea in the mind of girls who feel
themselves oppressed by imputations of sexual guilt, – which was the
case with Dora. A first suspicion of this connection came to me while
I was working as a physician at the Psychiatric Clinic of the University.
I there came across a case of confusional insanity with hallucinations, in
which the attack, which ran a rapid course, turned out to be a reaction
to a reproach made against the patient by her *fiancé*. – If the analysis had
been continued, Dora's maternal longing for a child would probably
have been revealed as an obscure though powerful motive in her behaviour. – The numerous questions which she had been raising latterly
seem to have been belated derivatives of questions inspired by the
sexual curiosity which she had tried to gratify with the encyclopaedia.
The subjects which she read up in it were presumably pregnancy,
childbirth, virginity, and so on. – In reproducing the dream Dora had
forgotten one of the questions which need to be inserted into the course
of the second situation in the dream. This question could only be: 'Does
Herr— live here?' or 'Where does Herr— live?' There must have been
some reason for her having forgotten this apparently innocent question,
especially as she need not have brought it into the dream at all. This
reason, it seems to me, lay in her surname itself, which also denoted an
object and in fact more than one kind of object, and which could
therefore be regarded as an 'ambiguous' word. Unluckily I cannot give
the name and show how well designed it was to indicate something
'ambiguous' and 'improper'. This interpretation was supported by the
discovery of a similar play upon words in another part of the dream,
where the material was derived from Dora's recollections of her aunt's
death ('they have already gone to the cemetery') and where there was
similarly a play upon her aunt's *name*. These improper words seemed to
point to a second and *oral* source of information, since the encyclopaedia
would not cover them. I should not have been surprised to hear that
this source had been Frau K. herself, Dora's calumniator. [Cf. p. 97.]
In that case she would have been the one person whom Dora generously
spared, while she pursued the others with an almost malignant

The labour of elucidating the second dream had so far occupied two hours. At the end of the second session, when I expressed my satisfaction at the result, Dora replied in a depreciatory tone: 'Why, has anything so very remarkable come out?' These words prepared me for the advent of fresh revelations.

She opened the third session with these words: 'Do you know that I am here for the last time today?' – 'How can I know, as you have said nothing to me about it?' – 'Yes, I made up my mind to put up with it till the New Year.[1] But I shall wait no longer than that to be cured.' – 'You know that you are free to stop the treatment at any time. But for today we will go on with our work. When did you come to this decision?' – 'A fortnight ago, I think.' – 'That sounds just like a maidservant or a governess – a fortnight's notice.' – 'There was a governess who gave notice with the K.s, when I was on my visit to them that time at L—, by the lake.' – 'Really? You have never told me about her. Tell me.'

'Well, there was a young girl in the house, who was the children's governess; and she behaved in the most extraordinary way to Herr K. She never said good morning to him, never answered his remarks, never handed him anything at table when he asked for it, and in short treated him like thin air. For that matter he was hardly any politer to her. A day or two before the scene by the lake, the girl took me aside and said she had something to tell me. She then told me that Herr K. had made advances to her at a time when his wife was away for several weeks; he had made violent love to her and had implored her to yield to his entreaties, saying that he got nothing from his wife, and so on.' – 'Why, those are the very words he used afterwards, when he made his proposal to you and you

vindictiveness. Behind the almost limitless series of displacements which were thus brought to light, it was possible to divine the operation of a single simple factor – Dora's deep-rooted homosexual love for Frau K. [Cf. pages 94 ff. and 162 *n*.]

1. It was December 31st.

gave him the slap in his face' [p. 138]. – 'Yes. She had given way to him, but after a little while he had ceased to care for her, and since then she hated him.' – 'And this governess had given notice?' – 'No. She meant to give notice. She told me that as soon as she felt she was thrown over she had told her parents what had happened. They were respectable people living in Germany somewhere. Her parents said that she must leave the house instantly; and, as she failed to do so, they wrote to her saying that they would have nothing more to do with her, and that she was never to come home again.' – 'And why had she not gone away?' – 'She said she meant to wait a little longer, to see if there might not be some change in Herr K. She could not bear living like that any more, she said, and if she saw no change she should give notice and go away.' – 'And what became of the girl?' – 'I only know that she went away.' – 'And she did not have a child as a result of the adventure?' – 'No.'

Here, therefore (and quite in accordance with the rules), was a piece of material information coming to light in the middle of the analysis and helping to solve problems which had previously been raised. I was able to say to Dora: 'Now I know your motive for the slap in the face with which you answered Herr K.'s proposal. It was not that you were offended at his suggestions; you were actuated by jealousy and revenge. At the time when the governess was telling you her story you were still able to make use of your gift for putting on one side everything that is not agreeable to your feelings. But at the moment when Herr K. used the words "I get nothing out of my wife" – which were the same words he had used to the governess – fresh emotions were aroused in you and tipped the balance. "Does he dare", you said to yourself, "treat me like a governess, like a servant?" Wounded pride added to jealousy and to the conscious motives of common sense – it was too much.[1] To

1. It is not a matter of indifference, perhaps, that Dora may have heard her father make the same complaint about his wife, just as I myself did from his own lips [p. 57]. She was perfectly well aware of its meaning.

prove to you how deeply impressed you were by the governess's story, let me draw your attention to the repeated occasions upon which you have identified yourself with her both in your dream and in your conduct. You told your parents what happened – a fact which we have hitherto been unable to account for – just as the governess wrote and told *her* parents. You give me a fortnight's notice, just like a governess. The letter in the dream which gave you leave to go home is the counterpart of the governess's letter from her parents forbidding her to do so.'

'Then why did I not tell my parents at once?'

'How much time did you allow to elapse?'

'The scene took place on the last day of June; I told my mother about it on July 14th.'

'Again a fortnight, then – the time characteristic for a person in service. Now I can answer your question. You understood the poor girl very well. She did not want to go away at once, because she still had hopes, because she expected that Herr K.'s affections would return to her again. So that must have been your motive too. You waited for that length of time so as to see whether he would repeat his proposals; if he had, you would have concluded that he was in earnest, and did not mean to play with you as he had done with the governess.'

'A few days after I had left he sent me a picture post-card.'[1]

'Yes, but when after that nothing more came, you gave free rein to your feelings of revenge. I can even imagine that at that time you were still able to find room for a subsidiary intention, and thought that your accusation might be a means of inducing him to travel to the place where you were living. – 'As he actually offered to do at first,' Dora threw in. – 'In that way your longing for him would have been appeased' – here she nodded assent, a thing which I had not expected – 'and he might have made you the amends you desired.'

1. Here is the point of contact with the engineer [p. 135], who was concealed behind the figure of Dora herself in the first situation in the dream.

'What amends?'

'The fact is, I am beginning to suspect that you took the affair with Herr K. much more seriously than you have been willing to admit so far. Had not the K.s often talked of getting a divorce?'

'Yes, certainly. At first she did not want to, on account of the children. And now she wants to, but he no longer does.'

'May you not have thought that he wanted to get divorced from his wife so as to marry you? And that now he no longer wants to because he has no one to replace her? It is true that two years ago you were very young. But you told me yourself that your mother was engaged at seventeen and then waited two years for her husband. A daughter usually takes her mother's love-story as her model. So you too wanted to wait for him, and you took it that he was only waiting till you were grown up enough to be his wife.[1] I imagine that this was a perfectly serious plan for the future in your eyes. You have not even got the right to assert that it was out of the question for Herr K. to have had any such intention; you have told me enough about him that points directly towards his having such an intention.[2] Nor does his behaviour at L— contradict this view. After all, you did not let him finish his speech and do not know what he meant to say to you. Incidentally, the scheme would by no means have been so impracticable. Your father's relations with Frau K. - and it was probably only for this reason that you lent them your support for so long – made it certain that her consent to a divorce could be obtained; and you can get anything you like out of your father. Indeed, if your temptation at L— had had a different upshot, this would have been the only possible solution for all the parties concerned. And I think that

1. The theme of waiting till the goal is reached occurs in the content of the first situation in the dream. I recognize in this phantasy of waiting for a fiancée a portion of the third component of that situation. I have already alluded [p. 140, *n*. 1] to the existence of this third component.

2. In particular there was a speech which he had made in presenting Dora with a letter-case for Christmas in the last year in which they lived together at B—.

is why you regretted the actual event so deeply and emended it in the phantasy which made its appearance in the shape of the appendicitis. So it must have been a bitter piece of disillusionment for you when the effect of your charges against Herr K. was not that he renewed his proposals but that he replied instead with denials and slanders. You·will agree that nothing makes you so angry as having it thought that you merely fancied the scene by the lake. [Cf. p. 79.] I know now – and this is what you do not want to be reminded of – that you *did* fancy that Herr K.'s proposals were serious, and that he would not leave off until you had married him.'

Dora had listened to me without any of her usual contradictions. She seemed to be moved; she said good-bye to me very warmly, with the heartiest wishes for the New Year, and – came no more. Her father, who called on me two or three times afterwards, assured me that she would come back again, and said it was easy to see that she was eager for the treatment to continue. But it must be confessed that Dora's father was never entirely straightforward. He had given his support to the treatment so long as he could hope that I should 'talk' Dora out of her belief that there was something more than a friendship between him and Frau K. His interest faded when he observed that it was not my intention to bring about that result. I knew Dora would not come back again. Her breaking off so unexpectedly, just when my hopes of a successful termination of the treatment were at their highest, and her thus bringing those hopes to nothing – this was an unmistakable act of vengeance on her part. Her purpose of self-injury also profited by this action. No one who, like me, conjures up the most evil of those half-tamed demons that inhabit the human breast, and seeks to wrestle with them, can expect to come through the struggle unscathed. Might I perhaps have kept the girl under my treatment if I myself had acted a part, if I had exaggerated the importance to me of her staying on, and had shown a warm personal interest in her – a course which, even after allowing for my position as her physician, would have been tantamount to providing her with a substitute for the affection she longed for? I do not know. Since in every case a portion of the factors that are encountered under the form of resistance remains unknown, I have always avoided acting a part, and have contented myself with practising the humbler arts of psychology. In spite of every theoretical interest and of every endeavour to be of assistance as a physician, I keep the fact in mind that there must be some limits set to the extent to which psychological influence may be used, and I respect as one of these limits the patient's own will and understanding.

Nor do I know whether Herr K. would have done any better if it had been revealed to him that the slap Dora gave him by no means signified a final 'No' on her part, but that it expressed the jealousy which had lately been roused in her, while her strongest feelings were still on his side. If he had disregarded that first 'No', and had continued to press his suit with a passion which left room for no doubts, the result might very well have been a triumph of the girl's affection for him over all her internal difficulties. But I think she might just as well have been merely provoked into satisfying her craving for revenge upon him all the more thoroughly. It is never possible to calculate towards which side the decision will incline in such a conflict of motives: whether towards the removal of the repression or towards its reinforcement. Incapacity for meeting a *real* erotic demand is one of the most essential features of a neurosis. Neurotics are dominated by the opposition between reality and phantasy. If what they long for the most intensely in their phantasies is presented them in reality, they none the less flee from it; and they abandon themselves to their phantasies the most readily where they need no longer fear to see them realized. Nevertheless, the barrier erected by repression can fall before the onslaught of a violent emotional excitement produced by a real cause; it is possible for a neurosis to be overcome by reality. But we have no general means of calculating through what person or what event such a cure can be effected.[1]

1. I will add a few remarks on the structure of this dream, though it is not possible to understand it thoroughly enough to allow of a synthesis being attempted. A prominent piece of the dream is to be seen in the phantasy of revenge against her father, which stands out like a façade in front of the rest. (She had gone away from home by her own choice; her father was ill, and then dead ... Then she went home; all the others were already at the cemetery. She went to her room, not the least sadly, and calmly began reading the encyclopaedia.) This part of the material also contained two allusions to her other act of revenge, which she had actually carried out, when she let her parents discover a farewell letter from her. (The letter – from her mother, in the dream – and the mention of the funeral of the aunt who had always been her model.) – Behind this phantasy lie concealed her thoughts of revenge against Herr K., for which she found an outlet in her behaviour to me. (The maidservant, the invitation, the wood, the two and a half hours – all these came from material connected with the events at L—.) Her recollection of the governess, and of the latter's exchange of letters with her parents, is related, no less than her farewell letter, to the letter in the dream allowing her to come home. Her refusal to let herself be accompanied and her decision to go alone may perhaps be translated into these words: 'Since you have treated me like a servant, I shall take no more notice of you, I shall go my own way by myself, and not marry.' – Screened by these thoughts of revenge, glimpses can be caught in other places of material derived from tender phantasies based upon the love for Herr K. which still persisted unconsciously in Dora. ('I would have waited for you till I could be your wife' – defloration – childbirth.) – Finally, we can see the action of the fourth and most deeply buried group of thoughts – those relating to her love for Frau K. – in the fact that the phantasy of defloration is represented from the man's point of view (her identification of herself with her admirer who lived abroad) and in the fact that in two places there are the clearest allusions to ambiguous speeches ('Does Herr— live here?') and to that source of her sexual knowledge which had not been oral (the encyclopaedia). – Cruel and sadistic tendencies find satisfaction in this dream.

POSTSCRIPT

IT is true that I have introduced this paper as a fragment of an analysis; but the reader will have discovered that it is incomplete to a far greater degree than its title might have led him to expect. It is therefore only proper that I should attempt to give a reason for the omissions – which are by no means accidental.

A number of the results of the analysis have been omitted, because at the time when work was broken off they had either not been established with sufficient certainty or they required further study before any general statement could be made about them. At other points, where it seemed to be permissible, I have indicated the direction along which some particular solution would probably have been found to lie. I have in this paper left entirely out of account the technique, which does not at all follow as a matter of course, but by whose means alone the pure metal of valuable unconscious thoughts can be extracted from the raw material of the patient's associations. This brings with it the disadvantage of the reader being given no opportunity of testing the correctness of my procedure in the course of this exposition of the case. I found it quite impracticable, however, to deal simultaneously with the technique of analysis and with the internal structure of a case of hysteria : I could scarcely have accomplished such a task, and if I had, the result would have been almost unreadable. The technique of analysis demands an entirely separate exposition, which would have to be illustrated by numerous examples chosen from a very great variety of cases and which would not have to take the results obtained in each particular case into account. Nor have I attempted in this paper to substantiate the psychological postulates which will be seen to underlie my descriptions of mental phenomena. A cursory attempt to do so would have effected nothing; an exhaustive one would have been a volume in itself. I can only assure the reader that I approached the study of the phenomena revealed by observation of the psychoneuroses without being pledged to any particular psychological system, and that I then proceeded to adjust my views until they seemed adapted for giving an account of the collection of facts which had been observed. I take no pride in having avoided speculation; the material for my hypotheses was collected by the most extensive and laborious series of observations. The decidedness of my attitude on the subject of the unconscious is perhaps specially likely to cause offence, for I handle unconscious ideas, unconscious trains of thought, and unconscious impulses as though they were no less valid and unimpeachable psychological data than conscious ones. But of this I am certain – that any one who sets out to investigate the same region of phenomena and employs the same method will find himself compelled to take up the same position, however much philosophers may expostulate.

Some of my medical colleagues have looked upon my theory of hysteria as a purely psychological one, and have for that reason pronounced it *ipso facto* incapable of solving a pathological problem. They may perhaps discover from this paper that their objection was based upon their having unjustifiably transferred what is a characteristic of the technique on to the theory itself. It is the therapeutic technique alone that is purely psychological; the theory does not by any means fail to point out that neuroses have an organic basis – though it is true that it does not look for that basis in any pathological anatomical changes, and provisionally substitutes the conception of organic functions for the chemical changes which we should expect to find but which we are at present unable to apprehend. No one, probably, will be inclined to deny the sexual function the character of an organic factor, and it is the sexual function that I look upon as the foundation of hysteria and of the psychoneuroses in general. No theory of sexual life will, I suspect, be able to avoid assuming the existence of some definite sexual substances having an excitant action. Indeed, of all the clinical pictures which we meet with in clinical medicine, it is the phenomena of intoxication and abstinence in connection with the use of certain chronic poisons that most closely resemble the genuine psychoneuroses.[1]

But, once again, in the present paper I have not gone fully into all that might be said today about 'somatic compliance', about the infantile germs of perversion, about the erotogenic zones, and about our predisposition towards bisexuality; I have merely drawn attention to the points at which the analysis comes into contact with these organic bases of the symptoms. More than this could not be done with a single case. And I had the same reasons that I have already mentioned for wishing to avoid a cursory discussion of these factors. There is a rich opportunity here for further works, based upon the study of a large number of analyses.

Nevertheless, in publishing this paper, incomplete though it is, I had two objects in view. In the first place, I wished to supplement my book on the interpretation of dreams by showing how an art, which would otherwise be useless, can be turned to account for the discovery of the hidden and repressed parts of mental life. (Incidentally, in the process of analysing the two dreams dealt with in the paper, the technique of dream-interpretation, which is similar to that of psychoanalysis, has come under consideration.) In the second place, I wished to stimulate interest in a whole group of phenomena of which science is still in complete ignorance today because they can only be brought to light by the use of this particular method. No one, I believe, can have had any true conception of the complexity of the psychological events in a case of hysteria – the juxtaposition of the most dissimilar tendencies, the mutual dependence of contrary ideas, the repressions and displacements, and so on. The emphasis laid by Janet upon the 'idée fixe' which becomes transformed into a symptom amounts to

1. [Cf. the third of Freud's *Three Essays* (1905*d*), and his second paper on sexuality and the aetiology of the neuroses (1906*a*), *P.F.L.*, 7, 137–8 and *P.F.L.*, 10, 80 f.]

no more than an extremely meagre attempt at schematization.[1] Moreover, it is impossible to avoid the suspicion that, when the ideas attaching to certain excitations are incapable of becoming conscious, those excitations must act upon one another differently, run a different course, and manifest themselves differently from those other excitations which we describe as 'normal' and which have ideas attaching to them of which we become conscious. When once things have been made clear up to this point, no obstacle can remain in the way of an understanding of a therapeutic method which removes neurotic symptoms by transforming ideas of the former kind into normal ones.

I was further anxious to show that sexuality does not simply intervene, like a *deus ex machina*, on one single occasion, at some point in the working of the processes which characterize hysteria, but that it provides the motive power for every single symptom, and for every single manifestation of a symptom. The symptoms of the disease are nothing else than *the patient's sexual activity*. A single case can never be capable of proving a theorem so general as this one; but I can only repeat over and over again – for I never find it otherwise – that sexuality is the key to the problem of the psychoneuroses and of the neuroses in general. No one who disdains the key will ever be able to unlock the door. I still await news of the investigations which are to make it possible to contradict this theorem or to limit its scope. What I have hitherto heard against it have been expressions of personal dislike or disbelief. To these it is enough to reply in the words of Charcot: '*Ça n'empêche pas d'exister.*'[2]

Nor is the case of whose history and treatment I have published a fragment in these pages well calculated to put the value of psychoanalytic therapy in its true light. Not only the briefness of the treatment (which hardly lasted three months) but

---

1. [See, for instance, Chapter II ('Les idées fixes') of Janet, 1894.]
2. [One of Freud's favourite quotations. Charcot's dictum in full was: 'La théorie c'est bon, mais ça n'empêche pas d'exister.' ('Theory is good, but it doesn't prevent things from existing.')]

another factor inherent in the nature of the case prevented results being brought about such as are attainable in other instances, where the improvement will be admitted by the patient and his relatives and will approximate more or less closely to a complete recovery. Satisfactory results of this kind are reached when the symptoms are maintained solely by the internal conflict between the impulses concerned with sexuality. In such cases the patient's condition will be seen improving in proportion as he is helped towards a solution of his mental problems by the translation of pathogenic into normal material. The course of events is very different when the symptoms have become enlisted in the service of external motives, as had happened with Dora during the two preceding years. It is surprising, and might easily be misleading, to find that the patient's condition shows no noticeable alteration even though considerable progress has been made with the work of analysis. But in reality things are not as bad as they seem. It is true that the symptoms do not disappear while the work is proceeding; but they disappear a little while later, when the relations between patient and physician have been dissolved. The postponement of recovery or improvement is really only caused by the physician's own person.

I must go back a little, in order to make the matter intelligible. It may be safely said that during psychoanalytic treatment the formation of new symptoms is invariably stopped. But the productive powers of the neurosis are by no means extinguished; they are occupied in the creation of a special class of mental structures, for the most part unconscious, to which the name of 'transferences' may be given.

What are transferences? They are new editions or facsimiles of the impulses and phantasies which are aroused and made conscious during the progress of the analysis; but they have this peculiarity, which is characteristic for their species, that they replace some earlier person by the person of the physician. To put it another way: a whole series of psychological experiences are revived, not as belonging to the past, but as applying to the person of the physician at the present moment. Some of these transferences have a content which differs from that of their model in no respect whatever except for the substitution. These then – to keep to the same metaphor – are merely new impressions or reprints. Others are more ingeniously constructed; their content has been subjected to a moderating influence – to *sublimation*, as I call it – and they may even become conscious, by cleverly taking advantage of some real peculiarity in the physician's person or circumstances and attaching themselves to that. These, then, will no longer be new impressions, but revised editions.

If the theory of analytic technique is gone into, it becomes evident that transference is an inevitable necessity. Practical experience, at all events, shows conclusively that there is no means of avoiding it, and that this latest creation of the disease must be combated like all the earlier ones. This happens, however, to be by far the hardest part of the whole task. It is easy to learn how to interpret dreams, to extract from the patient's associations his unconscious thoughts and memories, and to practise similar explanatory arts: for these the patient himself will always provide the text. Transference is the one thing the presence of which has to be detected almost without assistance and with only the slightest clues to go upon, while at the same time the risk of making arbitrary inferences has to be avoided. Nevertheless, transference cannot be evaded, since use is made of it in setting up all the obstacles that make the material inaccessible to treatment, and since it is only after the transference has been resolved that a patient arrives at a sense of conviction of the validity of the connections which have been constructed during the analysis.

Some people may feel inclined to look upon it as a serious objection to a method which is in any case troublesome enough that it itself should multiply the labours of the physician by creating a new species of pathological mental products. They may even be tempted to infer from the existence of transferences that the patient will be injured by analytic treatment.

Both these suppositions would be mistaken. The physician's labours are not multiplied by transference; it need make no difference to him whether he has to overcome any particular impulse of the patient's in connection with himself or with some one else. Nor does the treatment force upon the patient, in the shape of transference, any new task which he would not otherwise have performed. It is true that neuroses may be cured in institutions from which psychoanalytic treatment is excluded, that hysteria may be said to be cured not by the method but by the physician, and that there is usually a sort of blind dependence and a permanent bond between a patient and the physician who has removed his symptoms by hypnotic suggestion; but the scientific explanation of all these facts is to be found in the existence of 'transferences' such as are regularly directed by patients on to their physicians. Psychoanalytic treatment does not *create* transferences, it merely brings them to light, like so many other hidden psychical factors. The only difference is this – that spontaneously a patient will only call up affectionate and friendly transferences to help towards his recovery; if they cannot be called up, he feels the physician is 'antipathetic' to him, and breaks away from him as fast as possible and without having been influenced by him. In psychoanalysis, on the other hand, since the play of motives is different, all the patient's tendencies, including hostile ones, are aroused; they are then turned to account for the purposes of the analysis by being made conscious, and in this way the transference is constantly being destroyed. Transference, which seems ordained to be the greatest obstacle to psychoanalysis, becomes its most powerful ally, if its presence can be detected each time and explained to the patient.[1]

1. [*Footnote added* 1923:] A continuation of these remarks upon transference is contained in my technical paper on 'transference-love' (1915*a*). [Freud had already discussed transference at some length near the end of his chapter on 'The Psychotherapy of Hysteria' in *Studies on Hysteria* (Breuer and Freud, 1895, *P.F.L.*, 3, 389–92). But the present passage is the first one in which he indicates the importance of transference as a factor in the therapeutic process of psychoanalysis.]

I have been obliged to speak of transference, for it is only by means of this factor that I can elucidate the peculiarities of Dora's analysis. Its great merit, namely, the unusual clarity which makes it seem so suitable as a first introductory publication, is closely bound up with its great defect, which led to its being broken off prematurely. I did not succeed in mastering the transference in good time. Owing to the readiness with which Dora put one part of the pathogenic material at my disposal during the treatment, I neglected the precaution of looking out for the first signs of transference, which was being prepared in connection with another part of the same material – a part of which I was in ignorance. At the beginning it was clear that I was replacing her father in her imagination, which was not unlikely, in view of the difference between our ages. She was even constantly comparing me with him consciously, and kept anxiously trying to make sure whether I was being quite straightforward with her, for her father 'always preferred secrecy and roundabout ways'. But when the first dream came, in which she gave herself the warning that she had better leave my treatment just as she had formerly left Herr K.'s house, I ought to have listened to the warning myself. 'Now,' I ought to have said to her, 'it is from Herr K. that you have made a transference on to me. Have you noticed anything that leads you to suspect me of evil intentions similar (whether openly or in some sublimated form) to Herr K.'s? Or have you been struck by anything about me or got to know anything about me which has caught your fancy, as happened previously with Herr K.?' Her attention would then have been turned to some detail in our relations, or in my person or circumstances, behind which there lay concealed something analogous but immeasurably more important concerning Herr K. And when this transference had been cleared up, the analysis would have obtained access to new memories, dealing, probably, with actual events. But I was deaf to this first note of warning, thinking I had ample time before me, since no further stages of transference developed and the material for the analysis had not yet run dry. In this way the transference took me unawares, and, because of the unknown quantity in me which reminded Dora of Herr K., she took her revenge on me as she wanted to take her revenge on him, and deserted me as she believed herself to have been deceived and deserted by him. Thus she *acted out* an essential part of her recollections and phantasies instead of reproducing it in the treatment. What this unknown quantity was I naturally cannot tell. I suspect that it had to do with money, or with jealousy of another patient who had kept up relations with my family after her recovery. When it is possible to work tranferences into the analysis at an early stage, the course of the analysis is retarded and obscured, but its existence is better guaranteed against sudden and overwhelming resistances.

In Dora's second dream there are several clear allusions to transference. At the time she was telling me the dream I was still unaware (and did not learn until two days later) that we had only *two hours* more work before us. This was the same length of time which she had spent in front of the Sistine Madonna [p. 135 f.], and which (by making a correction and putting 'two hours' instead of 'two and a half hours') she had taken as the length of the walk which she had not made round the lake [p. 138]. The striving and waiting in the dream, which related to the young man in Germany, and had their origin in her waiting till Herr K. could marry her, had been expressed in the transference a few days before. The treatment, she had thought, was too long for her; she would never have the patience to wait so long. And yet in the first few weeks she had had discernment enough to listen without making any such objections when I informed her that her complete recovery would require perhaps a year. Her refusing in the dream to be accompanied, and preferring to go alone, also originated from her visit to the gallery at Dresden, and I was myself to experience them on the appointed day. What they meant was, no doubt: 'Men are all so detestable that I would rather not marry. This is my revenge.'[1]

If cruel impulses and revengeful motives, which have already been used in the patient's ordinary life for maintaining her symptoms, become transferred on to the physician during treatment, before he has had time to detach them from himself by tracing them back to their sources, then it is not to be wondered at if the patient's condition is unaffected by his therapeutic efforts. For how could the patient take a more effective revenge than by demonstrating upon her own person the helplessness and incapacity of the physician? Nevertheless, I am not inclined to put too low a value on the therapeutic results even of such a fragmentary treatment as Dora's.

It was not until fifteen months after the case was over and this paper composed that I had news of my patient's condition and the effects of my treatment. On a date which is not a matter of

1. The longer the interval of time that separates me from the end of this analysis, the more probable it seems to me that the fault in my technique lay in this omission: I failed to discover in time and to inform the patient that her homosexual (gynaecophilic) love for Frau K. was the strongest unconscious current in her mental life. I ought to have guessed that the main source of her knowledge of sexual matters could have been no one but Frau K. – the very person who later on charged her with being interested in those same subjects. Her knowing all about such things and, at the same time, her always pretending not to know where her knowledge came from was really too remarkable. [Cf. p. 62.] I ought to have attacked this riddle and looked for the motive of such an extraordinary piece of repression. If I had done this, the second dream would have given me my answer. The remorseless craving for revenge expressed in that dream was suited as nothing else was to conceal the current of feeling that ran contrary to it – the magnanimity with which she forgave the treachery of the friend she loved and concealed from everyone the fact that it was this friend who had herself revealed to her the knowledge which had later been the ground of the accusations against her. Before I had learnt the importance of the homosexual current of feeling in psychoneurotics, I was often brought to a standstill in the treatment of my cases or found myself in complete perplexity.

complete indifference, on the first of April (times and dates, as
we know, were never without significance for her), Dora came
to see me again: to finish her story and to ask for help once
more. One glance at her face, however, was enough to tell me
that she was not in earnest over her request. For four or five
weeks after stopping the treatment she had been 'all in a
muddle', as she said. A great improvement had then set in; her
attacks had become less frequent and her spirits had risen. In the
May of that year one of the K.'s two children (it had always been
delicate) had died. She took the opportunity of their loss to pay
them a visit of condolence, and they received her as though
nothing had happened in the last three years. She made it up
with them, she took her revenge on them, and she brought her
own business to a satisfactory conclusion. To the wife she said:
'I know you have an affair with my father'; and the other did
not deny it. From the husband she drew an admission of the
scene by the lake which he had disputed, and brought the news
of her vindication home to her father. Since then she had not
resumed her relations with the family.

After this she had gone on quite well till the middle of
October, when she had had another attack of aphonia which
had lasted for six weeks. I was surprised at this news, and, on
my asking her whether there had been any exciting cause, she
told me that the attack had followed upon a violent fright. She
had seen some one run over by a carriage. Finally she came out
with the fact that the accident had occurred to no less a person
than Herr K. himself. She had come across him in the street one
day; they had met in a place where there was a great deal of
traffic; he had stopped in front of her as though in bewilderment, and in his abstraction he had allowed himself to be
knocked down by a carriage.[1] She had been able to convince
herself, however, that he escaped without serious injury. She
still felt some slight emotion if she heard any one speak of her

---

1. We have here an interesting contribution to the problem of indirect attempts at suicide, which I have discussed in my *Psychopathology
of Everyday Life* [1901b, Chapter VIII, *P.F.L.*, 5, 233–8].

father's affair with Frau K., but otherwise she had no further concern with the matter. She was absorbed in her work, and had no thoughts of marrying.

She went on to tell me that she had come for help on account of a right-sided facial neuralgia, from which she was now suffering day and night. 'How long has it been going on?' 'Exactly a fortnight.'[1] I could not help smiling; for I was able to show her that exactly a fortnight earlier she had read a piece of news that concerned me in the newspaper. (This was in 1902.)[2] And this she confirmed.

Her alleged facial neuralgia was thus a self-punishment – remorse at having once given Herr K. a box on the ear, and at having transferred her feelings of revenge on to me. I do not know what kind of help she wanted from me, but I promised to forgive her for having deprived me of the satisfaction of affording her a far more radical cure for her troubles.

Years have again gone by since her visit. In the meantime the girl has married, and indeed – unless all the signs mislead me – she has married the young man who came into her associations at the beginning of the analysis of the second dream.[3] Just as the first dream represented her turning away from the man she loved to her father – that is to say, her flight from life into disease – so the second dream announced that she was about to tear herself free from her father and had been reclaimed once more by the realities of life.

1. For the significance of this period of time and its relation to the theme of revenge, see the analysis of the second dream [p. 146 ff.].

2. [No doubt the news was of Freud's appointment to a Professorship in March of that year.]

3. [P. 135. – In the editions of 1909, 1912 and 1921 the following footnote appeared at this point: 'This, as I afterwards learnt, was a mistaken notion.']

ANALYSIS OF A PHOBIA IN A
FIVE-YEAR-OLD BOY
'Little Hans'
(1909)

EDITOR'S NOTE

ANALYSE DER PHOBIE EINES FÜNFJÄHRIGEN KNABEN

(A) German Editions:

1909 *Jb. psychoanalyt. psychopath. Forsch.*, **1** (1), 1–109.
1913 *S.K.S.N.*, **3**, 1–122. (1921, 2nd ed.)
1924 *Gesammelte Schriften*, **8**, 129–263. (Revised ed.)
1932 *Vier Krankengeschichten*, 142–281.
1941 *Gesammelte Werke*, **7**, 243–377.
1922 'Nachschrift zur Analyse des kleinen Hans', *Int. Z. Psychoanal.*, **8** (3), 321.
1924 *Gesammelte Schriften*, **8**, 264–5.
1932 *Vier Krankengeschichten*, 282–3.
1940 *Gesammelte Werke*, **13**, 431–2.

(B) English Translations:

'Analysis of a Phobia in a Five-Year-Old Boy'
1925 *Collected Papers*, **3**, 149–287. – 'Postscript (1922)', ibid., 288–9. (Tr. Alix and James Strachey.)
1955 *Standard Edition*, **10**, 1–149.

The present edition is a corrected reprint of the *Standard Edition* translation, with some editorial changes.

Some records of the earlier part of little Hans's life had already been published by Freud two years before, in his paper on 'The Sexual Enlightenment of Children' (1907c). In the earlier editions of that paper, however, the boy was referred to as 'little Herbert'; but the name was changed to 'little Hans' after the publication of the present work. This case history is also briefly mentioned in, and in fact largely forms the basis of, another of Freud's previous papers, 'On the Sexual Theories of Children' (1908c), in which many of the most important theories discussed in the present case history were already published. It is worth mentioning that on its first publication in the *Jahrbuch* the present paper was described not as 'by' Freud, but as 'communicated by' him. In a footnote added by Freud for the eighth volume of the *Gesammelte Schriften* (1924), which contained this and the four other long case histories, he remarks that this one was published with the express consent of little Hans's father. This footnote will be found at the end of the 'Prefatory Remarks' to the case of 'Dora' (1905e, cf. above, pp. 42–3).

The case history of little Hans was later used by Freud as a basis for discussing the nature of anxiety in Chapters IV and VII of *Inhibitions, Symptoms and Anxiety* (1926d). It was also quoted in connection with totemism and animal phobias in *Totem and Taboo* (1912–13), Essay IV, Section 3. Further discussions of anxiety and phobias in children will be found in Lecture 25 of the *Introductory Lectures* (1916–17) and in Chapter III of *Inhibitions, Symptoms and Anxiety*, as well as in the 'Wolf Man' case history (1918b).

This chronological table, based on data derived from the case history, may help the reader to follow the story:

1903   (April) Hans born.
1906   (*Aet.* 3–3¾) First reports.
        (*Aet.* 3¼–3½) (Summer) First visit to Gmunden.
        (*Aet.* 3½) Castration threat.
        (*Aet.* 3½) (October) Hanna born.
1907   (*Aet.* 3¾) First dream.
        (*Aet.* 4) Removal to new flat.
        (*Aet.* 4¼–4½) (Summer) Second visit to Gmunden. Episode of biting horse.
1908   (*Aet.* 4¾) (January) Episode of falling horse. Outbreak of phobia.
        (*Aet.* 5) (May) End of analysis.

I
INTRODUCTION

In the following pages I propose to describe the course of the illness and recovery of a very youthful patient. The case history is not, strictly speaking, derived from my own observation. It is true that I laid down the general lines of the treatment, and that on one single occasion, when I had a conversation with the boy, I took a direct share in it; but the treatment itself was carried out by the child's father, and it is to him that I owe my sincerest thanks for allowing me to publish his notes upon the case. But his services go further than this. No one else, in my opinion, could possibly have prevailed on the child to make any such avowals; the special knowledge by means of which he was able to interpret the remarks made by his five-year-old son was indispensable, and without it the technical difficulties in the way of conducting a psychoanalysis upon so young a child would have been insuperable. It was only because the authority of a father and of a physician were united in a single person, and because in him both affectionate care and scientific interest were combined, that it was possible in this one instance to apply the method to a use to which it would not otherwise have lent itself.[1]

But the peculiar value of this observation lies in the considerations which follow. When a physician treats an adult neurotic by psychoanalysis, the process he goes through of uncovering the psychical formations, layer by layer, eventually enables him to frame certain hypotheses as to the patient's infantile sexuality; and it is in the components of the latter that he believes he has discovered the motive forces of all the

1. [Later experience showed Freud that this limitation was unnecessary. (Cf. the works quoted in the footnote on p. 303 below.) Some further remarks on the theoretical value of child-analysis occur in the 'Wolf Man' case history (1918*b*), *P.F.L.*, **9**, 235–6.]

neurotic symptoms of later life. I have set out these hypotheses in my *Three Essays on the Theory of Sexuality* (1905*d*), and I am aware that they seem as strange to an outside reader as they seem incontrovertible to a psychoanalyst. But even a psycho-analyst may confess to the wish for a more direct and less roundabout proof of these fundamental theorems. Surely there must be a possibility of observing in children at first hand and in all the freshness of life the sexual impulses and wishes which we dig out so laboriously in adults from among their own débris – especially as it is also our belief that they are the common property of all men, a part of the human constitution, and merely exaggerated or distorted in the case of neurotics.

With this end in view I have for many years been urging my pupils and my friends to collect observations of the sexual life of children – the existence of which has as a rule been cleverly overlooked or deliberately denied. Among the material which came into my possession as a result of these requests, the reports which I received at regular intervals about little Hans soon began to take a prominent place. His parents were both among my closest adherents, and they had agreed that in bringing up their first child they would use no more coercion than might be absolutely necessary for maintaining good behaviour. And, as the child developed into a cheerful, good-natured and lively little boy, the experiment of letting him grow up and express himself without being intimidated went on satisfactorily. I shall now proceed to reproduce his father's records of little Hans just as I received them; and I shall of course refrain from any at-tempt at spoiling the *naïveté* and directness of the nursery by making any conventional emendations.

The first reports of Hans date from a period when he was not quite three years old. At that time, by means of various remarks and questions, he was showing a quite peculiarly lively interest in that portion of his body which he used to describe as his 'widdler'. Thus he once asked his mother this question:

Hans: 'Mummy, have you got a widdler too?'

Mother: 'Of course. Why?'

Hans: 'I was only just thinking.'

At the same age he went into a cow-shed once and saw a cow being milked. 'Oh, look!' he said, 'there's milk coming out of its widdler!'

Even these first observations begin to rouse an expectation that much, if not most, of what little Hans shows us will turn out to be typical of the sexual development of children in general. I once put forward the view[1] that there was no need to be too much horrified at finding in a woman the idea of sucking at a male organ. This repellent impulse, I argued, had a most innocent origin, since it was derived from sucking at the mother's breast; and in this connection, I went on, a cow's udder plays an apt part as an intermediate image, being in its nature a *mamma* and in its shape and position a penis. Little Hans's discovery confirms the latter part of my contention.

Meanwhile his interest in widdlers was by no means a purely theoretical one; as might have been expected, it also impelled him to *touch* his member. When he was three and a half his mother found him with his hand on his penis. She threatened him in these words: 'If you do that, I shall send for Dr A. to cut off your widdler. And then what'll you widdle with?'

Hans: 'With my bottom.'

He made this reply without having any sense of guilt as yet. But this was the occasion of his acquiring the 'castration complex', the presence of which we are so often obliged to infer in analysing neurotics, though they one and all struggle violently against recognizing it. There is much of importance to be said upon the significance of this element in the life of a child. The 'castration complex' has left marked traces behind it in myths

---

[1]. See my 'Fragment of an Analysis of a Case of Hysteria' (1905*e*) [p. 86 above].

(and not only in Greek myths); in a passage in my *Interpretation of Dreams* [1900*a*],[1] and elsewhere, I have touched upon the part it plays.[2]

At about the same age (three and a half), standing in front of the lions' cage at Schönbrunn,[3] little Hans called out in a joyful and excited voice: 'I saw the lion's widdler.'

Animals owe a good deal of their importance in myths and

1. [Within a couple of pages of the end of the book. The term 'castration complex' had been used by Freud for the first time in his paper on 'The Sexual Theories of Children' (1908*c*), published very shortly before the present one. Cf. the Editor's Note, p. 167 f. above.]

2. (*Footnote added* 1923:) – Since this was written, the study of the castration complex has been further developed in contributions to the subject by Lou Andreas-Salomé [1916], A. Stärcke [1921], F. Alexander [1922], and others. It has been urged that every time his mother's breast is withdrawn from a baby he is bound to feel it as castration (that is to say, as the loss of what he regards as an important part of his own body); that, further, he cannot fail to be similarly affected by the regular loss of his faeces; and, finally, that the act of birth itself (consisting as it does in the separation of the child from his mother, with whom he has hitherto been united) is the prototype of all castration. While recognizing all of these roots of the complex, I have nevertheless put forward the view that the term 'castration complex' ought to be confined to those excitations and consequences which are bound up with the loss of the *penis*. Any one who, in analysing adults, has become convinced of the invariable presence of the castration complex, will of course find difficulty in ascribing its origin to a chance threat – of a kind which is not, after all, of such universal occurrence; he will be driven to assume that children construct this danger for themselves out of the slightest hints, which will never be wanting. [Cf. Freud's discussion of 'primal phantasies' in Lecture 23 of his *Introductory Lectures* (1916–17) and in Sections V and VIII of his case history of the 'Wolf Man' (1918*b*).] This circumstance is also the motive, indeed, that has stimulated the search for those deeper roots of the complex which are universally forthcoming. But this makes it all the more valuable that in the case of little Hans the threat of castration is reported by his parents themselves, and moreoever at a date before there was any question of his phobia. [Cf. 'The Dissolution of the Oedipus Complex' (1924*d*), *P.F.L.*, 7, 317.]

3. [The imperial palace on the outskirts of Vienna. There was a zoological collection in the park.]

fairy tales to the openness with which they display their genitals and their sexual functions to the inquisitive little human child. There can be no doubt about Hans's sexual curiosity; but it also roused the spirit of enquiry in him and enabled him to arrive at genuine abstract knowledge.

When he was at the station once (aged three and three-quarters) he saw some water being let out of an engine. 'Oh, look,' he said, 'the engine's widdling. Where's it got its widdler?'

After a little he added in reflective tones: 'A dog and a horse have widdlers; a table and a chair haven't.' He had thus got hold of an essential characteristic for differentiating between animate and inanimate objects.

Thirst for knowledge seems to be inseparable from sexual curiosity. Hans's curiosity was particularly directed towards his parents.

Hans (aged three and three-quarters): 'Daddy, have you got a widdler too?'

Father: 'Yes, of course.'

Hans: 'But I've never seen it when you were undressing.'

Another time he was looking on intently while his mother undressed before going to bed. 'What are you staring like that for?' she asked.

Hans: 'I was only looking to see if you'd got a widdler too.'

Mother: 'Of course. Didn't you know that?'

Hans: 'No. I thought you were so big you'd have a widdler like a horse.'

This expectation of little Hans's deserves to be borne in mind; it will become important later on.

But the great event of Hans's life was the birth of his little sister Hanna when he was exactly three and a half.[1] His behaviour on that occasion was noted down by his father on the spot: 'At five in the morning', he writes, 'labour began, and Hans's bed was moved into the next room. He woke up there

1. April 1903 to October 1906.

at seven, and, hearing his mother groaning, asked: "Why's Mummy coughing?" Then, after a pause, "The stork's coming today for certain."

'Naturally he has often been told during the last few days that the stork is going to bring a little girl or a little boy; and he quite rightly connected the unusual sounds of groaning with the stork's arrival.

'Later on he was taken into the kitchen. He saw the doctor's bag in the front hall and asked: "What's that?" "A bag," was the reply. Upon which he declared with conviction: "The stork's coming today." After the baby's delivery the midwife came into the kitchen and Hans heard her ordering some tea to be made. At this he said: "I know! Mummy's to have some tea because she's coughing." He was then called into the bedroom. He did not look at his mother, however, but at the basins and other vessels, filled with blood and water, that were still standing about the room. Pointing to the blood-stained bed-pan, he observed in a surprised voice: "But blood doesn't come out of *my* widdler."

'Everything he says shows that he connects what is strange in the situation with the arrival of the stork. He meets everything he sees with a very suspicious and intent look, and *there can be no question that his first doubts about the stork have taken root.*

'Hans is very jealous of the new arrival, and whenever any one praises her, says she is a lovely baby, and so on, he at once declares scornfully: "But she's not got any teeth yet."[1] And in fact when he saw her for the first time he was very much surprised that she was unable to speak, and decided that this was because she had no teeth. During the first few days he was naturally put very much in the background. He was suddenly taken ill with a sore throat. In his fever he was heard saying: "But I don't *want* a baby sister!"

'Some six months later he had got over his jealousy, and his

---

1. This again is a typical mode of behaviour. Another little boy, only two years his sister's senior, used to parry similar remarks with an angry cry of 'Too 'ickle! too 'ickle!'

brotherly affection for the baby was only equalled by his sense
of his own superiority over her.[1]

'A little later Hans was watching his seven-day-old sister
being given a bath. "But her widdler's still quite small," he
remarked; and then added, as though by way of consolation:
"When she grows up it'll get bigger all right."[2]

1. Another child, rather older than Hans, welcomed his younger
brother with the words: 'The stork can take him away again.' Compare
in this connection my remarks in *The Interpretation of Dreams* [1900a,
Chapter V, Section D (β), *P.F.L.*, 4, 347 ff.] on dreams of the death of
loved relatives.

2. Two other boys were reported to me as having made the same
judgement, expressed in identical words and followed by the same
anticipation, when they were allowed to satisfy their curiosity and look
at their baby sister's body for the first time. One might well feel horrified at such signs of the premature decay of a child's intellect. Why was
it that these young enquirers did not report what they really saw –
namely, that there was no widdler there? In little Hans's case, at all
events, we can account completely for the faulty perception. We are
aware that by a process of careful induction he had arrived at the
general proposition that every animate object, in contradistinction to
inanimate ones, possesses a widdler. His mother had confirmed him in
this conviction by giving him corroborative information in regard to
persons inaccessible to his own observation. He was now utterly incapable of surrendering what he had achieved merely on the strength
of this single observation made upon his little sister. He therefore made
a judgement that in that instance also there was a widdler present, only
that it was still very small, but that it would grow till it was as big as
a horse's.

We can go a step further in vindicating little Hans's honour. As a
matter of fact, he was behaving no worse than a philosopher of the
school of Wundt. In the view of that school, consciousness is the invariable characteristic of what is mental, just as in the view of little Hans
a widdler is the indispensable criterion of what is animate. If now the
philosopher comes across mental processes whose existence cannot but
be inferred, but about which there is not a trace of consciousness to be
detected – for the subject, in fact, knows nothing of them, although it is
impossible to avoid inferring their existence – then, instead of saying
that they are *un*conscious mental processes, he calls them *semi*-conscious.
The widdler's still very small! And in this comparison the advantage is

'At the same age (when he was three and three-quarters) Hans produced his first account of a dream: "Today when I was asleep I thought I was at Gmunden[1] with Mariedl."

'Mariedl was the thirteen-year-old daughter of our landlord and used often to play with him.'

As Hans's father was telling his mother the dream in his presence, he corrected him, saying: 'Not with Mariedl, but quite alone with Mariedl.'

In this connection we learn: 'In the summer of 1906 Hans was at Gmunden, and used to run about all day long with our landlord's children. When we left Gmunden we thought he would be very much upset by having to come away and move back to town. To our surprise this was not so. He seemed glad of the change, and for several weeks he talked very little about Gmunden. It was not until after some weeks had passed that there began to emerge reminiscences – often vividly coloured – of the time he had spent at Gmunden. During the last four weeks or so he has been working these reminiscences up into phantasies. He imagines that he is playing with the other children, with Berta, Olga, and Fritzl; he talks to them as though they were really with him, and he is capable of amusing himself in this way for hours at a time. Now that he has got a sister and is obviously taken up with the problem of the origin of children, he always calls Berta and Olga "his children"; and once he added: "my children Berta and Olga were brought by the stork too". The dream, occurring now, after six months'

---

in favour of little Hans. For, as is so often the case with the sexual researches of children, behind the mistake a piece of genuine knowledge lies concealed. Little girls *do* possess a small widdler, which we call a clitoris, though it does not grow any larger but remains permanently stunted. Compare my short paper on 'The Sexual Theories of Children' (1908c) [and the Section on' The Sexual Researches of Childhood' in the second of Freud's *Three Essays on the Theory of Sexuality* (1905d), P.F.L., 7, 112 ff. and 195].

1. [A summer resort on one of the Upper Austrian lakes. – Mariedl, Franzl, Fritzl, and similar forms are the characteristically Austrian affectionate diminutives of Marie, Franz, Fritz, etc.]

absence from Gmunden, is evidently to be read as an expression of a longing to go back there.'

Thus far his father. I will anticipate what is to come by adding that when Hans made this last remark about his children having been brought by the stork, he was contradicting aloud a doubt that was lurking within him.

His father luckily made a note of many things which turned out later on to be of unexpected value. [See p. 199 ff.] 'I drew a giraffe for Hans, who has been to Schönbrunn several times lately. He said to me: "Draw its widdler too." "Draw it yourself," I answered; whereupon he added this line to my picture (see Fig. 1). He began by drawing a short stroke, and

widdler

FIG. I.

then added a bit on to it, remarking: "Its widdler's longer."

'Hans and I walked past a horse that was micturating, and he said: "The horse has got its widdler underneath like me."

'He was watching his three-months-old sister being given a bath, and said in pitying tones: "She *has* got a tiny little widdler."

'He was given a doll to play with and undressed it. He examined it carefully and said: "Her widdler's ever so tiny."'

As we already know, this formula made it possible for him to go on believing in his discovery [of the distinction between animate and inanimate objects] (see p. 173 [and 175, n. 2]).

Every investigator runs the risk of falling into an occasional error. It is some consolation for him, if, like little Hans in the next example, he does not err alone but can quote a common linguistic usage in his support. For Hans saw a monkey in his picture-book one day, and pointing to its up-curled tail, said: 'Daddy, look at its widdler!'

His interest in widdlers led him to invent a special game of his own. 'Leading out of the front hall there is a lavatory and also a dark storeroom for keeping wood in. For some time past Hans had been going into this wood-cupboard and saying: "I'm going to my W.C." I once looked in to see what he was doing in the dark storeroom. He showed me his parts and said: "I'm widdling." That is to say, he has been "playing" at W.C. That it is in the nature of a game is shown not merely by the fact that he was only pretending to widdle, but also by the fact that he does not go into the W.C., which would after all be far simpler, but prefers the wood-cupboard and calls it "his W.C."'

We should be doing Hans an injustice if we were to trace only the auto-erotic features of his sexual life. His father has detailed information to give us on the subject of his love relationships with other children. From these we can discern the existence of an 'object-choice' just as in the case of an adult; and also, it must be confessed, a very striking degree of inconstancy and a disposition to polygamy.

'In the winter (at the age of three and three-quarters) I took Hans to the skating rink and introduced him to my friend N.'s two little daughters, who were about ten years old. Hans sat down beside them, while they, in the consciousness of their mature age, looked down on the little urchin with a good deal of contempt; he gazed at them with admiration, though this proceeding made no great impression on them. In spite of this Hans always spoke of them afterwards as "my little girls". "Where are my little girls? When are my little girls coming?" And for some weeks he kept tormenting me with the question: "When am I going to the rink again to see my little girls?"

'A five-year-old boy cousin came to visit Hans, who had by then reached the age of four. Hans was constantly putting his arms round him, and once, as he was giving him one of these tender embraces, said: "I *am* so fond of you."'

This is the first trace of homosexuality that we have come across in him, but it will not be the last. Little Hans seems to be a positive paragon of all the vices.

'When Hans was four years old we moved into a new flat. A door led out of the kitchen on to a balcony, from which one could see into a flat on the opposite side of the courtyard. In this flat Hans discovered a little girl of about seven or eight. He would sit on the step leading on to the balcony so as to admire her, and would stop there for hours on end. At four o'clock in the afternoon in particular, when the little girl came home from school, he was not to be kept in the room, and nothing could induce him to abandon his post of observation. Once, when the little girl failed to make her appearance at the window at her usual hour, Hans grew quite restless, and kept pestering the servants with questions – "When's the little girl coming? Where's the little girl?" and so on. When she did appear at last, he was quite blissful and never took his eyes off the flat opposite. The violence with which this "long-range love"[1] came over him is to be explained by his having no playmates of either sex. Spending a good deal of time with other children clearly forms part of a child's normal development.

'Hans obtained some companionship of this kind when, shortly afterwards (he was by then four and a half)[2], we moved to Gmunden for the summer holidays. In our house there his playmates were our landlord's children: Franzl (about twelve years old), Fritzl (eight), Olga (seven), and Berta (five). Besides these there were the neighbour's children, Anna (ten), and two other little girls of nine and seven whose names I have

1. Und die Liebe per Distanz,
   Kurzgesagt, missfällt mir ganz.
                Wilhelm Busch.
  [Long-range love, I must admit, Does not suit my taste a bit.]
2. [This is a slip for 'four and a quarter'.]

forgotten. Hans's favourite was Fritzl; he often hugged him and made protestations of his love. Once when he was asked: "Which of the girls are you fondest of?" he answered: "Fritzl!" At the same time he treated the girls in a most aggressive, masculine and arrogant way, embracing them and kissing them heartily – a process to which Berta in particular offered no objection. When Berta was coming out of the room one evening he put his arms round her neck and said in the fondest tones: "Berta, you *are* a dear!" This, by the way, did not prevent his kissing the others as well and assuring them of his love. He was fond, too, of the fourteen-year-old Mariedl – another of our landlord's daughters – who used to play with him. One evening as he was being put to bed he said: "I want Mariedl to sleep with me." On being told that would not do, he said: "Then she shall sleep with Mummy or with Daddy." He was told that would not do either, but that Mariedl must sleep with her own father and mother. Upon which the following dialogue took place:

'*Hans*: "Oh, then I'll just go downstairs and sleep with Mariedl."

'*Mother*: "You really want to go away from Mummy and sleep downstairs?"

'*Hans*: "Oh, I'll come up again in the morning to have breakfast and do number one."

'*Mother*: "Well, if you really want to go away from Daddy and Mummy, then take your coat and knickers and – goodbye!"

'Hans did in fact take his clothes and go towards the staircase, to go and sleep with Mariedl, but, it need hardly be said, he was fetched back.

'(Behind his wish, "I want Mariedl to sleep with us," there of course[1] lay another one: "I want Mariedl" (with whom he liked to be so much) "to become one of our family." But Hans's father and mother were in the habit of taking him into their bed, though only occasionally, and there can be no doubt that

1. ['Of course' was omitted (perhaps inadvertently) after the first

lying beside them had aroused erotic feelings in him; so that his wish to sleep with Mariedl had an erotic sense as well. Lying in bed with his father or mother was a source of erotic feelings in Hans just as it is in every other child.)'

In spite of his accesses of homosexuality, little Hans bore himself like a true man in the face of his mother's challenge.

'In the next instance, too, Hans said to his mother: "I say, I *should* so like to sleep with the little girl." This episode has given us a great deal of entertainment, for Hans has really behaved like a grown-up person in love. For the last few days a pretty little girl of about eight has been coming to the restaurant where we have lunch. Of course Hans fell in love with her on the spot. He keeps constantly turning round in his chair to take furtive looks at her; when he has finished eating, he stations himself in her vicinity so as to flirt with her, but if he finds he is being observed, he blushes scarlet. If his glances are returned by the little girl, he at once looks shamefacedly the other way. His behaviour is naturally a great joy to every one lunching at the restaurant. Every day as he is taken there he says: "Do you think the little girl will be there today?" And when at last she appears, he goes quite red, just as a grown-up person would in such a case. One day he came to me with a beaming face and whispered in my ear: "Daddy, I know where the little girl lives. I saw her going up the steps in such-and-such a place." Whereas he treats the little girls at home aggressively, in this other affair he appears in the part of a platonic and languishing admirer. Perhaps this has to do with the little girls at home being village children, while the other is a young lady of

_____

edition. – In the editions before 1924 this whole paragraph was enclosed in square brackets. The translators, in 1923, inferred from this fact, and from the references to Hans's parents being in the third person, that the paragraph was a comment of Freud's. On his being asked, however, he replied explicitly that the paragraph originated from Hans's father. From 1924 onwards the square brackets were replaced by round ones.]

refinement. As I have already mentioned, he once said he would like to sleep with her.

'Not wanting Hans to be left in the overwrought state to which he had been brought by his passion for the little girl, I managed to make them acquainted, and invited the little girl to come and see him in the garden after he had finished his afternoon sleep. Hans was so much excited at the prospect of the little girl coming, that for the first time he could not get off to sleep in the afternoon, but tossed about restlessly on his bed. When his mother asked, "Why aren't you asleep? Are you thinking about the little girl?" he said "Yes" with a happy look. And when he came home from the restaurant he said to every one in the house: "I say, my little girl's coming to see me today." The fourteen-year-old Mariedl reported that he had repeatedly kept asking her: "I say, do you think she'll be nice to me? Do you think she'll kiss me if I kiss her?" and so on.

'But in the afternoon it rained, so that the visit did not come off, and Hans consoled himself with Berta and Olga.'

Other observations, also made at the time of the summer holidays, suggest that all sorts of new developments were going on in the little boy.

'Hans, four and a quarter. This morning Hans was given his usual daily bath by his mother and afterwards dried and powdered. As his mother was powdering round his penis and taking care not to touch it, Hans said: "Why don't you put your finger there?"

'*Mother*: "Because that'd be piggish."

'*Hans*: "What's that? Piggish? Why?"

'*Mother*: "Because it's not proper."

'*Hans* (laughing): "But it's great fun."'[1]

1. Another mother, a neurotic, who was unwilling to believe in infantile masturbation, told me of a similar attempt at seduction on the part of her three-and-a-half-year-old daughter. She had had a pair of drawers made for the little girl, and was trying them on her to see whether they were not too tight for walking. To do this she passed her

At about the same period Hans had a dream which was in striking contrast with the boldness he had shown towards his mother. It was the first dream of his that was made unrecognizable by distortion. His father's penetration, however, succeeded in clearing it up.

'Hans, four and a quarter. *Dream*. This morning Hans woke up and said: "I say, last night I thought: *Some one said: 'Who wants to come to me?' Then some one said: 'I do.' Then he had to make him widdle*."

'Further questions made it clear that there was no visual content whatever in this dream, and that it was of the purely auditory type. During the last few days Hans has been playing parlour games and "forfeits" with our landlord's children, amongst whom are his friends Olga (aged seven) and Berta (aged five). (The game of forfeits is played in this way: *A*: "Whose is this forfeit in my hand?" *B*: "Mine." Then it is decided what *B* must do.) The dream was modelled on this game; only what Hans wished was that the person to whom the forfeit belonged should be condemned, not to give the usual kiss or be given the usual box on the ear, but to widdle, or rather to be made to widdle by someone.[1]

'I got him to tell me the dream again. He told it in the same words, except that instead of "then some one said" this time he said "then she said". This "she" is obviously Berta or Olga, one of the girls he had been playing with. Translated, the dream ran as follows: "I was playing forfeits with the little girls. I asked: 'Who wants to come to me?' She (Berta or Olga) replied: 'I do.' Then she had to make me widdle." (That is, she had to assist him in micturating, which is evidently agreeable for Hans.)

---

hand upwards along the inner surface of the child's thigh. Suddenly the little girl shut her legs together on her mother's hand, saying: 'Oh, Mummy, *do* leave your hand there. It feels so lovely.'

1. [So in the original. But, as will be seen, the sense requires 'or rather to make someone else widdle'.]

'It is clear that being made to widdle – having his knickers unbuttoned and his penis taken out – is a pleasurable process for Hans. On walks it is mostly his father who assists Hans in this way; and this gives the child an opportunity for the fixation of homosexual inclinations upon him.

'Two days ago, as I have already reported, while his mother was washing and powdering his genital region, he asked her: "Why don't you put your finger there?" Yesterday, when I was helping Hans to do number one, he asked me for the first time to take him to the back of the house so that no one should see him. He added: "Last year when I widdled, Berta and Olga watched me." This meant, I think, that last year he had enjoyed being watched by the girls, but that this was no longer so. His exhibitionism has now succumbed to repression. The fact that the wish that Berta and Olga should watch him widdling (or make him widdle) is now repressed in real life is the explanation of its appearance in the dream, where it was neatly disguised under the game of forfeits. – I have repeatedly observed since then that he does not like to be seen widdling.'

I will only add that this dream obeys the rule I have given in *The Interpretation of Dreams* [1900a, Chapter VI, Section F, (P.F.L., 4, 545)], to the effect that speeches occurring in dreams are derived from speeches heard or spoken by the dreamer during the preceding days.

Hans's father has noted down one other observation, dating from the period immediately after their return to Vienna: 'Hans (aged four and a half) was again watching his little sister being given her bath, when he began laughing. On being asked why he was laughing, he replied. "I'm laughing at Hanna's widdler." "Why?" "Because her widdler's so lovely."

'Of course his answer was a disingenuous one. In reality her widdler had seemed to him *funny*. Moreover, this is the first time he has recognized in this way the distinction between male and female genitals instead of denying it.'

CASE HISTORY AND ANALYSIS

'MY dear Professor, I am sending you a little more about Hans – but this time, I am sorry to say, material for a case history. As you will see, during the last few days he has developed a nervous disorder, which has made my wife and me most uneasy, because we have not been able to find any means of dissipating it. I shall venture to call upon you tomorrow, . . . but in the meantime . . . I enclose a written record of the material available.

'No doubt the ground was prepared by sexual over-excitation due to his mother's tenderness; but I am not able to specify the actual exciting cause. He is afraid *a horse will bite him in the street*, and this fear seems somehow to be connected with his having been frightened by a large penis. As you know from a former report, he had noticed at a very early age what large penises horses have, and at that time he inferred that as his mother was so large she must have a widdler like a horse. [Cf. p. 173.]

'I cannot see what to make of it. Has he seen an exhibitionist somewhere? Or is the whole thing simply connected with his mother? It is not very pleasant for us that he should begin setting us problems so early. Apart from his being afraid of going into the street and from his being in low spirits in the evening, he is in other respects the same Hans, as bright and cheerful as ever.'

We will not follow Hans's father either in his easily comprehensible anxieties or in his first attempts at finding an explanation; we will begin by examining the material before us. It is not in the least our business to 'understand' a case at once: this is only possible at a later stage, when we have received enough impressions of it. For the present we will suspend our judgement and give our impartial attention to everything that there is to observe.

The earliest accounts, dating from the first days in January of the present year (1908), run as follows:

'Hans (aged four and three-quarters) woke up one morning in tears. Asked why he was crying, he said to his mother: "When I was asleep I thought you were gone and I had no Mummy to coax with."[1]

'An anxiety dream, therefore.

'I had already noticed something similar at Gmunden in the summer. When he was in bed in the evening he was usually in a very sentimental state. Once he made a remark to this effect: "Suppose I was to have no Mummy", or "Suppose you were to go away", or something of the sort; I cannot remember the exact words. Unfortunately, when he got into an elegiac mood of that kind, his mother used always to take him into bed with her.

'On about January 5th he came into his mother's bed in the morning, and said: "Do you know what Aunt M. said? She said: 'He *has* got a dear little thingummy.'"[2] (Aunt M. was stopping with us four weeks ago. Once while she was watching my wife giving the boy a bath she did in fact say these words to her in a low voice. Hans had overheard them and was now trying to put them to his own uses.)

'On January 7th he went to the Stadtpark[3] with his nurse-maid as usual. In the street he began to cry and asked to be taken home, saying that he wanted to "coax" with his Mummy. At home he was asked why he had refused to go any farther and had cried, but he would not say. Till the evening he was

1. 'Hans's expression for "to caress".'
2. Meaning his penis. It is one of the commonest things – psycho-analyses are full of such incidents – for children's genitals to be caressed, not only in word but in deed, by fond relatives, including even parents themselves.
3. [Public gardens near the centre of Vienna.]

cheerful, as usual. But in the evening he grew visibly frightened; he cried and could not be separated from his mother, and
wanted to "coax" with her again. Then he grew cheerful
again, and slept well.

'On January 8th my wife decided to go out with him herself,
so as to see what was wrong with him. They went to Schönbrunn, where he always likes going. Again he began to cry,
did not want to start, and was frightened. In the end he did
go; but was visibly frightened in the street. On the way back
from Schönbrunn he said to his mother, after much internal
struggling: "*I was afraid a horse would bite me.*" (He had, in fact,
become uneasy at Schönbrunn when he saw a horse.) In the
evening he seems to have had another attack similar to that of
the previous evening, and to have wanted to be "coaxed"
with. He was calmed down. He said, crying: "I know I shall
have to go for a walk again tomorrow." And later: "The
horse'll come into the room."

'On the same day his mother asked: "Do you put your hand
to your widdler?" and he answered: "Yes. Every evening,
when I'm in bed." The next day, January 9th, he was warned,
before his afternoon sleep, not to put his hand to his widdler.
When he woke up he was asked about it, and said he had put it
there for a short while all the same.'

Here, then, we have the beginning of Hans's anxiety as well
as of his phobia. As we see, there is good reason for keeping
the two separate. Moreover, the material seems to be amply
sufficient for giving us our bearings; and no moment of time
is so favourable for the understanding of a case as its initial
stage, such as we have here, though unluckily that stage is as
a rule neglected or passed over in silence. The disorder set in
with thoughts that were at the same time fearful and tender,
and then followed an anxiety dream on the subject of losing his
mother and so not being able to coax with her any more. His
affection for his mother must therefore have become enor-
mously intensified. This was the fundamental phenomenon in
his condition. In support of this, we may recall his two attempts

at seducing his mother, the first of which dated back to the summer [p. 182], while the second (a simple commendation of his penis) occurred immediately before the outbreak of his street-anxiety. It was this increased affection for his mother which turned suddenly into anxiety – which, as we should say, succumbed to repression. We do not yet know from what quarter the impetus towards repression may have come. Perhaps it was merely the result of the intensity of the child's emotions, which had become greater than he could control; or perhaps other forces which we have not yet recognized were also at work. This we shall learn as we go on. Hans's anxiety, which thus corresponded to a repressed erotic longing, was, like every infantile anxiety, without an object to begin with: it was still anxiety and not yet fear. The child cannot tell [at first] what he is afraid of; and when Hans, on the first walk with the nursemaid, would not say what he was afraid of, it was simply that he himself did not yet know. He said all that he knew, which was that in the street he missed his mother, whom he could coax with, and that he did not want to be away from her. In saying this he quite straightforwardly confessed the primary meaning of his dislike of streets.

Then again, there were the states into which he fell on two consecutive evenings before going to sleep, and which were characterized by anxiety mingled with clear traces of tenderness. These states show that at the beginning of his illness there was as yet no phobia whatever present, whether of streets or of walking or even of horses. If there had been, his evening states would be inexplicable; for who bothers at bedtime about streets and walking? On the other hand it becomes quite clear why he was so fearful in the evening, if we suppose that at bedtime he was overwhelmed by an intensification of his libido – for its object was his mother, and its aim may perhaps have been to sleep with her. He had besides learnt from his experience that *at Gmunden* his mother could be prevailed upon, when he got into such moods, to take him into her bed, and he wanted to gain the same ends here in Vienna. Nor must we forget that for part of the time at Gmunden he had been alone with his mother, as his father had not been able to spend the whole of the holidays there, and further, that in the country his affections had been divided among a number of playmates and friends of both sexes, while in Vienna he had none, so that his libido was in a position to return undivided to his mother.

His anxiety, then, corresponded to repressed longing. But it was not the same thing as the longing: the repression must be taken into account too. Longing can be completely transformed into satisfaction if it is presented with the object longed for. Therapy of that kind is no longer effective in dealing with anxiety. The anxiety remains even when the longing can be satisfied. It can no longer be completely retransformed into libido; there is something that keeps the libido back under repression.[1] This was shown to be so in the case of Hans on the occasion of his next walk, when his mother went with him. He was with his mother, and yet he still suffered from anxiety – that is to say, from an unsatisfied longing for her. It is true that the anxiety was less; for he did allow himself to be induced to go for the walk, whereas he had obliged the nursemaid to turn back. Nor is a street quite the right place for 'coaxing', or whatever else this young lover may have wanted. But his anxiety had stood the test; and the next thing for it to do was to find an object. It was on this walk that he first expressed a fear that a horse would bite him. Where did the material for this phobia come from? Probably from the complexes, as yet unknown to us, which had contributed to the repression and were keeping under repression his libidinal feelings towards his mother. That is an unsolved problem, and we shall now have to follow the development of the case in order to arrive at its solution. Hans's father has already given us certain clues, prob-

1. To speak quite frankly, this is actually the criterion according to which we decide whether such feelings of mingled apprehension and longing are normal or not: we begin to call them 'pathological anxiety' from the moment at which they can no longer be relieved by the attainment of the object longed for.

ably trustworthy ones, such as that Hans had always observed horses with interest on account of their large widdlers, that he had supposed that his mother must have a widdler like a horse, and so on. We might thus be led to think that the horse was merely a substitute for his mother. But if so, what would be the meaning of his being afraid in the evening that a horse would come into the room? A small boy's foolish fears, it will be said. But a neurosis never says foolish things, any more than a dream. When we cannot understand something, we always fall back on abuse. An excellent way of making a task lighter.

There is another point in regard to which we must avoid giving way to this temptation. Hans admitted that every night before going to sleep he amused himself with playing with his penis. 'Ah!' the family doctor will be inclined to say, 'now we have it. The child masturbated: hence his pathological anxiety.' But gently. That the child was getting pleasure for himself by masturbating does not by any means explain his anxiety; on the contrary, it makes it more problematical than ever. States of anxiety are not produced by masturbation or by getting satisfaction in any shape. Moreover, we may presume that Hans, who was now four and three-quarters, had been indulging in this pleasure every evening for at least a year (see p. 171). And we shall find [pp. 193–4] that at this moment he was actually engaged in a struggle to break himself of the habit – a state of things which fits in much better with repression and the generation of anxiety.

We must say a word, too, on behalf of Hans's excellent and devoted mother. His father accuses her, not without some show of injustice, of being responsible for the outbreak of the child's neurosis, on account of her excessive display of affection for him and her too frequent readiness to take him into her bed. We might as easily blame her for having precipitated the process of repression by her energetic rejection of his advances ('that'd be piggish' [p. 182]). But she had a predestined part to play, and her position was a hard one.

I arranged with Hans's father that he should tell the boy that all this business about horses was a piece of nonsense and nothing more. The truth was, his father was to say, that he was very fond of his mother and wanted to be taken into her bed. The reason he was afraid of horses now was that he had taken so much interest in their widdlers. He himself had noticed that it was not right to be so very much preoccupied with widdlers, even with his own, and he was quite right in thinking this. I further suggested to his father that he should begin giving Hans some enlightenment in the matter of sex knowledge. The child's past behaviour justified us in assuming that his libido was attached to a wish to see his mother's widdler; so I proposed to his father that he should take away this aim from Hans by informing him that his mother and all other female beings (as he could see from Hanna) had no widdler at all. This last piece of enlightenment was to be given him on a suitable occasion when it had been led up to by some question or some chance remark on Hans's part.

The next batch of news about Hans covers the period from March 1st to March 17th. The interval of more than a month will be accounted for directly.

'After Hans had been enlightened,[1] there followed a fairly quiet period, during which he could be induced without any particular difficulty to go for his daily walk in the Stadtpark. [See p. 258.] His fear of horses became transformed more and more into a compulsion to look at them. He said: "I have to look at horses, and then I'm frightened."

'After an attack of influenza, which kept him in bed for two weeks, his phobia increased again so much that he could not be induced to go out, or at any rate no more than on to the balcony. Every Sunday he went with me to Lainz,[2] because on

1. As to the meaning of his anxiety; not yet as to women having no widdlers.

2. A suburb of Vienna [just beyond Schönbrunn] where Hans's grandparents lived.

that day there is not much traffic in the streets, and it is only a short way to the station. On one occasion in Lainz he refused to go for a walk outside the garden because there was a carriage standing in front of it. After another week which he has had to spend indoors because he has had his tonsils out, the phobia has grown very much worse again. He goes out on to the balcony, it is true, but not for a walk. As soon as he gets to the street door he hurriedly turns round.

'On Sunday, March 1st, the following conversation took place on the way to the station. I was once more trying to explain to him that horses do not bite. *He*: "But white horses bite. There's a white horse at Gmunden that bites. If you hold your finger to it it bites." (I was struck by his saying "finger" instead of "hand".) He then told me the following story, which I give here in a connected form: "When Lizzi had to go away, there was a cart with a white horse in front of her house, to take her luggage to the station." (Lizzi, he tells me, was a little girl who lived in a neighbouring house.) "Her father was standing near the horse, and the horse turned its head round (to touch him), and he said to Lizzi: *'Don't put your finger to the white horse or it'll bite you.'*" Upon this I said: "I say, it strikes me that it isn't a horse you mean, but a widdler, that one mustn't put one's hand to."

'*He*: "But a widdler doesn't bite."

'*I*: "Perhaps it does, though." He then went on eagerly to try and prove to me that it really was a white horse.[1]

'On March 2nd, as he again showed signs of being afraid, I said to him: "Do you know what? This nonsense of yours" (that is how he speaks of his phobia) "will get better if you go for more walks. It's so bad now because you haven't been able to go out because you were ill."

---

1. Hans's father had no reason to doubt that it was a real event that the boy was describing. – I may also mention that the sensations of itching in the glans penis, which lead children to touch their genitals, are usually described by them in the phrase '*Es beisst mich*' ['I'm itching', literally 'it bites me'].

'*He*: "Oh no, it's so bad because I still put my hand to my widdler every night."'

Doctor and patient, father and son, were therefore at one in ascribing the chief share in the pathogenesis of Hans's present condition to his habit of masturbating. Indications were not wanting, however, of the presence of other significant factors.

'On March 3rd we got in a new maid, whom he is particularly pleased with. She lets him ride on her back while she cleans the floor, and so he always calls her "my horse", and holds on to her dress with cries of "Gee-up". On about March 10th he said to this new nursemaid: "If you do such-and-such a thing you'll have to undress altogether, and take off your chemise even." (He meant this as a punishment, but it is easy to recognize the wish behind it.)

'*She*: "And what'd be the harm? I'd just say to myself I haven't got any money to spend on clothes."

'*He*: "Why, it'd be shameful. People'd see your widdler."'

Here we have the same curiosity again, but directed on to a new object, and (appropriately to a period of repression) cloaked under a moralizing purpose.

'On March 13th in the morning I said to Hans: "You know, if you don't put your hand to your widdler any more, this nonsense of yours'll soon get better."

'*Hans*: "But I don't put my hand to my widdler any more."

'*I*: "But you still want to."

'*Hans*: "Yes, I do. But wanting's not doing, and doing's not wanting." (!!)

'*I*: "Well, but to prevent your wanting to, this evening you're going to have a bag to sleep in."

'After this we went out in front of the house. Hans was still afraid, but his spirits were visibly raised by the prospect of having his struggles made easier for him, and he said: "Oh, if I have a bag to sleep in my nonsense'll have gone tomorrow." And, in fact, he was *much* less afraid of horses, and was fairly calm when vehicles drove past.

'Hans had promised to go with me to Lainz the next Sunday,

March 15th. He resisted at first, but finally went with me all the same. He obviously felt all right in the street, as there was not much traffic, and said: "How sensible! God's done away with horses now." On the way I explained to him that his sister has not got a widdler like him. Little girls and women, I said, have no widdlers: Mummy has none, Anna has none, and so on.

'*Hans*: "Have you got a widdler?"

'*I*: "Of course. Why, what do you suppose?"

'*Hans* (after a pause): "But how do little girls widdle, if they have no widdlers?"

'*I*: "They don't have widdlers like yours. Haven't you noticed already, when Hanna was being given her bath?"

'All day long he was in very high spirits, went tobogganing, and so on. It was only towards evening that he fell into low spirits again and seemed to be afraid of horses.

'That evening his attack of nerves and his need for being coaxed with were less pronounced than on previous days. Next day his mother took him with her into town and he was very much frightened in the streets. The day after, he stopped at home and was very cheerful. Next morning he woke up in a fright at about six o'clock. When he was asked what was the matter he said: "I put my finger to my widdler just a very little. I saw Mummy quite naked in her chemise, and she let me see her widdler. I showed Grete,[1] my Grete, what Mummy was doing, and showed her my widdler. Then I took my hand away from my widdler quick." When I objected that he could only mean "in her chemise" *or* "quite naked", Hans said: "She was in her chemise, but the chemise was so short that I saw her widdler."'

This was none of it a dream, but a masturbatory phantasy, which was, however, equivalent to a dream. What he made his mother do was evidently intended as a piece of self-justification: 'If Mummy shows her widdler, I may too.'

---

1. 'Grete is one of the little girls at Gmunden about whom Hans is having phantasies just now; he talks and plays with her.'

We can gather two things from this phantasy: first, that his mother's reproof had produced a powerful result on him at the time it was made,[1] and secondly, that the enlightenment he had been given to the effect that women have no widdlers was not accepted by him at first. He regretted that it should be so, and in his phantasy he stuck to his former view. He may also perhaps have had his reasons for refusing to believe his father for the moment.

Weekly Report from Hans's Father: 'My dear Professor, I enclose the continuation of Hans's story – quite an interesting instalment. I shall perhaps take the liberty of calling upon you during your consulting hours on Monday and if possible of bringing Hans with me – assuming that he will come. I said to him today: "Will you come with me on Monday to see the Professor, who can take away your nonsense for you?"

'*He*: "No."

'*I*: "But he's got a very pretty little girl." – Upon which he willingly and gladly consented.

'Sunday, March 22nd. With a view to extending the Sunday programme, I proposed to Hans that we should go first to Schönbrunn, and only go on from there to Lainz at midday. He had, therefore, to make his way not only from our house to the Hauptzollamt station on the Stadtbahn,[2] but also from the Hietzing station to Schönbrunn, and again from there to the Hietzing steam tramway station. And he managed all this, looking hurriedly away whenever any horses came along, for he was evidently feeling nervous. In looking away he was following a piece of advice given him by his mother.

'At Schönbrunn he showed signs of fear at animals which on other occasions he had looked at without any alarm. Thus he

---

1. [This presumably refers to her threat (p. 171). But see the qualification of this on pp. 197-8.]

2. [The Head Customs House station on the Vienna local and sub-urban railway. Hietzing is a suburb which adjoins the palace of Schönbrunn.]

absolutely refused to go into the house in which the *giraffe* is kept, nor would he visit the elephant, which used formerly to amuse him a great deal. He was afraid of all the large animals, whereas he was very much entertained by the small ones. Among the birds, he was also afraid of the pelican this time – which had never happened before – evidently because of its size again.

'I therefore said to him: "Do you know why you're afraid of big animals? Big animals have big widdlers, and you're really afraid of big widdlers."

'*Hans*: "But I've never seen the big animals' widdlers yet."[1]

'*I*: "But you *have* seen a horse's, and a horse is a big animal."

'*Hans*: "O, a horse's often. Once at Gmunden when the cart was standing at the door, and once in front of the Head Customs House."

'*I*: "When you were small, you most likely went into a stable at Gmunden . . ."

'*Hans* (interrupting): "Yes, I went into the stable every day at Gmunden when the horses had come home."

'*I*: ". . . and you were most likely frightened when you saw the horse's big widdler one time. But there's no need for you to be frightened of it. Big animals have big widdlers, and little animals have little widdlers."

'*Hans*: "And every one has a widdler. And my widdler will get bigger as I get bigger; it's fixed in, of course."

'Here the talk came to an end. During the next few days it seemed as though his fears had again somewhat increased. He hardly ventured out of the front door, to which he was taken after luncheon.'

Hans's last words of comfort throw a light upon the situation and allow us to make some small corrections in his father's assertions. It is true that he was afraid of big animals because

---

1. This was untrue. See his exclamation in front of the lions' cage on p. 172. It was probably the beginning of amnesia resulting from repression.

he was obliged to think of their big widdlers; but it cannot really be said that he was afraid of big widdlers themselves. Formerly the idea of them had been decidedly pleasurable to him, and he used to make every effort to get a glimpse of one. Since that time this enjoyment had been spoiled for him, owing to the general reversal of pleasure into unpleasure which had come over the whole of his sexual researches – in a way which has not yet been explained – and also owing to something which is clearer to us, namely, to certain experiences and reflections which had led to distressing conclusions. We may infer from his self-consolatory words ('my widdler will get bigger as I get bigger') that during his observations he had constantly been making comparisons, and that he had remained extremely dissatisfied with the size of his own widdler. Big animals reminded him of his defect, and were for that reason disagreeable to him. But since the whole train of thought was probably incapable of becoming clearly conscious, this distressing feeling, too, was transformed into anxiety, so that his present anxiety was erected both upon his former pleasure and his present unpleasure. When once a state of anxiety establishes itself, the anxiety swallows up all other feelings; with the progress of repression, and the more those ideas which are charged with affect and which have been conscious move down into the unconscious, all affects are capable of being changed into anxiety.

Hans's singular remark, 'it's fixed in, of course', makes it possible to guess many things in connection with his consolatory speech which he could not express in words and did not express during the course of the analysis. I shall bridge the gap for a little distance by means of my experiences in the analyses of grown-up people; but I hope the interpolation will not be considered arbitrary or capricious. 'It's fixed in, of course': if the motives of the thought were solace and defiance, we are reminded of his mother's old threat that she should have his widdler cut off if he went on playing with it. [See p. 171.] At the time it was made, when he was three and a half, this threat had no effect. He calmly replied that then he should widdle with his bottom. It would be the most completely typical procedure if the threat of castration were to have a *deferred* effect, and if he were now, a year and a quarter later, oppressed by the fear of having to lose this precious piece of his ego. In other cases of illness we can observe a similar deferred operation of commands and threats made in childhood, where the interval covers as many decades or more. I even know cases in which a 'deferred obedience' under the influence of repression has had a principal share in determining the symptoms of the disease.[1]

The piece of enlightenment which Hans had been given a short time before to the effect that women really do not possess a widdler was bound to have had a shattering effect upon his self-confidence and to have aroused his castration complex. For this reason he resisted the information, and for this reason it had no therapeutic results. Could it be that living beings really did exist which did not possess widdlers? If so, it would no longer be so incredible that they could take his own widdler away, and, as it were, make him into a woman![2]

---

1. [Another instance of 'deferred obedience' will be found in the Schreber analysis (1911c). A sociological application of the concept appears in *Totem and Taboo* (1912–13), *P.F.L.*, **9**, 191 and n.3; ibid., **13**, 205 and n.1.]

2. I cannot interrupt the discussion so far as to demonstrate the typical character of the unconscious train of thought which I think there is here reason for attributing to little Hans. The castration complex is the deepest unconscious root of anti-semitism; for even in the nursery little boys hear that a Jew has something cut off his penis – a piece of his penis, they think – and this gives them a right to despise Jews. And there is no stronger unconscious root for the sense of superiority over women. Weininger (the young philosopher who, highly gifted but sexually deranged, committed suicide after producing his remarkable book, *Geschlecht und Charakter* [1903]), in a chapter that attracted much attention, treated Jews and women with equal hostility and overwhelmed them with the same insults. Being a neurotic, Weininger was completely under the sway of his infantile complexes; and from that standpoint what is common to Jews and women is their relation to the

'During the night of 27th-28th Hans surprised us by getting out of bed while it was quite dark and coming into our bed. His room is separated from our bedroom by another small room. We asked him why: whether he had been afraid, perhaps. "No," he said; "I'll tell you tomorrow." He went to sleep in our bed and was then carried back to his own.

'Next day I questioned him closely to discover why he had come in to us during the night; and after some reluctance the following dialogue took place, which I immediately took down in shorthand:

'*He*: "*In the night there was a big giraffe in the room and a crumpled one; and the big one called out because I took the crumpled one away from it. Then it stopped calling out; and then I sat down on top of the crumpled one.*"

'*I* (puzzled): "What? A crumpled giraffe? How was that?"

'*He*: "Yes." (He quickly fetched a piece of paper, crumpled it up, and said:) "It was crumpled like that."

'*I*: "And you sat down on top of the crumpled giraffe? How?"

'He again showed me, by sitting down on the ground.

'*I*: "Why did you come into our room?"

'*He*: "I don't know myself."

'*I*: "Were you afraid?"

'*He*: "No. Of course not."

'*I*: "Did you dream about the giraffe?"

'*He*: "No. I didn't dream. I thought it. I thought it all. I'd woken up earlier."

'*I*: "What can it mean: a crumpled giraffe? You know you can't squash a giraffe together like a piece of paper."

'*He*: "Of course I know. I just thought it. Of course there aren't any really and truly.[1] The crumpled one was all lying on

_____

castration complex. [A more elaborate analysis of anti-semitism will be found in one of Freud's last writings, *Moses and Monotheism* (1939*a*), P.F.L., **13**, 334 ff.]

1. In his own language Hans was saying quite definitely that it was a phantasy.

the floor, and I took it away – took hold of it with my hands."

'*I*: "What? Can you take hold of a big giraffe like that with your hands?'

'*He*: "I took hold of the crumpled one with my hand."

'*I*: "Where was the big one meanwhile?"'

'*He*: "The big one just stood farther off."

'*I*: "What did you do with the crumpled one?"'

'*He*: "I held it in my hand for a bit, till the big one had stopped calling out. And when the big one had stopped calling out, I sat down on top of it."

'*I*: "Why did the big one call out?"'

'*He*: "Because I'd taken away the little one from it." (He noticed that I was taking everything down, and asked:) "Why are you writing that down?"'

'*I*: "Because I shall send it to a Professor, who can take away your 'nonsense' for you."'

'*He*: "Oho! So you've written down as well that Mummy took off her chemise, and you'll give that to the Professor too."

'*I*: "Yes. But he won't understand how you can think that a giraffe can be crumpled up."'

'*He*: "Just tell him I don't know myself, and then he won't ask. But if he asks what the crumpled giraffe is, then he can write to us, and we can write back, or let's write at once that I don't know myself."

'*I*: "But why did you come in in the night?"'

'*He*: "I don't know."

'*I*: "Just tell me quickly what you're thinking of."'

'*He* (jokingly): "Of raspberry syrup." ⎫

'*I*: "What else?" ⎬ His wishes.

'*He*: "A gun for shooting people dead with."[1] ⎭

'*I*: "You're sure you didn't dream it?"'

---

1. At this point his father in his perplexity was trying to practise the classical technique of psychoanalysis. This did not lead to much; but the result, such as it was, can be given a meaning in the light of later disclosures. [See pp. 258 and 270 *n*. 2.]

'*He*: "Quite sure; no, I'm quite certain of it."'

'He proceeded: "Mummy begged me so long to tell her why I came in in the night. But I didn't want to say, because I felt ashamed with Mummy at first."'

'*I*: "Why?"'

'*He*: "I didn't know."'

'My wife had in fact examined him all the morning, till he had told her the giraffe story.'

That same day his father discovered the solution of the giraffe phantasy.

'The big giraffe is myself, or rather my big penis (the long neck), and the crumpled giraffe is my wife, or rather her genital organ. It is therefore the result of the enlightenment he has had [p. 194].

'Giraffe: see the expedition to Schönbrunn. [Cf. pp. 177 and 195 f.]. Moreover, he has a picture of a giraffe and an elephant hanging over his bed.

'The whole thing is a reproduction of a scene which has been gone through almost every morning for the last few days. Hans always comes in to us in the early morning, and my wife cannot resist taking him into bed with her for a few minutes. Thereupon I always begin to warn her not to take him into bed with her ("the big one called out because I'd taken the crumpled one away from it"); and she answers now and then, rather irritated, no doubt, that it's all nonsense, that after all one minute is of no importance, and so on. Then Hans stays with her a little while. ("Then the big giraffe stopped calling out; and then I sat down on top of the crumpled one.")

'Thus the solution of this matrimonial scene transposed into giraffe life is this: he was seized in the night with a longing for his mother, for her caresses, for her genital organ, and came into our bedroom for that reason. The whole thing is a continuation of his fear of horses.'

I have only this to add to his father's penetrating interpretation. The '*sitting* down on top of' was probably Hans's representation of taking *possession*.[1] But the whole thing was a phantasy of defiance connected with his satisfaction at the triumph over his father's resistance. 'Call out as much as you like! But Mummy takes me into bed all the same, and Mummy belongs to me!' It is therefore justifiable, as his father suspected, to divine behind the phantasy a fear that his mother did not like him, because his widdler was not comparable to his father's.

Next morning his father was able to get his interpretation confirmed.

'On Sunday, March 29th, I went with Hans to Lainz. I jokingly took leave of my wife at the door with the words: "Good-bye, big giraffe!" "Why giraffe?" asked Hans. "Mummy's the big giraffe," I replied; to which Hans rejoined: "Oh yes! And Hanna's the crumpled giraffe, isn't she?"

'In the train I explained the giraffe phantasy to him, upon which he said: "Yes, that's right." And when I said to him that I was the big giraffe, and that its long neck had reminded him of a widdler, he said: "Mummy has a neck like a giraffe, too. I saw, when she was washing her white neck."[2]

'On Monday, March 30th, in the morning, Hans came to me and said: "I say! I thought two things this morning!" "What was the first?" "I was with you at Schönbrunn where the sheep are; and then we crawled through under the ropes, and then we told the policeman at the end of the garden, and he grabbed hold of us." He had forgotten the second thing.

'I can add the following comment on this. When we wanted to visit the sheep on Sunday, we found that a space in the gardens was shut off by a rope, so that we were unable to get to them. Hans was very much astonished that the space should be

---

1. [The German word for 'possession' ('*Besitz*') shows its etymological connection with the phrase used by little Hans ('*sich draufsetzen*') more obviously than the English.]

2. Háns only confirmed the interpretation of the two giraffes as his father and mother, and not the sexual symbolism, according to which the giraffe itself represented the penis. This symbolism was probably correct, but we really cannot ask more of Hans.

shut off only with a rope, which it would be quite easy to slip under. I told him that respectable people didn't crawl under the rope. He said it would be quite easy; whereupon I replied that a policeman might come along and take one off. There is a lifeguardsman on duty at the entrance of Schönbrunn; and I once told Hans that he arrested naughty children.

'After we returned from our visit to you, which took place the same day, Hans confessed to yet another little bit of craving to do something forbidden: "I say, I thought something this morning again." "What?" "I went with you in the train, and we smashed a window and the policeman took us off with him." '

A most suitable continuation of the giraffe phantasy. He had a suspicion that to take possession of his mother was forbidden; he had come up against the barrier against incest.[1] But he regarded it as forbidden *in itself*. His father was with him each time in the forbidden exploits which he carried out in his imagination, and was locked up with him. His father, he thought, also did that enigmatic forbidden something with his mother which he replaced by an act of violence such as smashing a window-pane or forcing a way into an enclosed space.

That afternoon the father and son visited me during my consulting hours. I already knew the funny little fellow, and with all his self-assurance he was yet so amiable that I had always been glad to see him. I do not know whether he remembered me, but he behaved irreproachably and like a perfectly reasonable member of human society. The consultation was a short one. His father opened it by remarking that, in spite of all the pieces of enlightenment we had given Hans, his fear of horses had not yet diminished. We were also forced to confess that the connections between the horses he was afraid of and the affectionate feelings towards his mother which had been revealed were by no means abundant. Certain details which I now learnt – to the effect that he was particularly bothered by

1. [See the last section of the third of Freud's *Three Essays on the Theory of Sexuality* (1905d), P.F.L., **7**, 148.]

what horses wear in front of their eyes and by the black round their mouths – were certainly not to be explained from what we knew. But as I saw the two of them sitting in front of me and at the same time heard Hans's description of his anxiety-horses, a further piece of the solution shot through my mind, and a piece which I could well understand might escape his father. I asked Hans jokingly whether his horses wore eye-glasses, to which he replied that they did not. I then asked him whether his father wore eyeglasses, to which, against all the evidence, he once more said no. Finally I asked him whether by 'the black round the mouth' he meant a moustache; and I then disclosed to him that he was afraid of his father, precisely because he was so fond of his mother. It must be, I told him, that he thought his father was angry with him on that account; but this was not so, his father was fond of him in spite of it, and he might admit everything to him without any fear. Long before he was in the world, I went on, I had known that a little Hans would come who would be so fond of his mother that he would be bound to feel afraid of his father because of it; and I had told his father this. 'But why do you think I'm angry with you?' his father interrupted me at this point; 'have I ever scolded you or hit you?' Hans corrected him: 'Oh yes! You have hit me.' 'That's not true. When was it, anyhow?' 'This morning,' answered the little boy; and his father recollected that Hans had quite unexpectedly butted his head into his stomach, so that he had given him as it were a reflex blow with his hand. It was remarkable that he had not brought this detail into connection with the neurosis; but he now recognized it as an expression of the little boy's hostile disposition towards him, and perhaps also as a manifestation of a need for getting punished for it.[1]

'Does the Professor talk to God,' Hans asked his father on the way home, 'as he can tell all that beforehand?' I should be

1. Later on the boy repeated his reaction towards his father in a clearer and more complete manner, by first hitting his father on the hand and then affectionately kissing the same hand. – [Cf. in this connection the third part of Freud's paper on 'Character Types' (1916*d*).]

extraordinarily proud of this recognition out of the mouth of a child, if I had not myself provoked it by my joking boastfulness. From the date of this consultation I received almost daily reports of the alterations in the little patient's condition. It was not to be expected that he should be freed from his anxiety at a single blow by the information I gave him; but it became apparent that a possibility had now been offered him of bringing forward his unconscious productions and of unfolding his phobia. From that time forward he carried out a programme which I was able to announce to his father in advance.

'April 2nd. The *first real improvement* is to be noted. While formerly he could never be induced to go out of the street-door for very long, and always ran back into the house with every sign of fright if horses came along, this time he stayed in front of the street-door for an hour – even while carts were driving past, which happens fairly often in our street. Every now and then he ran into the house when he saw a cart approaching in the distance, but he turned round at once as though he were changing his mind. In any case there is only a trace of the anxiety left, and the progress since his enlightenment is unmistakable.

'In the evening he said: "We get as far as the street-door now, so we'll go into the Stadtpark too."

'On April 3rd, in the morning he came into bed with me, whereas for the last few days he had not been coming any more and had even seemed to be proud of not doing so. "And why have you come today?" I asked.

'*Hans*: "When I'm not frightened I shan't come any more."

'*I*: "So you come in to me because you're frightened?"

'*Hans*: "When I'm not with you I'm frightened; when I'm not in bed with you, then I'm frightened. When I'm not frightened any more I shan't come any more."

'*I*: "So you're fond of me and you feel anxious when you're in your bed in the morning? and that's why you come in to me?"

'*Hans*: "Yes. Why did you tell me I'm fond of *Mummy* and that's why I'm frightened, when I'm fond of *you*?"'

Here the little boy was displaying a really unusual degree of clarity. He was bringing to notice the fact that his love for his father was wrestling with his hostility towards him in his capacity of rival with his mother; and he was reproaching his father with not having yet drawn his attention to this interplay of forces, which was bound to end in anxiety. His father did not entirely understand him as yet, for during this conversation he only succeeded in convincing himself of the little boy's hostility towards him, the existence of which I had asserted during our consultation. The following dialogue, which I nevertheless give without alteration, is really of more importance in connection with the progress of the father's enlightenment than with the little patient.

'Unfortunately I did not immediately grasp the meaning of this reproach. Because Hans is fond of his mother he evidently wants to get me out of the way, and he would then be in his father's place. This suppressed hostile wish is turned into anxiety *about* his father, and he comes in to me in the morning to see if I have gone away. Unfortunately at the moment I did not understand this, and said to him:

'"When you're alone, you're just anxious for me and come in to me."

'*Hans*: "When you're away, I'm afraid you're not coming home."

'*I*: "And have I ever threatened you that I shan't come home?"

'*Hans*: "Not you, but Mummy. Mummy's told me she won't come back." (He had probably been naughty, and she had threatened to go away.)

'*I*: "She said that because you were naughty."

'*Hans*: "Yes."

'*I*: "So you're afraid I'm going away because you were naughty; that's why you come in to me."

'When I got up from table after breakfast Hans said:

"Daddy, don't trot away from me!" I was struck by his saying "trot" instead of "run", and replied: "Oho! So you're afraid of the horse trotting away from you." Upon which he laughed.'

We know that this portion of Hans's anxiety had two constituents: there was fear *of* his father and fear *for* his father. The former was derived from his hostility towards his father, and the latter from the conflict between his affection, which was exaggerated at this point by way of compensation, and his hostility.

His father proceeds: 'This is no doubt the beginning of an important phase. His motive for at the most just venturing outside the house but not going away from it, and for turning round at the first attack of anxiety when he is half-way, is his fear of not finding his parents at home because they have gone away. He sticks to the house from love of his mother, and he is afraid of my going away because of the hostile wishes that he nourishes against me – for then *he* would be the father.

'In the summer I used to be constantly leaving Gmunden for Vienna on business, and he was then the father. You will remember that his fear of horses is connected with the episode at Gmunden when a horse was to take Lizzi's luggage to the station [p. 192]. The repressed wish that I should drive to the station, for then he would be alone with his mother (the wish that "the horse should drive off"), is turned into fear of the horse's driving off; and in fact nothing throws him into greater alarm than when a cart drives off from the courtyard of the Head Customs House (which is just opposite our flat) and the horses start moving.

'This new phase (hostile sentiments towards his father) could only come out after he knew that I was not angry because he was so fond of his mother.

'In the afternoon I went out in front of the street-door with him again; he again went out in front of the house, and stayed there even when carts went past. In the case of a few carts only he was afraid, and ran into the entrance-hall. He also said to me in explanation: "Not all white horses bite." That is to say: owing to the analysis some white horses have already been recognized as "Daddy", and they no longer bite; but there are others still left over which *do* bite.

'The position of our street-door is as follows: Opposite it is the warehouse of the Office for the Taxation of Food-Stuffs, with a loading dock at which carts are driving up all day long to fetch away boxes, packing-cases, etc. This courtyard is cut off from the street by railings; and the entrance gates to the courtyard are opposite our house (Fig. 2). I have noticed for

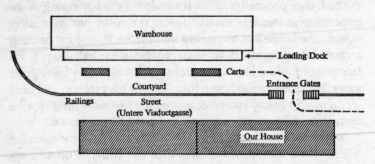

FIG. 2.

some days that Hans is specially frightened when carts drive into or out of the yard, a process which involves their taking a corner. I asked at the time why he was so much afraid, and he replied: "*I'm afraid the horses will fall down when the cart turns*" (a). He is equally frightened when carts standing at the loading dock start moving in order to drive off (b). Further (c), he is more frightened of large dray-horses than of small horses, and of rough farm-horses than of smart horses (such as those in a carriage and pair). He is also more frightened when a vehicle drives past quickly (d) than when the horses trot up slowly. These differentiations have, of course, only come to light clearly during the last few days.'

I should be inclined to say that, in consequence of the analysis, not only the patient but his phobia too had plucked up courage and was venturing to show itself. [Cf. p. 281.]

'On April 5th Hans came in to our bedroom again, and was sent back to his own bed. I said to him: "As long as you come into our room in the mornings, your fear of horses won't get better." He was defiant, however, and replied: "I shall come in all the same, even if I *am* afraid." So he will not let himself be forbidden to visit his mother.

'After breakfast we were to go downstairs. Hans was delighted, and planned that, instead of stopping in front of the street-door as usual, he should go across the street into the yard, where he had often enough seen street-boys playing. I told him I should be pleased if he were to go across, and took the opportunity of asking him why he is so much afraid when the loaded carts at the loading dock start moving (b).

'*Hans*: "I'm afraid of standing by the cart and the cart driving off quick, and of my standing on it and wanting to get on to the board (the loading dock), and my driving off in the cart."

'*I*: "And if the cart stands still? Aren't you afraid then? Why not?"

'*Hans*: "If the cart stands still, then I can get on to the cart quick and get on to the board." [Fig. 3.]

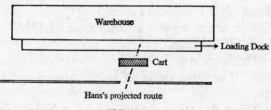

FIG. 3.

'(So Hans is planning to climb over a cart on to the loading dock, and is afraid of the cart driving away, while he is on it.)

'*I*: "Perhaps you're afraid you won't come home any more if you drive away in the cart?"

'*Hans*: "Oh no! I can always come back to Mummy, in the cart or in a cab. I can tell him the number of the house too."

'*I*: "Then why *are* you afraid?"

'*Hans*: "I don't know. But the Professor'll know. D'you think he'll know?"

'*I*: "And why do you want to get over on to the board?"

'*Hans*: "Because I've never been up there, and I should so much like to be there; and d'you know why I should like to go there? Because I should like to load and unload the boxes, and I should like to climb about on the boxes there. I should so like to climb about there. D'you know who I learnt the climbing about from? Some boys climbed on the boxes, and I saw them, and I want to do it too."

'His wish was not fulfilled. For when Hans ventured once more in front of the street-door, the few steps across the street and into the courtyard awoke too great resistances in him, because carts were constantly driving into the yard.'

The Professor only knows that the game which Hans intended to play with the loaded carts must have stood in the relation of a symbolic substitute to some other wish as to which he had so far uttered no word. But, if it did not seem too daring, this wish might already, even at this stage, be constructed.

'In the afternoon we again went out in front of the street-door, and when I returned I asked Hans:

'"Which horses are you actually most afraid of?"

'*Hans*: "All of them."

'*I*: "That's not true."

'*Hans*: "I'm most afraid of horses with a thing on their mouths."

'*I*: "What do you mean? The piece of iron they have in their mouths?"

'*Hans*: "No. They have something black on their mouths." (He covered his mouth with his hand.)

'*I*: "What? A moustache, perhaps?"

'*Hans* (laughing): "Oh no!"

'*I*: "Have they all got it?"

'*Hans*: "No, only a few of them."

'*I*: "What is it that they've got on their mouths?"

'*Hans*: "A black thing." (I think in reality it must be the thick piece of harness that dray-horses wear over their noses.) [Fig. 4.]

FIG. 4.

'"And I'm most afraid of furniture-vans, too."

'*I*: "Why?"

'*Hans*: "I think when furniture-horses are dragging a heavy van they'll fall down."

'*I*: "So you're not afraid with a small cart?"

'*Hans*: "No. I'm not afraid with a small cart or with a post-office van. I'm most afraid too when a bus comes along."

'*I*: "Why? Because it's so big?"

'*Hans*: "No. Because once a horse in a bus fell down."

'*I*: "When?"

'*Hans*: "Once when I went out with Mummy in spite of my 'nonsense', when I bought the waistcoat." (This was subsequently confirmed by his mother.)

'*I*: "What did you think when the horse fell down?"

'*Hans*: "Now it'll always be like this. All horses in buses'll fall down."

'*I*: "In all buses?"

'*Hans*: "Yes. And in furniture-vans too. Not often in furniture-vans."

'*I*: "You had your nonsense already at that time?"

'*Hans*: "No. I only got it then. When the horse in the bus fell down, it gave me such a fright, really! That was when I got the nonsense."

'*I*: "But the nonsense was that you thought a horse would bite you. And now you say you were afraid a horse would fall down."

'*Hans*: "Fall down and bite."[1]

'*I*: "Why did it give you such a fright?"

'*Hans*: "Because the horse went like this with its feet." (He lay down on the ground and showed me how it kicked about.) "It gave me a fright *because it made a row with its feet*."

'*I*: "Where did you go with Mummy that day?"

'*Hans*: "First to the Skating Rink, then to a *café*, then to buy a waistcoat, then to the pastry-cook's with Mummy, and then home in the evening; we went back through the Stadtpark." (All of this was confirmed by my wife, as well as the fact that the anxiety broke out immediately afterwards.)

'*I*: "Was the horse dead when it fell down?"

'*Hans*: "Yes!"

'*I*: "How do you know that?"

'*Hans*: "Because I saw it." (He laughed.) "No, it wasn't a bit dead."

'*I*: "Perhaps you thought it was dead?"

'*Hans*: "No. Certainly not. I only said it as a joke." (His expression at the moment, however, had been serious.)

'As he was tired, I let him run off. He only told me besides this that he had first been afraid of bus-horses, then of all others, and only in the end of furniture-van horses.

'On the way back from Lainz there were a few more questions:

'*I*: "When the bus-horse fell down, what colour was it? White, red, brown, grey?"

'*Hans*: "Black. Both horses were black."

'*I*: "Was it big or little?"

'*Hans*: "Big."

'*I*: "Fat or thin?"

---

1. Hans was right, however improbable this collocation may sound. The train of thought, as we shall see, was that the horse (his father) would bite him because of his wish that it (his father) should fall down.

'*Hans*: "Fat. Very big and fat."

'*I*: "When the horse fell down, did you think of your daddy?"

'*Hans*: "Perhaps. Yes. It's possible."'

His father's investigations may have been without success at some points; but it does no harm to make acquaintance at close quarters with a phobia of this sort – which we may feel inclined to name after its new objects. [Cf. p. 282.] For in this way we get to see how diffuse it really is. It extends on to horses and on to carts, on to the fact that horses fall down and that they bite, on to horses of a particular character, on to carts that are heavily loaded. I will reveal at once that all these characteristics were derived from the circumstance that the anxiety originally had no reference at all to horses but was transposed on to them secondarily and had now become fixed upon those elements of the horse-complex which showed themselves well adapted for certain transferences.[1] We must specially acknowledge one most important result of the boy's examination by his father. We have learned the immediate precipitating cause after which the phobia broke out. This was when the boy saw a big heavy horse fall down; and one at least of the interpretations of this impression seems to be that emphasized by his father, namely, that Hans at that moment perceived a wish that his father might fall down in the same way – and be dead. His serious expression as he was telling the story no doubt referred to this unconscious meaning. May there not have been yet another meaning concealed behind all this? And what can have been the significance of the making a row with its legs?

'For some time Hans has been playing horses in the room; he trots about, falls down, kicks about with his feet, and neighs. Once he tied a small bag on like a nose-bag. He has repeatedly run up to me and bitten me.'

In this way he was accepting the last interpretations more

1. [Here 'transference' has a wider meaning than the one more usual in Freud's later writings.]

decidedly than he could in words, but naturally with a change of parts, for the game was played in obedience to a wishful phantasy. Thus *he* was the horse, and bit his father, and in this way was identifying himself with his father.

'I have noticed for the last two days that Hans has been defying me in the most decided manner, not impudently, but in the highest spirits. Is it because he is no longer afraid of me – the horse?

'April 6th. Went out with Hans in front of the house in the afternoon. At every horse that passed I asked him if he saw the "black on its mouth"; he said "no" every time. I asked him what the black really looked like; he said it was black iron. My first idea, that he meant the thick leather straps that are part of the harness of dray-horses, is therefore unconfirmed. I asked him if the "black" reminded him of a moustache, and he said: "Only by its colour." So I do not yet know what it really is.

'The fear has diminished; this time he ventured as far as the next-door house, but turned round quickly when he heard the sound of horses' hooves in the distance. When a cart drew up at our door and came to a stop, he became frightened and ran into the house, because the horse began pawing with its foot. I asked him why he was afraid, and whether perhaps he was nervous because the horse had done like this (and I stamped with my foot). He said: "Don't make such a row with your feet!" Compare his remark about the fallen bus-horse.

'He was particularly terrified by a furniture-van passing by. At that he ran right inside the house. "Doesn't a furniture-van like that," I asked him unconcernedly, "really look like a bus?" He said nothing. I repeated the question, and he then said: "Why, of course! Otherwise I shouldn't be so afraid of a furniture-van."

'April 7th. I asked again today what the "black on the horses' mouths" looked like. Hans said: "Like a muzzle." The curious thing is that for the last three days not a single horse has passed on which he could point out this "muzzle". I myself have seen no such horses on any of my walks, although Hans asseverates that such horses do exist. I suspect that some sort of horses' bridle – the thick piece of harness round their mouths, perhaps – really reminded him of a moustache, and that after I alluded to this this fear disappeared as well.

'Hans's improvement is constant. The radius of his circle of activity with the street-door as its centre grows ever wider. He has even accomplished the feat, which has hitherto been impossible for him, of running across to the pavement opposite. All the fear that remains is connected with the bus scene, the meaning of which is not yet clear to me.

'April 9th. This morning Hans came in to me while I was washing and bare to the waist.

'*Hans*: "Daddy, you *are* lovely! You're so white."

'*I*: "Yes. Like a white horse."

'*Hans*: "The only black thing's your moustache." (Continuing) "Or perhaps it's a black muzzle?"

'I told him then that I had been to see the Professor the evening before, and said: "There's one thing he wants to know." "I *am* curious," remarked Hans.

'I told him I knew on what occasions it was that he made a row with his feet. "Oh, yes!" he interrupted me, "when I'm cross, or when I have to do 'lumf' and would rather play." (He has a habit, it is true, of making a row with his feet, i.e. of stamping, when he is angry. – "Doing lumf" means doing number two. When Hans was small he said one day when he got off the chamber: "Look at the lumf [German: '*Lumpf*']." He meant "stocking" [German: "*Strumpf*"], because of its shape and colour. This designation has been preserved to this day. – In very early days, when he had to be put on the chamber, and refused to leave off playing, he used to stamp his feet in a rage, and kick about, and sometimes throw himself on the ground.)

'"And you kick about with your feet as well, when you have

to widdle and don't want to go, because you'd rather go on playing."

'*He*: "Oh, I must widdle." And he went out of the room – by way of confirmation, no doubt.'

In the course of his visit his father had asked me what Hans could have been reminded of by the fallen horse kicking about with its feet. I had suggested that that may have been his own reaction when he retained his urine. Hans now confirmed this by means of the re-emergence during the conversation of a desire to micturate; and he added some other meanings of the making a row with the feet.

'We then went out in front of the street-door. When a coal-cart came along, he said to me: "Daddy. I'm very much afraid of coal-carts, too."

'*I*: "Perhaps that's because they're as big as buses, too."

'*Hans*: "Yes; and because they're so heavily loaded, and the horses have so much to drag and might easily fall down. If a cart's empty, I'm not afraid." It is a fact, as I have already remarked, that only heavy vehicles throw him into a state of anxiety.'

Nevertheless, the situation was decidedly obscure. The analysis was making little progress; and I am afraid the reader will soon begin to find this description of it tedious. Every analysis, however, has dark periods of this kind. But Hans was now on the point of leading us into an unexpected region.

'I came home and was speaking to my wife, who had made various purchases which she was showing me. Among them was a pair of yellow ladies' drawers. Hans exclaimed "Ugh!" two or three times, threw himself on the ground, and spat. My wife said he had done this two or three times already when he had seen the drawers.

'"Why do you say 'Ugh'?" I asked.

'*Hans*: "Because of the drawers."

'*I*: "Why? Because of their colour? Because they're yellow, and remind you of lumf or widdle?"

'*Hans*: "Lumf isn't yellow. It's white or black." – Immediately afterwards: "I say, is it easy to do lumf if you eat cheese?" (I had once told him so, when he asked me why I ate cheese.)

'*I*: "Yes."

'*Hans*: "That's why you go straight off every morning and do lumf? I should so much like to eat cheese with my bread-and-butter."

'He had already asked me yesterday as he was jumping about in the street: "I say, it's true, isn't it, if you jump about a lot you can do lumf easily?" – There has been trouble with his stools from the very first; and aperients and enemas have frequently been necessary. At one time his habitual constipation was so great that my wife called in Dr L. He was of opinion that Hans was overfed, which was in fact the case, and recommended a more moderate diet – and the condition was at once brought to an end. Recently the constipation has again made its appearance more frequently.

'After luncheon I said to him: "We'll write to the Professor again," and he dictated to me: "When I saw the yellow drawers I said 'Ugh! that makes me spit!' and threw myself down and shut my eyes and didn't look."

'*I*: "Why?"

'*Hans*: "Because I saw the yellow drawers; and I did the same sort of thing with the black drawers too.[1] The black ones are the same sort of drawers, only they were black." (Interrupting himself) "I say, I *am* glad. I'm always so glad when I can write to the Professor."

'*I*: "Why did you say 'Ugh'? Were you disgusted?"

'*Hans*: "Yes, because I saw that. I thought I should have to do lumf."

'*I*: "Why?"

'*Hans*: "I don't know."

'*I*: "When did you see the black drawers?"

'*Hans*: "Once, when Anna (our maid) had been here a long

1. 'For the last few weeks my wife has possessed a pair of black bloomers for wearing on cycling tours.'

time – with Mummy – she brought them home just after she'd bought them." (This statement was confirmed by my wife.)

'*I*: "Were you disgusted then, too?"

'*Hans*: "Yes."

'*I*: "Have you seen Mummy in drawers like that?"

'*Hans*: "No."

'*I*: "When she was dressing?"

'*Hans*: "When she bought the yellow ones I'd seen them once before already." (This is contradicted. He saw the yellow ones for the first time when his mother bought them.) "She's got the black ones on today too" (correct), "because I saw her take them off in the morning."

'*I*: "What? She took off the black drawers in the morning?"

'*Hans*: "In the morning when she went out she took off the black drawers, and when she came back she put the black ones on again."

'I asked my wife about this, as it seemed to me absurd. She said it was entirely untrue. Of course she had not changed her drawers when she went out.

'I at once asked Hans about it: "You told me that Mummy had put on some black drawers, and that when she went out she took them off, and that when she came back she put them on again. But Mummy says it's not true."

'*Hans*: "I think perhaps I may have forgotten she didn't take them off." (Impatiently) "Oh, do let me alone."'

I have a few comments to make at this point on the business of the drawers. It was obviously mere hypocrisy on Hans's part to pretend to be so glad of the opportunity of giving an account of the affair. In the end he threw the mask aside and was rude to his father. It was a question of things which had once afforded him *a great deal of pleasure*, but of which, now that repression had set in, he was very much ashamed, and at which he professed to be disgusted. He told some downright lies so as to disguise the circumstances in which he had seen his mother change her drawers. In reality, the putting on and taking off of her drawers belonged to the 'lumf' context. His father was perfectly aware of what it was all about and of what Hans was trying to conceal.

'I asked my wife whether Hans was often with her when she went to the W.C. "Yes," she said, "often. He goes on pestering me till I let him. Children are all like that."'

Nevertheless, it is worth bearing carefully in mind the desire, which Hans had already repressed, for seeing his mother doing lumf.

'We went out in front of the house. He was in very good spirits and was prancing about all the time like a horse. So I said: "Now, who is it that's the bus-horse? Me, you or Mummy?"

'*Hans* (promptly): "I am; I'm a young horse."

'During the period when his anxiety was at its height, and he was frightened at seeing horses frisking, he asked me why they did it; and to reassure him I said: "Those are young horses, you see, and they frisk about like little boys. You frisk about too, and you're a little boy." Since then, whenever he has seen horses frisking, he has said: "That's right; those are young horses!"

'As we were going upstairs I asked him almost without thinking: "Used you to play at horses with the children at Gmunden?"

'*He*: "Yes." (Thoughtfully) "I think that was how I got the nonsense."

'*I*: "Who was the horse?"

'*He*: "I was; and Berta was the coachman."

'*I*: "Did you fall down by any chance, when you were a horse?"

'*Hans*: "No. When Berta said 'Gee-up', I ran ever so quick; I just raced along."[1]

'*I*: "You never played at buses?"

'*Hans*: "No. At ordinary carts, and horses without carts. When a horse has a cart, it can go without a cart just as well, and the cart can stay at home."

'*I*: "Used you often to play at horses?"

1. 'Hans had a set of toy harness with bells.'

'Hans: "Very often. Fritzl[1] was the horse once, too, and Franzl the coachman; and Fritzl ran ever so fast and all at-once he hit his foot on a stone and bled."

'I: "Perhaps he fell down?"

'Hans: "No. He put his foot in some water and then wrapped it up."[2]

'I: "Were you often the horse?"

'Hans: "Oh, yes."

'I: "And that was how you got the nonsense?"

'Hans: "Because they kept on saying ''cos of the horse,' ''cos of the horse'" (he put a stress on the ''cos'); "so perhaps I got the nonsense because they talked like that; ''cos of the horse.'''[3]

For a while Hans's father pursued his enquiry fruitlessly along other paths.

'I: "Did they tell you anything about horses?"

'Hans: "Yes."

'I: "What?"

'Hans: "I've forgotten."

'I: "Perhaps they told you about their widdlers?"

'Hans: "Oh, no."

1. Another of the landlord's children, as we already know [see p. 179].

2. See below [p. 242]. His father was quite right in suspecting that Fritzl fell down.

3. ['*Wegen dem Pferd*'.] I may explain that Hans was not maintaining that he had got the nonsense *at that time* but *in that connection*. Indeed, it must have been so, for theoretical considerations require that what is today the object of a phobia must at one time in the past have been the source of a high degree of pleasure. I may at the same time complete what the child was unable to express, and add that the little word '*wegen*' ['because of', "cos of'] was the means of enabling the phobia to extend from horses on to '*Wagen*' ['vehicles'] or, as Hans was accustomed to pronounce the word and hear it pronounced, '*Wägen*' [pronounced exactly like '*wegen*']. It must never be forgotten how much more concretely children treat words than grown-up people do, and consequently how much more significant for them are similarities of sound in words. [This point was remarked upon by Freud in *The Interpretation of Dreams* (1900*a*), Chapter VI (near the end of Section A), *P.F.L.*, 4, 412.]

'*I*: "Were you frightened of horses already then?"
'*Hans*: "Oh, no. I wasn't frightened at all."
'*I*: "Perhaps Berta told you that horses —"
'*Hans* (interrupting): "— widdle? No."

'On April 10th I took up our conversation of the day before, and tried to discover what his "'cos of the horse" meant. Hans could not remember; he only knew that some children had stood outside the front door one morning and had said, "'cos of the horse, 'cos of the horse!" He had been there himself. When I pressed him more closely, he declared that they had not said "'cos of the horse" at all, but that he had remembered wrong.

'*I*: "But you and the others were often in the stables. You must surely have talked about horses there." – "We didn't." – "What did you talk about?" – "Nothing." – "Such a lot of children, and nothing to talk about?" – "We did talk about something, but not about horses." – "Well, what was it?" – "I don't remember any more."

'I allowed the matter to drop, as the resistances were evidently too great,[1] and went on to the following question: "Did you like playing with Berta?"

'*He*: "Yes, very much; but not with Olga. D'you know what Olga did? I was given a paper ball once by Grete up there at Gmunden, and Olga tore it all to pieces. Berta would never have torn my ball. I liked playing with Berta very much."

'*I*: "Did you see what Berta's widdler looked like?"

'*He*: "No, but I saw the horses'; because I was always in the stables, and so I saw the horses' widdlers."

'*I*: "And so you were curious and wanted to know what Berta's and Mummy's widdlers looked like?"

'*He*: "Yes."

'I reminded him of how he had once complained to me that

1. In point of fact there was nothing more to be got out of it than Hans's verbal association, and this had escaped his father. Here is a good instance of conditions under which an analyst's efforts are wasted.

the little girls always wanted to look on while he was widdling [p. 184].

'*He*: "Berta always looked on at me too" (he spoke with great satisfaction and not at all resentfully); "often she did. I used to widdle in the little garden where the radishes were, and she stood outside the front door and looked on at me."

'*I*: "And when she widdled, did you look on?"

'*He*: "She used to go to the W.C."

'*I*: "And you were curious?"

'*He*: "I was inside the W.C. when she was in it."

'(This was a fact. The servants told us about it once, and I recollect that we forbade Hans to do it.)

'*I*: "Did you tell her you wanted to go in?"

'*He*: "I went in alone and because Berta let me. There's nothing shameful in that."

'*I*: "And you'd have liked to see her widdler?"

'*He*: "Yes, but I didn't see it."

'I then reminded him of the dream about playing forfeits that he had had at Gmunden [p. 183], and said: "When you were at Gmunden did you want Berta to make you widdle?"

'*He*: "I never said so to her."

'*I*: "Why didn't you ever say so to her?"

'*He*: "Because I didn't think of it." (Interrupting himself) "If I write everything to the Professor, my nonsense'll soon be over, won't it?"

'*I*: "Why did you want Berta to make you widdle?"

'*He*: "I don't know. Because she looked on at me."

'*I*: "Did you think to yourself she should put her hand to your widdler?"

'*He*: "Yes." (Changing the subject) "It was such fun at Gmunden. In the little garden where the radishes were there was a little sand-heap; I used to play there with my spade."

'(This was the garden where he used always to widdle.)

'*I*: "Did you put your hand to your widdler at Gmunden, when you were in bed?"

'*He*: "No. Not then; I slept so well at Gmunden that I

never thought of it at all. The only times I did was at — Street[1] and now."

    'I: "But Berta never put her hand to your widdler?"

    'He: "She never did, no; because I never told her to."

    'I: "Well, and when was it you wanted her to?"

    'He: "Oh, at Gmunden once."

    'I: "Only once?"

    'He: "Well, now and then."

    'I: "She used always to look on at you when you widdled; perhaps she was curious to know how you did it?"

    'He: "Perhaps she was curious to know what my widdler looked like."

    'I: "But you were curious too. Only about Berta?"

    'He: "About Berta, and about Olga."

    'I: "About who else?"

    'He: "About no one else."

    'I: "You know that's not true. About Mummy too."

    'He: "Oh, yes, about Mummy."

    'I: "But now you're not curious any more. You know what Hanna's widdler looks like, don't you?"

    'He: "It'll grow, though, won't it?"[2]

    'I: "Yes, of course. But when it's grown it won't look like yours."

    'He: "I know that. It'll be the same" (sc. as it now is) "only bigger."

    'I: "When we were at Gmunden, were you curious when your Mummy undressed?"

    'He: "Yes. And then when Hanna was in her bath I saw her widdler."

    'I: "And Mummy's too?"

    'He: "No."

    'I: "You were disgusted when you saw Mummy's drawers?"

    'He: "Only when I saw the black ones – when she bought them – then I spat. But I don't spit when she puts her drawers

---

1. The flat they were in before the move [p. 179].
2. Hans wants to be assured that his own widdler will grow.

on or takes them off. *I spit because the black drawers are black like a lumf and the yellow ones like a widdle, and then I think I've got to widdle.* When Mummy has her drawers on I don't see them; she's got her clothes on over them."

'*I*: "And when she takes off her clothes?"

'*He*: "I don't spit then either. But when her drawers are new they look like a lumf. When they're old, the colour goes away and they get dirty. When you buy them they're quite clean, but at home they've been made dirty. When they're bought they're new, and when they're not bought they're old."

'*I*: "Then you aren't disgusted by old ones?"

'*He*: "When they're old they're much blacker than a lumf, aren't they? They're just a bit blacker."[1]

'*I*: "Have you often been into the W.C. with Mummy?"

'*He*: "Very often."

'*I*: "And were you disgusted?"

'*He*: "Yes . . . No."

'*I*: "You like being there when Mummy widdles or does lumf?"

'*He*: "Yes, very much."

'*I*: "Why do you like it so much?"

'*He*: "I don't know."

'*I*: "Because you think you'll see her widdler."

'*He*: "Yes, I do think that."

'*I*: "But why won't you ever go into the W.C. at Lainz?"

'(At Lainz he always begs me not to take him into the W.C.; he was frightened once by the noise of the flush.)

'*He*: "Perhaps it's because it makes a row when you pull the plug."

'*I*: "And then you're afraid."

---

1. Our young man was here wrestling with a subject of which he was not equal to giving a clear exposition; so that there is some difficulty in understanding him. He may perhaps have meant that the drawers only recalled his feelings of disgust when he saw them on their own account; as soon as his mother had them on, he ceased to connect them with lumf or widdle, and they then interested him in a different way.

'*He*: "Yes."

'*I*: "And what about our W.C. here?"

'*He*: "Here I'm not. At Lainz it gives me a fright when you pull the plug. And when I'm inside and the water rushes down, then it gives me a fright too."

'And, "just to show me that he wasn't frightened in our flat," he made me go into the W.C. and set the flush in motion. He then explained to me:

'"First there's a loud row, and then a loose one." (This is when the water comes down.) "When there's a loud row I'd rather stay inside, and when there's a soft one I'd rather go out."

'*I*: "Because you're afraid?"

'*He*: "Because if there's a loud row I always so much like to see it" – (correcting himself) "to hear it; so I'd rather stay inside and hear it properly."

'*I*: "What does a loud row remind you of?"

'*He*: "That I've got to do lumf in the W.C." (The same thing, that is, that the black drawers reminded him of.)

'*I*: "Why?"

'*He*: "I don't know. A loud row sounds as though you were doing lumf. A big row reminds me of lumf, and a little one of widdle." (Cf. the black and the yellow drawers.)

'*I*: "I say, wasn't the bus-horse the same colour as a lumf"? (According to his account it had been black [p. 212].)

'*He* (very much struck): "Yes."'

At this point I must put in a few words. Hans's father was asking too many questions, and was pressing the inquiry along his own lines instead of allowing the little boy to express his thoughts. For this reason the analysis began to be obscure and uncertain. Hans went his own way and would produce nothing if attempts were made to draw him off it. For the moment his interest was evidently centred upon lumf and widdle, but we cannot tell why. Just as little satisfactory light was thrown upon the business of the row as upon that of the yellow and black drawers. I suspect that the boy's sharp ears had clearly detected the difference between the sounds made by a man micturating and a woman. The analysis succeeded in forcing the material somewhat artificially into an expression of the distinction between the two different calls of nature. I can only advise those of my readers who have not as yet themselves conducted an analysis not to try to understand everything at once, but to give a kind of unbiassed attention to every point that arises and to await further developments.

'April 11th. This morning Hans came into our room again and was sent away, as he always has been for the last few days.

'Later on, he began: "Daddy, I thought something: *I was in the bath*,[1] *and then the plumber came and unscrewed it.*[2] *Then he took a big borer and stuck it into my stomach*."'

Hans's father translated this phantasy as follows: '"I was in bed with Mummy. Then Daddy came and drove me away. With his big penis he pushed me out of my place by Mummy."'

Let us suspend our judgement for the present.

'He went on to relate a second idea that he had had. "We were travelling in the train to Gmunden. In the station we put on our clothes; but we couldn't get it done in time, and the train carried us on."

'Later on, I asked: "Have you ever seen a horse doing lumf?"

'*Hans*: "Yes, very often."

'*I*: "Does it make a loud row when it does lumf?"

'*Hans*: "Yes."

'*I*: "What does the row remind you of?"

'*Hans*: "Like when lumf falls into the chamber."

'The bus-horse that falls down and makes a row with its feet is no doubt – a lumf falling and making a noise. His fear of defaecation and his fear of heavily loaded carts is equivalent to the fear of a heavily loaded stomach.'

In this roundabout way Hans's father was beginning to get a glimmering of the true state of affairs.

1. 'Hans's mother gives him his bath.'
2. 'To take it away to be repaired.'

'April 11th. At luncheon Hans said: "If only we had a bath at Gmunden, so that I didn't have to go to the public baths!" It is a fact that at Gmunden he was always taken to the neighbouring public baths to be given a hot bath – a proceeding against which he used to protest with passionate tears. And in Vienna, too, he always screams if he is made to sit or lie in the big bath. He must be given his bath kneeling or standing.'

Hans was now beginning to bring fuel to the analysis in the shape of spontaneous utterances of his own. This remark of his established the connection between his two last phantasies – that of the plumber who unscrewed the bath and that of the unsuccessful journey to Gmunden. His father had correctly inferred from the latter that Hans had some aversion to Gmunden. This, by the way, is another good reminder of the fact that what emerges from the unconscious is to be understood in the light not of what goes before but of what comes after.

'I asked him whether he was afraid, and if so of what.

'*Hans*: "Because of falling in."

'*I*: "But why were you never afraid when you had your bath in the little bath?"

'*Hans*: "Why, I sat in that one. I couldn't lie down in it, it was too small."

'*I*: "When you went in a boat at Gmunden weren't you afraid of falling into the water?"

'*Hans*: "No, because I held on, so I coudn't fall in. It's only in the big bath that I'm afraid of falling in."

'*I*: "But Mummy baths you in it. Are you afraid of Mummy dropping you in the water?"

'*Hans*: "I'm afraid of her letting go and my head going in."

'*I*: "But you know Mummy's fond of you and won't let go of you."

'*Hans*: "I only just thought it."

'*I*: "Why?"

'*Hans*: "I don't know at all."

'*I*: "Perhaps it was because you'd been naughty and thought she didn't love you any more?"

'*Hans*: "Yes."

'*I*: "When you were watching Mummy giving Hanna her bath, perhaps you wished she would let go of her so that Hanna should fall in?"

'*Hans*: "Yes."'

Hans's father, we cannot help thinking, had made a very good guess.

'April 12th. As we were coming back from Lainz in a second-class carriage, Hans looked at the black leather upholstery of the seats, and said: "Ugh! that makes me spit! Black drawers and black horses make me spit too, because I have to do lumf."

'*I*: "Perhaps you saw something of Mummy's that was black, and it frightened you?"

'*Hans*: "Yes."

'*I*: "Well, what was it?"

'*Hans*: "I don't know. A black blouse or black stockings."

'*I*: "Perhaps it was black hair near her widdler, when you were curious and looked."

'*Hans* (defending himself): "But I didn't see her widdler."

'Another time, he was frightened once more at a cart driving out of the yard gates opposite. "Don't the gates look like a behind?" I asked.

'*He*: "And the horses are the lumfs!" Since then, whenever he sees a cart driving out, he says: "Look, there's a 'lumfy' coming!" This form of the word ("lumfy") is quite a new one to him; it sounds like a term of endearment. My sister-in-law always calls her child "Wumfy".

'On April 13th he saw a piece of liver in the soup and exclaimed: "Ugh! A lumf!" Meat croquettes, too, he eats with evident reluctance, because their form and colour remind him of lumf.

'In the evening my wife told me that Hans had been out on the balcony and had said: "I thought to myself Hanna was on the balcony and fell down off it." I had once or twice told him to be careful that Hanna did not get too near the balustrade when she was out on the balcony; for the railing was designed in the most unpractical way (by a metal-worker of the Secessionist movement) and had big gaps in it which I had to have filled in with wire netting. Hans's repressed wish was very transparent. His mother asked him if he would rather Hanna were not there, to which he said "Yes".

'April 14th. The theme of Hanna is uppermost. As you may remember from earlier records, Hans felt a strong aversion to the new-born baby that robbed him of a part of his parents' love. This dislike has not entirely disappeared and is only partly overcompensated by an exaggerated affection.[1] He has already several times expressed a wish that the stork should bring no more babies and that we should pay him money not to bring any more "out of the big box" where babies are. (Compare his fear of furniture-vans. Does not a bus look like a big box?) Hanna screams such a lot, he says, and that's a nuisance to him.

'Once he suddenly said. "Can you remember when Hanna came? She lay beside Mummy in bed, so nice and good." (His praise rang suspiciously hollow.)

'And then as regards downstairs, outside the house. There is again great progress to be reported. Even drays cause him less alarm. Once he called out, almost with joy: "Here comes a horse with something black on its mouth!" And I was at last able to establish the fact that it was a horse with a leather muzzle. But Hans was not in the least afraid of this horse.

'Once he knocked on the pavement with his stick and said: "I say, is there a man underneath? – some one buried? – or is that only in the cemetery?" So he is occupied not only with the riddle of life but with the riddle of death.

'When we got indoors again I saw a box standing in the

1. The 'Hanna' theme immediately succeeded the 'lumf' theme, and the explanation of this at length begins to dawn upon us: Hanna was a lumf herself – babies were lumfs.

front hall, and Hans said: "Hanna travelled with us to Gmunden in a box like that. Whenever we travelled to Gmunden she
travelled with us in the box. You don't believe me again?
Really, Daddy. Do believe me. We got a big box and it was
full of babies; they sat in the bath." (A small bath had been
packed inside the box.) "I put them in it. Really and truly. I can
remember quite well."[1]

'*I*: "What can you remember?"

'*Hans*: "That Hanna travelled in the box; because I haven't
forgotten about it. My word of honour!"

'*I*: "But last year Hanna travelled with us in the railway
carriage."

'*Hans*: "*But before that she always travelled with us in the box.*"

'*I*: "Didn't Mummy have the box?"

'*Hans*: "Yes. Mummy had it."

'*I*: "Where?"

'*Hans*: "At home in the attic."

'*I*: "Perhaps she carried it about with her?"[2]

'*Hans*: "No. And when we travel to Gmunden this time
Hanna'll travel in the box again."

'*I*: "And how did she get out of the box, then?"

'*Hans*: "She was taken out."

'*I*: "By Mummy?"

'*Hans*: "Mummy and me. Then we got into the carriage,
and Hanna rode on the horse, and the coachman said 'Gee-up'.
The coachman sat up in front. Were you there too? Mummy
knows all about it. Mummy doesn't know; she's forgotten
about it already, but don't tell her anything!"

1. Hans was now going off into a phantasy. As we can see, a box and
a bath have the same meaning for him: they both represent the space
which contains the babies. We must bear in mind Hans's repeated
assurances on this point.

2. The box was of course the womb. (Hans's father was trying to let
him know that he understood this.) And the same is true of the caskets
in which so many of the heroes of mythology were exposed, from the
time of King Sargon of Agade onwards. – (*Added* 1923:) Cf. Rank's
study, *Der Mythus von der Geburt des Helden*, 1909.

'I made him repeat the whole of this.

'*Hans*: "Then Hanna got out."

'*I*: "Why, she couldn't walk at all then."

'*Hans*: "Well then, we lifted her down."

'*I*: "But how could she have sat on the horse? She couldn't sit up at all last year."

'*Hans*: "Oh yes, she sat up all right, and called out 'Gee-up', and whipped with her whip – 'Gee-up! Gee-up!' – the whip I used to have. The horse hadn't any stirrups, but Hanna rode it. I'm not joking, you know, Daddy."'

What can be the meaning of the boy's obstinate persistence in all this nonsense? Oh no, it was no nonsense: it was parody, it was Hans's revenge upon his father. It was as much as to say: '*If you really expect me to believe that the stork brought Hanna in October, when even in the summer, while we were travelling to Gmunden, I'd noticed how big Mother's stomach was, – then I expect you to believe my lies.*' What can be the meaning of the assertion that even the summer before the last Hanna had travelled with them to Gmunden 'in the box', except that he knew about his mother's pregnancy? His holding out the prospect of a re-petition of this journey in the box in each successive year exemplifies a common way in which unconscious thoughts from the past emerge into consciousness; or it may have special reasons and express his dread of seeing a similar pregnancy repeated on their next summer holiday. We now see, more-over, what the circumstances were that had made him take a dislike to the journey to Gmunden, as his second phantasy had indicated [p. 226].

'Later on, I asked him how Hanna had actually come into his mother's bed after she was born.'

This gave Hans a chance of letting himself go and fairly 'stuffing' his father.

'*Hans*: "Hanna just came. Frau Kraus" (the midwife) "put her in the bed. She couldn't walk, of course. But the stork carried her in his beak. Of course she couldn't walk." (He went on without a pause.) "The stork came up the stairs up to the landing, and then he knocked and everybody was asleep, and he had the right key and unlocked the door and put Hanna in *your*[1] bed, and Mummy was asleep – no, the stork put her in *her* bed. It was the middle of the night, and then the stork put her in the bed very quietly, he didn't trample about at all, and then he took his hat and went away again. No, he hadn't got a hat."

'*I*: "Who took his hat? The doctor, perhaps?"

'*Hans*: "Then the stork went away; he went home, and then he rang at the door, and every one in the house stopped sleeping. But don't tell this to Mummy or Tini" (the cook). "It's a secret."

'*I*: "Are you fond of Hanna?"

'*Hans*: "Oh yes, very fond."

'*I*: "Would you rather that Hanna weren't alive or that she were?"

'*Hans*: "I'd rather she weren't alive."

'*I*: "Why?"

'*Hans*: "At any rate she wouldn't scream so, and I can't bear her screaming."

'*I*: "Why, you scream yourself."

'*Hans*: "But Hanna screams too."

'*I*: "Why can't you bear it?"

'*Hans*: "Because she screams so loud."

'*I*: "Why, she doesn't scream at all."

'*Hans*: "When she's whacked on her bare bottom, then she screams."

'*I*: "Have you ever whacked her?"

'*Hans*: "When Mummy whacks her on her bottom, then she screams."

'*I*: "And you don't like that?"

'*Hans*: "No . . . Why? Because she makes such a row with her screaming."

'*I*: "If you'd rather she weren't alive, you can't be fond of her at all."

1. Ironical, of course. Like his subsequent request that none of the secret should be betrayed to his mother.

'*Hans* (assenting): "H'm, well."

'*I*: "That was why you thought when Mummy was giving her her bath, if only she'd let go, Hanna would fall into the water . . ."

'*Hans* (taking me up): ". . . and die."

'*I*: "And then you'd be alone with Mummy. A good boy doesn't wish that sort of thing, though."

'*Hans*: "*But he may* THINK *it*."

I: "But that isn't good."

'*Hans*: "*If he thinks it, it* IS *good all the same, because you can write it to the Professor.*"[1]

'Later on I said to him: "You know, when Hanna gets bigger and can talk, you'll be fonder of her."

'*Hans*: "Oh no. I *am* fond of her. In the autumn, when she's big, I shall go with her to the Stadtpark quite alone, and explain everything to her."

'As I was beginning to give him some further enlightenment, he interrupted me, probably with the intention of explaining to me that it was not so wicked of him to wish that Hanna was dead.

'*Hans*: "You know, all the same, she'd been alive a long time even before she was here. When she was with the stork she was alive too.'

'*I*: "No. Perhaps she wasn't with the stork after all."

'*Hans*: "Who brought her, then? The stork had got her."

'*I*: "Where did he bring her from, then?"

'*Hans*: "Oh – from him."

'*I*: "Where had he got her, then?"

'*Hans*: "In the box; in the *stork-box*."

'*I*: "Well, and what does the box look like?"

'*Hans*: "Red. Painted red." (Blood?)

'*I*: "Who told you that?"

'*Hans*: "Mummy . . . I thought it to myself . . . it's in the book."

1. Well done, little Hans! I could wish for no better understanding of psychoanalysis from any grown up.

'*I*: "In what book?"

'*Hans*: "In the picture-book." (I made him fetch his first picture-book. In it was a picture of a stork's nest with storks, on a red chimney. This was the box. Curiously enough, on the same page there was also a picture of a horse being shod.[1] Hans had transferred the babies into the box, as they were not to be seen in the nest.)

'*I*: "And what did the stork do with her?"

'*Hans*: "Then the stork brought Hanna here. In his beak. You know, the stork that's at Schönbrunn, and that bit the umbrella." (A reminiscence of an episode at Schönbrunn.)

'*I*: "Did you see how the stork brought Hanna?"

'*Hans*: "Why, I was still asleep, you know. A stork can never bring a little girl or a little boy in the morning."

'*I*: "Why?"

'*Hans*: "He can't. A stork can't do it. Do you know why? So that people shan't see. And then, all at once, in the morning, there's a little girl there."[2]

'*I*: "But, all the same, you were curious at the time to know how the stork did it?"

'*Hans*: "Oh yes."

'*I*: "What did Hanna look like when she came?"

'*Hans* (hypocritically): "All white and lovely. So pretty."

'*I*: "But when you saw her the first time you didn't like her."

'*Hans*: "Oh, I did; very much!"

'*I*: "You were surprised that she was so small, though."

'*Hans*: "Yes."

1. [In view of what follows presently it may be worth remarking that the German word for 'shod' ('*beschlagen*') differs in only a single letter from that for 'beaten' ('*geschlagen*').]

2. There is no need to find fault with Hans's inconsistencies. In the previous conversation his disbelief in the stork had emerged from his unconscious and had been coupled with the exasperation he felt against his father for making so many mysteries. But he had now become calmer and was answering his father's questions with official thoughts in which he had worked out glosses upon the many difficulties involved in the stork hypothesis.

'*I*: "How small was she?"

'*Hans*: "Like a baby stork."

'*I*: "Like what else? Like a lumf, perhaps?"

'*Hans*: "Oh no. A lumf's much bigger . . . a bit smaller than Hanna, really."'

I had predicted to his father that it would be possible to trace back Hans's phobia to thoughts and wishes occasioned by the birth of his baby sister. But I had omitted to point out that according to the sexual theory of children a baby is a 'lumf', so that Hans's path would lie through the excremental complex. It was owing to this neglect on my part that the progress of the case became temporarily obscured. Now that the matter had been cleared up, Hans's father attempted to examine the boy a second time upon this important point.

The next day, 'I got Hans to repeat what he had told me yesterday. He said: "Hanna travelled to Gmunden in the big box, and Mummy travelled in the railway carriage, and Hanna travelled in the luggage train with the box; and then when we got to Gmunden Mummy and I lifted Hanna out and put her on the horse. The coachman sat up in front, and Hanna had the old whip" (the whip he had last year) "and whipped the horse and kept on saying 'Gee-up', and it was such fun, and the coachman whipped too. – The coachman didn't whip at all, because Hanna had the whip. – The coachman had the reins – Hanna had the reins too." (On each occasion we drove in a carriage from the station to the house. Hans was here trying to reconcile fact and fancy.) "At Gmunden we lifted Hanna down from the horse, and she walked up the steps by herself." (Last year, when Hanna was at Gmunden, she was eight months old. The year before that – and Hans's phantasy evidently related to that time – his mother had been five months gone with child when we arrived at Gmunden.)

'*I*: "Last year Hanna was there."

'*Hans*: "Last year she drove in the carriage; but the year before that, when she was living with us . . ."

'*I*: "Was she with us already then?"

'*Hans*: "Yes. You were always there; you used always to go in the boat with me, and Anna was our servant."

'*I*: "But that wasn't last year. Hanna wasn't alive then."

'*Hans*: "*Yes, she was alive then.* Even while she was still travelling in the box she could run about and she could say 'Anna'." (She has only been able to do so for the last four months.)

'*I*: "But she wasn't with us at all then."

'*Hans*: "Oh yes, she was; she was with the stork."

'*I*: "How old is she, then?"

'*Hans*: "She'll be two years old in the autumn. Hanna *was* there, you know she was."

'*I*: "And when was she with the stork in the stork-box?"

'*Hans*: "A long time before she travelled in the box, a very long time."

'*I*: "How long has Hanna been able to walk, then? When she was at Gmunden she couldn't walk yet."

'*Hans*: "Not last year; but other times she could."

'*I*: "But Hanna's only been at Gmunden once."

'*Hans*: "No. She's been twice. Yes, that's it. I can remember quite well. Ask Mummy, she'll tell you soon enough."

'*I*: "It's not true, all the same."

'*Hans*: "Yes, it *is* true. *When she was at Gmunden the first time she could walk and ride, and later on she had to be carried.* – No. It was only later on that she rode, and last year she had to be carried."

'*I*: "But it's only quite a short time that she's been walking. At Gmunden she couldn't walk."

'*Hans*: "Yes. Just you write it down. I can remember quite well. – Why are you laughing?"

'*I*: "Because you're a fraud; because you know quite well that Hanna's only been at Gmunden once."

'*Hans*: "No, that isn't true. The first time she rode on the horse . . . and the second time . . ." (He showed signs of evident uncertainty.)

'*I*: "Perhaps the horse was Mummy?"

'*Hans*: "No, a real horse in a fly."

'*I*: "But we used always to have a carriage with two horses."

'*Hans*: "Well, then, it was a carriage and pair."

'*I*: "What did Hanna eat inside the box?"

'*Hans*: "They put in bread-and-butter for her, and herring, and radishes" (the sort of thing we used to have for supper at Gmunden), "and as Hanna went along she buttered her bread-and-butter and ate fifty meals."

'*I*: "Didn't Hanna scream?"

'*Hans*: "No."

'*I*: "What did she do, then?"

'*Hans*: "Sat quite still inside."

'*I*: "Didn't she push about?"

'*Hans*: "No, she kept on eating all the time and didn't stir once. She drank up two big mugs of coffee – by the morning it was all gone, and she left the bits behind in the box, the leaves of the two radishes and a knife for cutting the radishes. She gobbled everything up like a hare: one minute and it was all finished. It *was* a joke. Hanna and I really travelled together in the box; I slept the whole night in the box." (We did in fact, two years ago, make the journey to Gmunden by night.) "And Mummy travelled in the railway carriage. And we kept on eating all the time when we were driving in the carriage, too; it *was* jolly. – She didn't ride on a horse at all ..." (he now became undecided, for he knew that we had driven with two horses) "... she sat in the carriage. Yes, that's how it was, but Hanna and I drove quite by ourselves ... Mummy rode on the horse, and Karoline" (our maid last year) "on the other ... I say, what I'm telling you isn't a bit true."

'*I*: "What isn't true?"

'*Hans*: "None of it is. I say, let's put Hanna and me in the box[1] and I'll widdle into the box. I'll just widdle into my

1. 'The box standing in the front hall which we had taken to Gmunden as luggage.'

knickers; I don't care a bit; there's nothing at all shameful in it. I say, that isn't a joke, you know; but it's great fun, though."

'Then he told me the story of how the stork came – the same story as yesterday, except that he left out the part about the stork taking his hat when he went away.

'*I*: "Where did the stork keep his latch-key?"

'*Hans*: "In his pocket."

'*I*: "And where's the stork's pocket?"

'*Hans*: "In his beak."

'*I*: "It's in his beak! I've never seen a stork yet with a key in his beak."

'*Hans*: "How else could he have got in? How did the stork come in at the door, then? No, it isn't true; I just made a mistake. The stork rang at the front door and some one let him in."

'*I*: "And how did he ring?"

'*Hans*: "He rang the bell."

'*I*: "How did he do that?"

'*Hans*: "He took his beak and pressed on it with his beak."

'*I*: "And did he shut the door again?"

'*Hans*: "No, a maid shut it. She was up already, you see, and opened the door for him and shut it."

'*I*: "Where does the stork live?"

'*Hans*: "Where? In the box where he keeps the little girls. At Schönbrunn, perhaps."

'*I*: "I've never seen a box at Schönbrunn."

'*Hans*: "It must be farther off, then. – Do you know how the stork opens the box? He takes his beak – the box has got a key, too – he takes his beak, lifts up one" (i.e. one-half of the beak) "and unlocks it like this." (He demonstrated the process on the lock of the writing-table.) "There's a handle on it too."

'*I*: "Isn't a little girl like that too heavy for him?"

'*Hans*: "Oh no."

'*I*: "I say, doesn't a bus look like a stork-box?"

'*Hans*: "Yes."

'*I*: "And a furniture-waggon?"

'*Hans*: "And a scallywaggon" ("scallywag" – a term of abuse for naughty children) "too."

'April 17th. Yesterday Hans carried out his long-premeditated scheme of going across into the courtyard opposite. He would not do it today, as there was a cart standing at the loading dock exactly opposite the entrance gates. "When a cart stands there," he said to me, "I'm afraid *I shall tease the horses* and they'll fall down and make a row with their feet."

'*I*: "How does one tease horses?"

'*Hans*: "When you're cross with them you tease them, and when you shout 'Gee-up'."[1]

'*I*: "Have you ever teased horses?"

'*Hans*: "Yes, quite often. I'm *afraid* I shall do it, but I don't *really*."

'*I*: "Did you ever tease horses at Gmunden?"

'*Hans*: "No."

'*I*: "But you like teasing them?"

'*Hans*: "Oh yes, very much."

'*I*: "Would you like to whip them?"

'*Hans*: "Yes."

'*I*: "Would you like to beat the horses as Mummy beats Hanna? You like that too, you know."

'*Hans*: "It doesn't do the horses any harm when they're beaten." (I said this to him once to mitigate his fear of seeing horses whipped.) "Once I really did it. Once I had the whip, and whipped the horse, and it fell down and made a row with its feet."

I: "When?"

'*Hans*: "At Gmunden."

'*I*: "A real horse? Harnessed to a cart?"

'*Hans*: "It wasn't in the cart."

---

1. 'Hans has often been very much terrified when drivers beat their horses and shout "Gee-up".'

'*I*: "Where was it, then?"

'*Hans*: "I just held it so that it shouldn't run away." (Of course, all this sounded most improbable.)

'*I*: "Where was that?"

'*Hans*: "Near the trough."

'*I*: "Who let you? Had the coachman left the horse standing there?"

'*Hans*: "It was just a horse from the stables."

'*I*: "How did it get to the trough?"

'*Hans*: "I took it there."

'*I*: "Where from? Out of the stables?"

'*Hans*: "I took it out because I wanted to beat it."

'*I*: "Was there no one in the stables?"

'*Hans*: "Oh yes, Loisl." (The coachman at Gmunden.)

'*I*: "Did he let you?"

'*Hans*: "I talked nicely to him, and he said I might do it."

'*I*: "What did you say to him?"

'*Hans*: "Could I take the horse and whip it and shout at it. And he said 'Yes'."

'*I*: "Did you whip it a lot?"

'*Hans*: "*What I've told you isn't the least true.*"

'*I*: "How much of it's true?"

'*Hans*: "None of it's true; I only told it you for fun."

'*I*: "You never took a horse out of the stables?"

'*Hans*: "Oh no."

'*I*: "But you wanted to."

'*Hans*: "Oh yes, wanted to. I've thought it to myself."

'*I*: "At Gmunden?"

'*Hans*: "No, only here. I thought it in the morning when I was quite undressed; no, in the morning in bed."

'*I*: "Why did you never tell me about it?"

'*Hans*: "I didn't think of it."

'*I*: "You thought it to yourself because you saw it in the street."

'*Hans*: "Yes."

'*I*: "Which would you really like to beat? Mummy, Hanna, or me?"

'*Hans*: "Mummy."

'*I*: "Why?"

'*Hans*: "I should just like to beat her."

'*I*: "When did you ever see any one beating their Mummy?"

'*Hans*: "I've never seen any one do it, never in all my life."

'*I*: "And yet you'd just like to do it. How would you like to set about it?"

'*Hans*: "With a carpet-beater." (His mother often threatens to beat him with the carpet-beater.)

'I was obliged to break off the conversation for today.

'In the street Hans explained to me that buses, furniture-vans, and coal-carts were stork-box carts.'

That is to say, pregnant women. Hans's access of sadism immediately before cannot be unconnected with the present theme.

'April 21st. This morning Hans said that he had thought as follows: "There was a train at Lainz and I travelled with my Lainz Grandmummy to the Hauptzollamt station. You hadn't got down from the bridge yet, and the second train was already at St Veit.[1] When you came down, the train was there already, and we got in."

'(Hans was at Lainz yesterday. In order to get on to the departure platform one has to cross a bridge. From the platform one can see along the line as far as St Veit station. The whole thing is a trifle obscure. Hans's original thought had no doubt been that he had gone off by the first train, which I had missed, and that then a second train had come in from Unter St Veit and that I had gone after him in it. But he had distorted a part

1. [Unter St Veit: one station farther away from Vienna than Lainz. Owing to the straightness of the line, a traveller waiting on the platform at Lainz for a train to Vienna can see it approaching all the way from Unter St Veit and even beyond.]

of this runaway phantasy, so that he said finally: "Both of us only got away by the second train."

'This phantasy is related to the last one [p. 226], which was not interpreted, and according to which we took too long to put on our clothes in the station at Gmunden, so that the train carried us on.)

'Afternoon, in front of the house. Hans suddenly ran indoors as a carriage with two horses came along. I could see nothing unusual about it, and asked him what was wrong. "The horses are so proud," he said, "that I'm afraid they'll fall down." (The coachmen was reining the horses in tight, so that they were trotting with short steps and holding their heads high. In fact their action *was* "proud".)

'I asked him who it really was that was so proud.

'*He*: "You are, when I come into bed with Mummy."

'*I*: "So you want me to fall down?"

'*Hans*: "Yes. You've got to be naked" (meaning "barefoot", as Fritzl had been) "and knock up against a stone and bleed, and then I'll be able to be alone with Mummy for a little bit at all events. When you come up into our flat I'll be able to run away quick so that you don't see."

'*I*: "Can you remember who it was that knocked up against the stone?"

'*He*: "Yes, Fritzl."

'*I*: "When Fritzl fell down, what did you think?"[1]

'*He*: "That *you* should hit the stone and tumble down."

'*I*: "So you'd like to go to Mummy?"

'*He*: "Yes."

'*I*: "What do I really scold you for?"

'*He*: "I don't know." (!!)

'*I*: "Why?"

'*He*: "Because you're cross."

---

1. So that in fact Fritzl *did* fall down – which he at one time denied. [See p. 220.]

'*I*: "But that's not true."

'*Hans*: "Yes, it *is* true. You're cross. I know you are. It must be true."

'Evidently, therefore, my explanation that only *little* boys come into bed with their Mummies and that *big* ones sleep in their own beds had not impressed him very much.

'I suspect that his desire to "tease" the horse, i.e. to beat it and shout at it, does not apply to his mother, as he pretended, but to me. No doubt he only put her forward because he was unwilling to admit the alternative to me. For the last few days he has been particularly affectionate to me.'

Speaking with the air of superiority which is so easily acquired after the event, we may correct Hans's father, and explain that the boy's wish to 'tease' the horse had two constituents; it was compounded of an obscure sadistic desire for his mother and of a clear impulse for revenge against his father. The latter could not be reproduced until the former's turn had come to emerge in connection with the pregnancy complex. In the process of the formation of a phobia from the unconscious thoughts underlying it, condensation takes place; and for that reason the course of the analysis can never follow that of the development of the neurosis.

'April 22nd. This morning Hans again thought something to himself: "A street-boy was riding on a truck, and the guard came and undressed the boy quite naked and made him stand there till next morning, and in the morning the boy gave the guard 50,000 florins so that he could go on riding on the truck."

'(The Nordbahn [Northern Railway] runs past opposite our house. In a siding there stood a trolley on which Hans once saw a street-boy riding. He wanted to do so too; but I told him it was not allowed, and that if he did the guard would be after him. A second element in this phantasy is Hans's repressed wish to be naked.)'

It has been noticeable for some time that Hans's imagination was being coloured by images derived from traffic, and was advancing systematically from horses, which draw vehicles, to railways. In the same way railway anxiety eventually becomes associated with every street-phobia.[1]

'At lunch-time I was told that Hans *had been playing all the morning with an india-rubber doll which he called Grete.* [Cf. p. 194.] *He had pushed a small penknife in through the opening to which the little tin squeaker had originally been attached, and had then torn the doll's legs apart so as to let the knife drop out. He had said to the nurse-maid, pointing between the doll's legs:* "Look, there's its widdler!"

'*I:* "What was it you were playing at with your doll today?"

'*Hans:* "I tore its legs apart. Do you know why? Because there was a knife inside it belonging to Mummy. I put it in at the place where the button[2] squeaks, and then I tore apart its legs and it came out there."

'*I:* "Why did you tear its legs apart? So that you could see its widdler?"

'*He:* "Its widdler was there before; I could have seen it anyhow."

'*I:* "What did you put the knife in for?"

'*He:* "I don't know."

'*I:* "Well, what does the knife look like?"

'He brought it to me.

'*I:* "Did you think it was a baby, perhaps?"

'*He:* "No, I didn't think anything at all; but I believe the stork got a baby once – or some one."

'*I:* "When?"

'*He:* "Once. I heard so – or didn't I hear it at all? – or did I say it wrong?"

'*I:* "What does 'say it wrong' mean?"

'*He:* "That it's not true."

1. [This characteristic of phobias is discussed below on p. 282.]

2. ['*Der Knopf.*' So in the first edition. In all subsequent ones '*der Kopf*' ('the head'). This latter is almost certainly wrong: see below, p. 288, where the hole is described as being 'in the body'.]

'*I*: "Everything one says is a bit true."

'*He*: "Well, yes, a little bit."

'*I*(after changing the subject): "How do you think chickens are born?"

'*He*: "The stork just makes them grow; the stork makes chickens grow – no, God does."

'I explained to him that chickens lay eggs, and that out of the eggs there come other chickens.

'Hans laughed.

'*I*: "Why do you laugh?"

'*He*: "Because I like what you've told me."

'He said he had seen it happen already.

'*I*: "Where?"

'*Hans*: "You did it."

'*I*: "Where did I lay an egg?"

'*Hans*: "At Gmunden; you laid an egg in the grass, and all at once a chicken came hopping out. You laid an egg once; I know you did, I know it for certain. Because Mummy said so."

'*I*: "I'll ask Mummy if that's true."

'*Hans*: "It isn't true a bit. But *I* once laid an egg, and a chicken came hopping out."

'*I*: "Where?"

'*Hans*: "At Gmunden I lay down in the grass – no, I knelt down – and the children didn't look on at me, and all at once in the morning I said: 'Look for it, children; I laid an egg yesterday.' And all at once they looked, and all at once they saw an egg, and out of it there came a little Hans. Well, what are you laughing for? Mummy didn't know about it, and Karoline didn't know, because no one was looking on, and all at once I laid an egg, and all at once it was there. Really and truly. Daddy, when does a chicken grow out of an egg? When it's left alone? Must it be eaten?"

'I explained the matter to him.

'*Hans*: "All right, let's leave it with the hen; then a chicken'll grow. Let's pack it up in the box and let's take it to Gmunden."'

As his parents still hesitated to give him the information

which was already long overdue, little Hans had by a bold
stroke taken the conduct of the analysis into his own hands.
By means of a brilliant symptomatic act, '*Look!*' he had said to
them, '*this is how I imagine that a birth takes place.*' What he had
told the maid-servant about the meaning of his game with the
doll had been insincere; to his father he explicitly denied that
he had only wanted to see its widdler. After his father had told
him, as a kind of payment on account, how chickens come out
of eggs, Hans gave a combined expression to his dissatisfaction,
his mistrust, and his superior knowledge in a charming piece
of persiflage, which culminated with his last words in an
unmistakable allusion to his sister's birth.

'*I*: "What were you playing at with your doll?"

'*Hans*: "I said 'Grete' to her."

'*I*: "Why?"

'*Hans*: "Because I said 'Grete' to her."

'*I*: "How did you play?"

'*Hans*: "I just looked after her like a real baby."

'*I*: "Would you like to have a little girl?"

'*Hans*: "Oh yes. Why not? I should like to have one, but
Mummy mustn't have one; I don't like that."

(He has often expressed this view before. He is afraid of losing
still more of his position if a third child arrives.)

'*I*: "But only women have children."

'*Hans*: "I'm going to have a little girl."

'*I*: "Where will you get her, then?"

'*Hans*: "Why, from the stork. *He takes the little girl out*, and
all at once the little girl lays an egg, and out of the egg there
comes another Hanna – another Hanna. Out of Hanna there
comes another Hanna. No, *one* Hanna comes out."

'*I*: "You'd like to have a little girl."

'*Hans*: "*Yes, next year I'm going to have one*, and she'll be
called Hanna too."

'*I*: "But why isn't Mummy to have a little girl?"

'*Hans*: "Because *I* want to have a little girl for once."

'*I*: "But you can't have a little girl."

'*Hans*: "Oh yes, boys have girls and girls have boys."[1]

'*I*: "Boys don't have children. Only women, only Mummies have children."

'*Hans*: "But why shouldn't I?"

'*I*: "Because God's arranged it like that."

'*Hans*: "But why don't *you* have one? Oh yes, you'll have one all right. Just you wait."

'*I*: "I shall have to wait some time."

'*Hans*: "But I belong to you."

'*I*: "But Mummy brought you into the world. So you belong to Mummy and me."

'*Hans*: "Does Hanna belong to me or to Mummy?"

'*I*: "To Mummy."

'*Hans*: "No, to me. *Why not to me and Mummy?*"

'*I*: "Hanna belongs to me, Mummy, and you."

'*Hans*: "There you are, you see."'

So long as the child is in ignorance of the female genitals, there is naturally a vital gap in his comprehension of sexual matters.

'On April 24th my wife and I enlighted Hans up to a certain point; we told him that children grow inside their Mummy, and are then brought into the world by being pressed out of her like a "lumf"', and that this involves a great deal of pain.

'In the afternoon we went out in front of the house. There was a visible improvement in his state. He ran after carts, and the only thing that betrayed a remaining trace of his anxiety was the fact that he did not venture away from the neighbourhood of the street-door and could not be induced to go for any considerable walk.

'On April 25th Hans butted me in the stomach with his head, as he has already done once before [p. 204]. I asked him if he was a goat.

1. Here is another bit of infantile sexual theory with an unsuspected meaning.

'"Yes," he said, "a ram." I enquired where he had seen a ram.

'*He*: "At Gmunden: Fritzl had one." (Fritzl had a real lamb to play with.)

'*I*: "You must tell me about the lamb. What did it do?"

'*Hans*: "You know, Fräulein Mizzi" (a school-mistress who lived in the house) "used always to put Hanna on the lamb, but it couldn't stand up then and it couldn't butt. If you went up to it it used to butt, because it had horns. Fritzl used to lead it on a string and tie it to a tree. He always tied it to a tree."

'*I*: "Did the lamb butt you?"

'*Hans*: "It jumped up at me; Fritzl took me up to it once . . . I went up to it once and didn't know, and all at once it jumped up at me. It was such fun – I wasn't frightened."

'This was certainly untrue.

'*I*: "Are you fond of Daddy?"

'*Hans*: "Oh yes."

'*I*: "Or perhaps not."

'Hans was playing with a little toy horse. At that moment the horse fell down, and Hans shouted out: "The horse has fallen down! Look what a row it's making!"

'*I*: "You're a little vexed with Daddy because Mummy's fond of him."

'*Hans*: "No."

'*I*: "Then why do you always cry whenever Mummy gives me a kiss? It's because you're jealous."

'*Hans*: "Jealous, yes."

'*I*: "You'd like to be Daddy yourself."

'*Hans*: "Oh yes."

'*I*: "What would you like to do if you were Daddy?"

'*Hans*: "And you were Hans? I'd like to take you to Lainz every Sunday – no, every weekday too. If I were Daddy I'd be ever so nice and good."

'*I*: "But what would you like to do with Mummy?"

'*Hans*: "Take her to Lainz, too."

'*I*: "And what besides?"

'*Hans*: "Nothing."

'*I*: "Then why were you jealous?"

'*Hans*: "I don't know."

'*I*: "Were you jealous at Gmunden, too?"

'*Hans*: "Not at Gmunden." (This is not true.) "At Gmunden I had my own things. I had a garden at Gmunden and children too."

'*I*: "Can you remember how the cow got a calf?"

'*Hans*: "Oh yes. It came in a cart." (No doubt he had been told this at Gmunden; another attack on the stork theory.) "And another cow pressed it out of its behind." (This was already the fruit of his enlightenment, which he was trying to bring into harmony with the cart theory.)

'*I*: "It isn't true that it came in a cart; it came out of the cow in the cow-shed."

'Hans disputed this, saying that he had seen the cart in the morning. I pointed out to him that he had probably been told this about the calf having come in a cart. In the end he admitted this, and said: "Most likely Berta told me, or not – or perhaps it was the landlord. He was there and it was at night, so it *is* true after all, what I've been telling you – or it seems to me nobody told me; I thought it to myself in the night."

'Unless I am mistaken, the calf was taken away in a cart; hence the confusion.

'*I*: "Why didn't you think it was the stork that brought it?"

'*Hans*: "I didn't want to think that."

'*I*: "But you thought the stork brought Hanna?"

'*Hans*: "In the morning" (of the confinement) "I thought so. – I say, Daddy, was Herr Reisenbichler" (our landlord) "there when the calf came out of the cow?"[1]

'*I*: "I don't know. Do you think he was?"

'*Hans*: "I think so . . . Daddy, have you noticed now and then that horses have something black on their mouths?"

---

1. Hans, having good reason to mistrust information given him by grown-up people, was considering whether the landlord might not be more trustworthy than his father.

'*I*: "I've noticed it now and then in the street at Gmunden."¹

'*I*: "Did you often get into bed with Mummy at Gmunden?"

'*Hans*: "Yes."

'*I*: "And you used to think to yourself you were Daddy?"

'*Hans*: "Yes."

'*I*: "And then you felt afraid of Daddy?"

'*Hans*: "*You know everything; I didn't know anything.*"

'*I*: "When Fritzl fell down you thought: 'If only Daddy would fall down like that!' And when the lamb butted you you thought: 'If only it would butt Daddy!' Can you remember the funeral at Gmunden?" (The first funeral that Hans had seen. He often recalls it, and it is no doubt a screen memory.)

'*Hans*: "Yes. What about it?"

'*I*: "You thought then that if only Daddy were to die you'd be Daddy."

'*Hans*: "Yes."

'*I*: "What carts are you still afraid of?"

'*Hans*: "All of them."

'*I*: "You know that's not true."

'*Hans*: "I'm not afraid of carriages and pair or cabs with one horse. I'm afraid of buses and luggage-carts, but only when they're loaded up, not when they're empty. When there's one horse and the cart's loaded full up, then I'm afraid; but when there are two horses and it's loaded full up, then I'm not afraid."

'*I*: "Are you afraid of buses because there are so many people inside?"

'*Hans*: "Because there's so much luggage on the top."

'*I*: "When Mummy was having Hanna, was she loaded full up too?"

'*Hans*: "Mummy'll be loaded full up again when she has another one, when another one begins to grow, when another one's inside her."

1. The train of thought is as follows. For a long time his father had refused to believe what he said about there being something black on horses' mouths, but finally it had been verified [p. 229].

'*I*: "And you'd like that?"

'*Hans*: "Yes."

'*I*: "You said you didn't want Mummy to have another baby."

'*Hans*: "Well, then she won't be loaded up again. Mummy said if Mummy didn't want one, God didn't want one either. If Mummy doesn't want one she won't have one." (Hans naturally asked yesterday if there were any more babies inside Mummy. I told him not, and said that if God did not wish it none would grow inside her.)

'*Hans*: "But Mummy told me if *she* didn't want it no more'd grow, and you say if *God* doesn't want it."

'So I told him it was as I had said, upon which he observed: "You were there, though, weren't you? You know better, for certain." He then proceeded to cross-question his mother, and she reconciled the two statements by declaring that if she didn't want it God didn't want it either.[1]

'*I*: "It seems to me that, all the same, you do wish Mummy would have a baby."

'*Hans*: "But I don't want it to happen."

'*I*: "But you wish for it?"

'*Hans*: "Oh yes, *wish*."

'*I*: "Do you know why you wish for it? It's because you'd like to be Daddy."

'*Hans*: "Yes . . . How does it work?"

'*I*: "How does what work?"

'*Hans*: "You say Daddies don't have babies; so how does it work, my wanting to be Daddy?"

'*I*: "You'd like to be Daddy and married to Mummy; you'd

---

1. *Ce que femme veut Dieu veut.* But Hans, with his usual acumen, had once more put his finger upon a most serious problem. [It seems likely that the whole passage from the words 'Hans naturally asked yesterday . . .' down to '. . . God didn't want it either' should be in brackets, and that it is all a report of what had happened the day before. When Freud was consulted on this point by the translators (in 1923), he agreed that this was probably so, but preferred to have the text left unaltered, since it was a transcript of Hans's father's report.]

like to be as big as me and have a moustache; and you'd like Mummy to have a baby."

'*Hans*: "And, Daddy, when I'm married I'll only have one if I want to, when I'm married to Mummy, and if I don't want a baby, God won't want it either, when I'm married."

'*I*: "Would you like to be married to Mummy?"

'*Hans*: "Oh yes."'

It is easy to see that Hans's enjoyment of his phantasy was interfered with by his uncertainty as to the part played by fathers and by his doubts as to whether the begetting of children would be under his control.

'On the evening of the same day, as Hans was being put to bed, he said to me: "I say, d'you know what I'm going to do now? Now I'm going to talk to Grete till ten o'clock; she's in bed with me. My children are always in bed with me. Can you tell me why that is?" – As he was very sleepy already, I promised him that we should write it down next day, and he went to sleep.

'I have already noticed in earlier records that since Hans's return from Gmunden he has constantly been having phantasies about "his children" [e.g. p. 176], has carried on conversations with them, and so on.[1]

'So on April 26th I asked him why he was always thinking of his children.

'*Hans*: "Why? *Because I should so like to have children; but I don't ever want it; I shouldn't like to have them.*"[2]

1. There is no necessity on this account to assume in Hans the presence of a feminine strain of desire for having children. It was with his mother that Hans had had his most blissful experience as a child, and he was now repeating them, and himself playing the active part, which was thus necessarily that of mother.

2. This startling contradiction was one between phantasy and reality, between wishing and having. Hans knew that in reality he was a child and that the other children would only be in his way; but in phantasy he was a mother and wanted children with whom he could repeat the endearments that he had himself experienced.

'*I*: "Have you always imagined that Berta and Olga and the rest were your children?"

'*Hans*: "Yes. Franzl, and Fritzl, and Paul too" (his playmates at Lainz), "and Lodi." This is an invented girl's name, that of his favourite child, whom he speaks of most often – I may here emphasize the fact that the figure of Lodi is not an invention of the last few days, but existed before the date of his receiving the latest piece of enlightenment (April 24th).

'*I*: "Who is Lodi? Is she at Gmunden?"

'*Hans*: "No."

'*I*: "Is there a Lodi?"

'*Hans*: "Yes, I know her."

'*I*: "Who is she, then?"

'*Hans*: "The one I've got here."

'*I*: "What does she look like?"

'*Hans*: "Look like? Black eyes, black hair . . . I met her once with Mariedl" (at Gmunden) "as I was going into the town."

'When I went into the matter it turned out that this was an invention.[1]

'*I*: "So you thought you were their Mummy?"

'*Hans*: "And really I *was* their Mummy."

'*I*: "What did you do with your children?"

'*Hans*: "I had them to sleep with me, the girls and the boys."

'*I*: "Every day?"

'*Hans*: "Why, of course."

'*I*: "Did you talk to them?"

'*Hans*: "When I couldn't get all the children into the bed, I put some of the children on the sofa, and some in the pram, and if there were still some left over I took them up to the attic and put them in the box, and if there were any more I put them in the other box."

'*I*: "So the stork-baby-boxes were in the attic?"

'*Hans*: "Yes."

1. It is possible, however, that Hans had exalted into his ideal some one whom he had met casually at Gmunden. The colour of this ideal's eyes and hair, by the way, was copied from his mother.

'*I*: "When did you get your children? Was Hanna alive already?"

'*Hans*: "Yes, she had been a long time."

'*I*: "But who did you think you'd got the children from?"

'*Hans*: "*Why, from me.*"¹

'*I*: "But at that time you hadn't any idea that children came from some one."

'*Hans*: "I thought the stork had brought them." (Clearly a lie and an evasion.)²

'*I*: "You had Grete in bed with you yesterday, but you know quite well that boys can't have children."

'*Hans*: "Well, yes. But I believe they can, all the same.'

'*I*: "How did you hit upon the name Lodi? No girl's called that. Lotti, perhaps?"

'*Hans*: "Oh no, Lodi. I don't know; but it's a beautiful name, all the same."

'*I* (jokingly): "Perhaps you mean a Schokolodi?"³

'*Hans* (promptly): "No, a Saffalodi,⁴ . . . because I like eating sausages so much, and salami⁵ too."

'*I*: "I say, doesn't a Saffalodi look like a lumf?"

'*Hans*: "Yes."

'*I*: "Well, what does a lumf look like?"

'*Hans*: "Black. You know" (pointing at my eyebrows and moustache), "like this and like this."

'*I*: "And what else? Round like a Saffaladi?"

'*Hans*: "Yes."

'*I*: "When you sat on the chamber and a lumf came, did you think to yourself you were having a baby?"

'*Hans* (laughing): "Yes. Even at — Street, and here as well."

1. Hans could not help answering from the auto-erotic point of view.

2. They were the children of his phantasy, that it to say, of his masturbation.

3. ['*Schokolade*' is the German for 'chocolate'.]

4. '"Saffaladi" means "*Zervelatwurst*" ["saveloy", a kind of sausage]. My wife is fond of relating how her aunt always calls it "Soffilodi". Hans may have heard this.'

5. [Another kind of sausage.]

'*I*: "You know when the bus-horses fell down? [Cf. p. 211 ff.] The bus looked like a baby-box, and when the black horse fell down it was just like . . ."

'*Hans* (taking me up): ". . . like having a baby."

'*I*: "And what did you think when it made a row with its feet?"

'*Hans*: "Oh, when I don't want to sit on the chamber and would rather play, then I make a row like this with my feet." [Cf. p. 215.] (He stamped his feet.)

'This was why he was so much interested in the question whether people *liked* or *did not like* having children.

'All day long today Hans has been playing at loading and unloading packing-cases; he said he wished he could have a toy waggon and boxes of that kind to play with. What used most to interest him in the courtyard of the Customs House opposite was the loading and unloading of the carts. And he used to be frightened most when a cart had been loaded up and was on the point of driving off. "The horses'll fall down,"[1] he used to say [p. 208]. He used to call the doors of the Head Customs House shed "holes" (e.g. the first hole, second hole, third hole, etc.). But now, instead of "hole", he says "behind-hole".

'The anxiety has almost completely disappeared, except that he likes to remain in the neighbourhood of the house, so as to have a line of retreat in case he is frightened. But he never takes flight into the house now, but stops in the street all the time. As we know, his illness began with his turning back in tears while he was out for a walk; and when he was obliged to go for a second walk he only went as far as the Hauptzollamt station on the Stadtbahn, from which our house can still be seen. At the time of my wife's confinement he was of course kept away from her; and his present anxiety, which prevents him from leaving the neighbourhood of the house, is in reality the longing for her which he felt then.

---

1. Do we not use the word '*niederkommen*' [literally, 'to come down'] when a woman is delivered?

'April 30th. Seeing Hans playing with his imaginary children again, "Hullo," I said to him, "are your children still alive? You know quite well a boy can't have any children."

'*Hans*: "I know. I was their Mummy before, *now I'm their Daddy*."

'*I*: "And who's the children's Mummy?"

'*Hans*: "Why, Mummy, and you're their *Grandaddy*."

'*I*: "So then you'd like to be as big as me, and be married to Mummy, and then you'd like her to have children."

'*Hans*: "Yes, that's what I'd like, and then my Lainz Grandmummy" (my mother) "will be their Grannie."'

Things were moving towards a satisfactory conclusion. The little Oedipus had found a happier solution than that prescribed by destiny. Instead of putting his father out of the way, he had granted him the same happiness that he desired himself: he made him a grandfather and married *him* to his own mother too.

'On May 1st Hans came to me at lunch-time and said: "D'you know what? Let's write something down for the Professor."

'*I*: "Well, and what shall it be?"

'*Hans*: "This morning I was in the W.C. with all my children. First I did lumf and widdled, and they looked on. Then I put them on the seat and they widdled and did lumf, and I wiped their behinds with paper. D'you know why? Because I'd so much like to have children; then I'd do everything for them – take them to the W.C., clean their behinds, and do everything one does with children."'

After the admission afforded by this phantasy, it will scarcely be possible to dispute the fact that in Hans's mind there was pleasure attached to the excretory functions.

'In the afternoon he ventured into the Stadtpark for the first time. As it is the First of May, no doubt there was less traffic than usual, but still quite enough to have frightened him up to now. He was very proud of his achievement, and after tea I was obliged to go with him to the Stadtpark once again. On the way we met a bus; Hans pointed it out to me, saying: "Look! a stork-box cart!" If he goes with me to the Stadtpark again tomorrow, as we have planned, we shall really be able to regard his illness as cured.

'On May 2nd Hans came to me in the morning. "I say," he said, "I thought something today." At first he had forgotten it; but later on he related what follows, though with signs of considerable resistance: "*The plumber came; and first he took away my behind with a pair of pincers, and then gave me another, and then the same with my widdler.* He said: 'Let me see your behind!' and I had to turn round, and he took it away; and then he said: 'Let me see your widdler!'"'

Hans's father grasped the nature of this wishful phantasy, and did not hesitate a moment as to the only interpretation it could bear.

'*I*: "He gave you a *bigger* widdler and a *bigger* behind."

'*Hans*: "Yes."

'*I*: "Like Daddy's; because you'd like to be Daddy."

'*Hans*: "Yes, and I'd like to have a moustache like yours and hairs like yours." (He pointed to the hairs on my chest.)

'In the light of this, we may review the interpetation of Hans's earlier phantasy to the effect that the plumber had come and unscrewed the bath and had stuck a borer into his stomach [p. 226]. The big bath meant a "behind", the borer or screwdriver was (as we explained at the time) a widdler.[1] The two

_____

1. Perhaps, too, the word 'borer' ['*Bohrer*'] was not chosen without regard for its connection with 'born' ['*geboren*'] and 'birth' ['*Geburt*']. If so, the child could have made no distinction between 'bored' ['*gebohrt*'] and 'born' ['*geboren*']. I accept this suggestion, made by an experienced fellow-worker, but I am not in a position to say whether we have before us here a deep and universal connection between the two ideas or merely the employment of a verbal coincidence peculiar to German [and English]. Prometheus (Pramantha), the creator of man, is also etymologically 'the borer'. (Cf. Abraham, *Traum und Mythus*, 1909.)

phantasies are identical. Moreover, a new light is thrown upon Hans's fear of the big bath. (This, by the way, has already diminished.) He dislikes his "behind" being too small for the big bath.'

In the course of the next few days Hans's mother wrote to me more than once to express her joy at the little boy's recovery.

A week later came a postscript from Hans's father.

'My dear Professor, I should like to make the following additions to Hans's case history:

'(1) The remission after he had been given his first piece of enlightenment was not so complete as I may have represented it [p. 191]. It is true that Hans went for walks; but only under compulsion and in a state of great anxiety. Once he went with me as far as the Hauptzollamt station, from which our house can still be seen, but could not be induced to go any farther.

'(2) As regards "raspberry syrup" and a "gun for shooting with" [p. 200]. Hans is given raspberry syrup when he is constipated. He also frequently confuses the words "shooting" and "shitting".[1]

'(3) Hans was about four years old when he was moved out of our bedroom into a room of his own.

'(4) A trace of his disorder still persists, though it is no longer in the shape of fear but only in that of the normal instinct for asking questions. The questions are mostly concerned with what things are made of (trams, machines, etc.), who makes things, etc. Most of his questions are characterized by the fact that Hans asks them although he has already answered them himself. He only wants to make sure. Once when he had tired me out with his questions and I had said to him: "Do you think I can answer every question you ask?" he replied: "Well, I thought as you knew that about the horse you'd know this too."

'(5) Hans only refers to his illness now as a matter of past history – "at the time when I had my nonsense".

1. [In German 'schiessen' and 'scheissen'.]

'(6) An unsolved residue remains behind; for Hans keeps cudgelling his brains to discover what a father has to do with his child, since it is the mother who brings it into the world. This can be seen from his questions, as, for instance: "I belong to *you*, too, don't I?" (meaning, not only to his mother). It is not clear to him in what way he belongs to me. On the other hand, I have no direct evidence of his having, as you suppose, overheard his parents in the act of intercourse.

'(7) In presenting the case one ought perhaps to insist upon the violence of his anxiety. Otherwise it might be said that the boy would have gone out for walks soon enough if he had been given a sound thrashing.'

In conclusion let me add these words. With Hans's last phantasy the anxiety which arose from his castration complex was also overcome, and his painful expectations were given a happier turn. Yes, the Doctor [see p. 171] (the plumber) *did* come, he *did* take away his penis, – but only to give him a bigger one in exchange for it. For the rest, our young investigator has merely come somewhat early upon the discovery that all knowledge is patchwork, and that each step forward leaves an unsolved residue behind.

III

DISCUSSION

I SHALL now proceed to examine this observation of the development and resolution of a phobia in a boy under five years of age, and I shall have to do so from three points of view. In the first place I shall consider how far it supports the assertions which I put forward in my *Three Essays on the Theory of Sexuality* (1905d). Secondly, I shall consider to what extent it can contribute towards our understanding of this very frequent form of disorder. And thirdly, I shall consider whether it can be made to shed any light upon the mental life of children or to afford any criticism of our educational aims.

I

My impression is that the picture of a child's sexual life presented in this observation of little Hans agrees very well with the account I gave of it (basing my views upon psychoanalytic examinations of adults) in my *Three Essays*. But before going into the details of this agreement I must deal with two objections which will be raised against my making use of the present analysis for this purpose. The first objection is to the effect that Hans was not a normal child, but (as events – the illness itself, in fact – showed) had a predisposition to neurosis, and was a young 'degenerate'; it would be illegitimate, therefore, to apply to other, normal children conclusions which might perhaps be true of him. I shall postpone consideration of this objection, since it only limits the value of the observation, and does not completely nullify it. According to the second and more uncompromising objection, an analysis of a child conducted by his father, who went to work instilled with *my* theoretical views and infected with *my* prejudices, must be entirely devoid of any objective worth. A child, it will be said, is necessarily highly suggestible, and in regard to no one, perhaps, more than to his own father; he will allow anything to be forced upon him, out of gratitude to his father for taking so much notice of him; none of his assertions can have any evidential value, and everything he produces in the way of associations, phantasies, and dreams will naturally take the direction into which they are being urged by every possible means. Once more, in short, the whole thing is simply 'suggestion' – the only difference being that in the case of a child it can be unmasked much more easily than in that of an adult.

A singular thing. I can remember, when I first began to meddle in the conflict of scientific opinions twenty-two years ago, with what derision the older generation of neurologists and psychiatrists of those days received assertions about suggestion and its effects.[1] Since then the situation has fundamentally changed. The former aversion has been converted into an only too ready acceptance; and this has happened not only as a consequence of the impression which the work of Liébeault and Bernheim and their pupils could not fail to create in the course of these two decades, but also because it has since been discovered how great an economy of thought can be effected by the use of the catchword 'suggestion'. Nobody knows and nobody cares what suggestion is, where it comes from, or when it arises, – it is enough that everything awkward in the region of psychology can be labelled 'suggestion'. I do not share the view which is at present fashionable that assertions made by children are invariably arbitrary and untrustworthy. The arbitrary has no existence in mental life. The untrustworthiness of the assertions of children is due to the predominance of their imagination, just as the untrustworthiness of the assertions of grown-up people is due to the predominance of their prejudices. For the rest, even children do not lie without a reason, and on the whole they are more inclined to a love of truth than are their elders. If we were to reject little Hans's

1. [Cf. the similar remarks at the end of the *Introductory Lectures* (1916–17), *P.F.L.*, 1, 516.]

statements root and branch we should certainly be doing him a grave injustice. On the contrary, we can quite clearly distinguish from one another the occasions on which he was falsifying the facts or keeping them back under the compelling force of a resistance, the occasions on which, being undecided himself, he agreed with his father (so that what he said must not be taken as evidence), and the occasions on which, freed from every pressure, he burst into a flood of information about what was really going on inside him and about things which until then no one but himself had known. Statements made by adults offer no greater certainty. It is a regrettable fact that no account of a psychoanalysis can reproduce the impressions received by the analyst as he conducts it, and that a final sense of conviction can never be obtained from reading about it but only from directly experiencing it. But this disability attaches in an equal degree to analyses of adults.

Little Hans is described by his parents as a cheerful, straightforward child, and so he should have been, considering the education given him by his parents, which consisted essentially in the omission of our usual educational sins. So long as he was able to carry on his researches in a state of happy *naïveté*, without a suspicion of the conflicts which were soon to arise out of them, he kept nothing back; and the observations made during the period before the phobia admit of no doubt or demur. It was with the outbreak of the illness and during the analysis that discrepancies began to make their appearance between what he said and what he thought; and this was partly because unconscious material, which he was unable to master all at once, was forcing itself upon him, and partly because the content of his thoughts provoked reservations on account of his relation to his parents. It is my unbiassed opinion that these difficulties, too, turned out no greater than in many analyses of adults.

It is true that during the analysis Hans had to be told many things that he could not say himself, that he had to be presented with thoughts which he had so far shown no signs of possessing, and that his attention had to be turned in the direction from which his father was expecting something to come. This detracts from the evidential value of the analysis; but the procedure is the same in every case. For a psychoanalysis is not an impartial scientific investigation, but a therapeutic measure. Its essence is not to prove anything, but merely to alter something. In a psychoanalysis the physician always gives his patient (sometimes to a greater and sometimes to a less extent) the conscious anticipatory ideas by the help of which he is put in a position to recognize and to grasp the unconscious material. For there are some patients who need more of such assistance and some who need less; but there are none who get through without some of it. Slight disorders may perhaps be brought to an end by the subject's unaided efforts, but never a neurosis – a thing which has set itself up against the ego as an element alien to it. To get the better of such an element another person must be brought in, and in so far as that other person can be of assistance the neurosis will be curable. If it is in the very nature of any neurosis to turn away from the 'other person' – and this seems to be one of the characteristics of the states grouped together under the name of dementia praecox – then for that very reason such a state will be incurable by any efforts of ours. It is true that a child, on account of the small development of his intellectual systems, requires especially energetic assistance. But, after all, the information which the physician gives his patient is itself derived in its turn from analytical experience; and indeed it is sufficiently convincing if, at the cost of this intervention by the physician, we are enabled to discover the structure of the pathogenic material and simultaneously to dissipate it.

And yet, even during the analysis, the small patient gave evidence of enough independence to acquit him upon the charge of 'suggestion'. Like all other children, he applied his childish sexual theories to the material before him without having received any encouragement to do so. These theories are extremely remote from the adult mind. Indeed, in this instance I actually omitted to warn Hans's father that the boy would be bound to approach the subject of childbirth by way of the excretory complex. This negligence on my part, though it led to an obscure phase in the analysis, was nevertheless the means of producing a good piece of evidence of the genuineness and independence of Hans's mental processes. He suddenly became occupied with 'lumf' [p. 215 ff.], without his father, who is supposed to have been practising suggestion upon him, having the least idea how he had arrived at that subject or what was going to come of it. Nor can his father be saddled with any responsibility for the production of the two plumber phantasies [pp. 226 and 257], which arose out of Hans's early acquired 'castration complex'. And I must here confess that, out of theoretical interest, I entirely concealed from Hans's father my expectation that there would turn out to be some such connection, so as not to interfere with the value of a piece of evidence such as does not often come within one's grasp.

If I went more deeply into the details of the analysis I could produce plenty more evidence of Hans's independence of 'suggestion'; but I shall break off the discussion of this preliminary objection at this point. I am aware that even with this analysis I shall not succeed in convincing any one who will not let himself be convinced, and I shall proceed with my discussion of the case for the benefit of those readers who are already convinced of the objective reality of unconscious pathogenic material. And I do this with the agreeable assurance that the number of such readers is steadily increasing.

The first trait in little Hans which can be regarded as part of his sexual life was a quite peculiarly lively interest in his 'widdler' – an organ deriving its name from that one of its two functions which, scarcely the less important of the two, is not to be eluded in the nursery. This interest aroused in him the spirit of enquiry, and he thus discovered that the presence or absence of a widdler made it possible to differentiate between animate and inanimate objects [p. 173]. He assumed that all animate objects were like himself, and possessed this important bodily organ; he observed that it was present in the larger animals, suspected that this was so too in both his parents, and was not deterred by the evidence of his own eyes from authenticating the fact in his new-born sister [p. 175]. One might almost say that it would have been too shattering a blow to his 'Weltanschauung' if he had had to make up his mind to forgo the presence of this organ in a being similar to him; it would have been as though it were being torn away from himself. It was probably on this account that a threat of his mother's [p. 171], which was concerned precisely with the loss of his widdler, was hastily dismissed from his thoughts and only succeeded in making its effects apparent at a later period. The reason for his mother's intervention had been that he used to like giving himself feelings of pleasure by touching his member: the little boy had begun to practise the commonest – and most normal – form of auto-erotic sexual activity.

The pleasure which a person takes in his own sexual organ may become associated with scopophilia (or sexual pleasure in looking) in its active and passive forms, in a manner which has been very aptly described by Alfred Adler (1908) as 'confluence of instincts'. So little Hans began to try to get a sight of other people's widdlers; his sexual curiosity developed, and at the same time he liked to exhibit his own widdler. One of his dreams, dating from the beginning of his period of repression, expressed a wish that one of his little girl friends should assist him in widdling, that is, that she should share the spectacle [p. 183]. The dream shows, therefore, that up till then this wish had subsisted unrepressed, and later information confirmed the fact that he had been in the habit of gratifying it. The active side of his sexual scopophilia soon became associated in him with a definite theme. He repeatedly expressed both to his father and his mother his regret that he had never yet seen their widdlers; and it was probably the need *for making a comparison* which impelled him to do this. The ego is always the standard by which one measures the external world; one learns to understand it by means of a constant comparison with oneself. Hans had observed that large animals had widdlers that were correspondingly larger than his; he consequently suspected that the same was true of his parents, and was anxious to make sure of this. His mother, he thought, must certainly have a widdler 'like a horse'. He was then prepared with the comforting reflection that his widdler would grow with him. It was as though the child's wish to be bigger had been concentrated on his genitals.

Thus in little Hans's sexual constitution the genital zone was from the outset the one among his erotogenic zones which afforded him the most intense pleasure. The only other similar pleasure of which he gave evidence was excretory pleasure, the pleasure attached to the orifices through which micturition and evacuation of the bowels are effected. In his final phantasy of bliss, with which his illness was overcome, he imagined he had children, whom he took to the W.C., whom he made to widdle, whose behinds he wiped – for whom, in short, he did 'everything one can do with children' [p. 256]; it therefore seems impossible to avoid the assumption that during the period when he himself had been looked after as an infant these same performances had been the source of pleasurable sensations for him. He had obtained this pleasure from his erotogenic zones with the help of the person who had looked after him – his mother, in fact; and thus the pleasure already pointed the way to object-choice. But it is just possible that at a still earlier date he had been in the habit of giving himself this pleasure auto-erotically – that he had been one of those children who like retaining their excreta till they can derive a voluptuous sensation from their evacuation. I say no more than that it is possible, because the matter was not cleared up in the analysis; the 'making a row with the legs' (kicking about), of which he was so much frightened later on, points in that direction. But in any case these sources of pleasure had no particularly striking importance with Hans, as they so often have with other children. He early became clean in his habits, and neither bed-wetting nor diurnal incontinence played any part during his first years; no trace was observed in him of any inclination to play with his excrement, a propensity which is so revolting in adults, and which commonly makes its reappearance at the termination of processes of psychical involution.

At this juncture it is as well to emphasize at once the fact that during his phobia there was an unmistakable repression of these two well-developed components of his sexual activity. He was ashamed of micturating before other people, accused himself of putting his finger to his widdler, made efforts to give up masturbating, and showed disgust at 'lumf' and 'widdle' and everything that reminded him of them. In his phantasy of looking after his children he undid this latter repression.

A sexual constitution like that of little Hans does not appear to carry with it a predisposition to the development either of perversions or of their negative (we will limit ourselves to a consideration of hysteria).[1] As far as my experience goes (and there is still a real need for speaking with caution on this point) the innate constitution of hysterics – that this is also true of perverts is almost self-evident – is marked by the genital zone being relatively less prominent than the other erotogenic zones. But we must expressly except from this rule one particular 'aberration' of sexual life. In those who later become homosexuals we meet with the same predominance in infancy of the genital zone (and especially of the penis) as in normal persons.[2] Indeed it is the high esteem felt by the homosexual for the male organ which decides his fate. In his childhood he chooses women as his sexual object, so long as he assumes that they too possess what in his eyes is an indispensable part of the body; when he becomes convinced that women have deceived him in this particular, they cease to be acceptable to him as a

1. [See the paragraphs on 'Neurosis and Perversion' at the end of Section 4 of the first of Freud's *Three Essays* (1905*d*, *P.F.L.*, **7**, 79 ff.).]

2. As my expectations led me to suppose, and as Sadger's observations [e.g. 1908 and 1909] have shown, all such people pass through an amphigenic phase in childhood.

sexual object. He cannot forgo a penis in any one who is to attract him to sexual intercourse; and if circumstances are favourable he will fix his libido upon the 'woman with a penis', a youth of feminine appearance. Homosexuals, then, are persons who, owing to the erotogenic importance of their own genitals, cannot do without a similar feature in their sexual object. In the course of their development from auto-erotism to object-love, they have remained fixated at a point between the two – a point which is closer to auto-erotism.[1]

There is absolutely no justification for distinguishing a special homosexual instinct. What constitutes a homosexual is a peculiarity not in his instinctual life but in his choice of an object. Let me recall what I have said in my *Three Essays* to the effect that we have mistakenly imagined the bond between instinct and object in sexual life as being more intimate than it really is.[2] A homosexual may have normal instincts, but he is unable to disengage them from a class of objects defined by a particular determinant. And in his childhood, since at that period this determinant is taken for granted as being of universal application, he is able to behave like little Hans, who showed his affection to little boys and girls indiscriminately, and once described his friend Fritzl as 'the girl he was fondest of' [p. 180]. Hans was a homosexual (as all children may very well be), quite consistently with the fact, which must always be kept in mind, that *he was acquainted with only one kind of genital organ* – a genital organ like his own.[3]

1. [The 'woman with a penis' had already appeared in Freud's paper 'The Sexual Theories of Children' (1908c), *P.F.L.*, **7**, 193–4. For a summary of his views on male homosexuality see the paragraph on the 'Sexual Object of Inverts' in Section 1 (A) of the first of the *Three Essays* (1905d), and especially the long footnote added in the course of the successive editions of that book (*P.F.L.*, **7**, 56–9).]

2. [Freud (1905d), *P.F.L.*, **7**, 59–60.]

3. (*Footnote added* 1923:) I have subsequently (1923e) drawn attention to the fact that the period of sexual development which our little patient was passing through is universally characterized by acquaintance with only *one* sort of genital organ, namely, the male one. In contrast to the

In his subsequent development, however, it was not to homosexuality that our young libertine proceeded, but to an energetic masculinity with traits of polygamy; he knew how to vary his behaviour, too, with his varying feminine objects – audaciously aggressive in one case, languishing and bashful in another. His affection had moved from his mother on to other objects of love, but at a time when there was a scarcity of these it returned to her, only to break down in a neurosis. It was not until this happened that it became evident to what a pitch of intensity his love for his mother had developed and through what vicissitudes it had passed. The sexual aim which he pursued with his girl playmates, of *sleeping* with them, had originated in relation to his mother. It was expressed in words which might be retained in maturity, though they would then bear a richer connotation.[1] The boy had found his way to object-love in the usual manner from the care he had received when he was an infant; and a new pleasure had now become the most important for him – that of sleeping beside his mother. I should like to emphasize the importance of pleasure derived from cutaneous contact as a component in this new aim of Hans's, which, according to the nomenclature (artificial to my mind) of Moll, would have to be described as satisfaction of the instinct of contrectation.[2]

In his attitude towards his father and mother Hans confirms in the most concrete and uncompromising manner what I have said in my *Interpretation of Dreams* [1900a, in Section D (β) of Chapter V; *P.F.L.*, **4**, 347 ff.] and in my *Three Essays* [1905d, *P.F.L.*, **7**, 144 ff.] with regard to the sexual relations of a child to his parents. Hans really was a little Oedipus who wanted to have his father 'out of the way', to get rid of him, so that he might be alone with his beautiful mother and sleep with her.

---

later period of maturity, this period is marked not by a *genital* primacy but by a primacy of the *phallus*. [*P.F.L.*, **7**, 308–10.]

  1. [The German '*bei jemandem schlafen*', literally 'to sleep with some one', is used (like the English) in the sense of 'to copulate with'.]

  2. [Moll (1898). Cf. *Three Essays*, *P.F.L.*, **7**, 84 *n*. 2.]

This wish had originated during his summer holidays, when the alternating presence and absence of his father had drawn Hans's attention to the condition upon which depended the intimacy with his mother which he longed for. At that time the form taken by the wish had been merely that his father should 'go away'; and at a later stage it became possible for his fear of being bitten by a white horse to attach itself directly on to this form of the wish, owing to a chance impression which he received at the moment of some one else's departure.[1] But subsequently (probably not until they had moved back to Vienna, where his father's absences were no longer to be reckoned on) the wish had taken the form that his father should be *permanently* away – that he should be 'dead'. The fear which sprang from this death-wish against his father, and which may thus be said to have had a normal motive, formed the chief obstacle to the analysis until it was removed during the conversation in my consulting-room [p. 204].[2]

But Hans was not by any means a bad character; he was not even one of those children who at his age still give free play to the propensity towards cruelty and violence which is a constituent of human nature. On the contrary, he had an unusually kind-hearted and affectionate disposition; his father reported that the transformation of aggressive tendencies into feelings of pity took place in him at a very early age. Long before the phobia he had become uneasy when he saw the horses in a merry-go-round being beaten; and he was never unmoved if

1. [In the editions before 1924 this read 'at the moment of the departure of another father'. The original account of the episode on p. 192 (as also the reference to it on p. 207) seemed, however, to imply that it was only Lizzi who was going away. Hence the correction and the similar one on p. 277.]

2. It is quite certain that Hans's two associations, 'raspberry-syrup' and 'a gun for shooting people dead with' [p. 200], must have had more than one set of determinants. They probably had just as much to do with his hatred of his father as with his constipation complex. His father, who himself guessed the latter connection [p. 258], also suggested that 'raspberry syrup' might be related to 'blood'.

any one wept in his presence. At one stage in the analysis a piece of suppressed sadism made its appearance in a particular context:[1] but it was *suppressed* sadism, and we shall presently have to discover from the context what it stood for and what it was meant to replace. And Hans deeply loved the father against whom he cherished these death-wishes; and while his intellect demurred to such a contradiction,[2] he could not help demonstrating the fact of its existence, by hitting his father and immediately afterwards kissing the place he had hit [p. 204 *n.*]. We ourselves, too, must guard against making a difficulty of such a contradiction. The emotional life of man is in general made up of pairs of contraries such as these.[3] Indeed, if it were not so, repressions and neuroses would perhaps never come about. In the adult these pairs of contrary emotions do not as a rule become simultaneously conscious except at the climaxes of passionate love; at other times they usually go on suppressing each other until one of them succeeds in keeping the other altogether out of sight. But in children they can exist peaceably side by side for quite a considerable time.

The most important influence upon the course of Hans's psychosexual development was the birth of a baby sister when he was three and a half years old. That event accentuated his relations to his parents and gave him some insoluble problems to think about; and later, as he watched the way in which the infant was looked after, the memory-traces of his own earliest experiences of pleasure were revived in him. This influence, too, is a typical one: in an unexpectedly large number of life histories, normal as well as pathological, we find ourselves obliged to take as our starting-point an outburst of sexual pleasure and sexual curiosity connected, like this one, with the

1. His wanting to beat and tease horses [p. 239].
2. See the critical question he addressed to his father (p. 206).
3. Das heisst, ich bin kein ausgeklügelt Buch.
    Ich bin ein Mensch mit seinem Widerspruch.
    C. F. Meyer, *Huttens letzte Tage* [xxvi, 'Homo Sum'].
        [In fact, I am no clever work of fiction;
        I am a man, with all his contradiction.]

birth of the next child. Hans's behaviour towards the new arrival was just what I have described in *The Interpretation of Dreams* [1900a, in Section D (β) of Chapter V; *P.F.L.* 4, 349 ff.]. In his fever a few days later he betrayed how little he liked the addition to the family [p. 174]. Affection for his sister might come later,[1] but his first attitude was hostility. From that time forward fear that yet another baby might arrive found a place among his conscious thoughts. In the neurosis, his hostility, already suppressed, was represented by a special fear – a fear of the bath [p. 227]. In the analysis he gave undisguised expression to his death-wish against his sister, and was not content with allusions which required supplementing by his father. His inner conscience did not consider this wish so wicked as the analogous one against his father; but it is clear that in his unconscious he treated both persons in the same way, because they both took his mummy away from him, and interfered with his being alone with her.

Moreover, this event and the feelings that were revived by it gave a new direction to his wishes. In his triumphant final phantasy [p. 256] he summed up all of his erotic wishes, both those derived from his auto-erotic phase and those connected with his object-love. In that phantasy he was married to his beautiful mother and had innumerable children whom he could look after in his own way.

2

One day while Hans was in the street he was seized with an attack of anxiety. He could not yet say what it was he was afraid of; but at the very beginning of this anxiety-state he betrayed to his father his motive for being ill, the gain from illness.[2] He

1. Cf. his plans of what he would do when his sister was old enough to speak (p. 233).

2. [The motives of illness and the gain from illness are discussed in the 'Dora' case history, pp. 75-9 above. Cf. in particular the long footnote on pp. 75-6, where further references are given.]

wanted to stay with his mother and to coax with her; his recollection that he had also been separated from her at the time of the baby's birth may also, as his father suggests [p. 255], have contributed to his longing. It soon became evident that his anxiety was no longer reconvertible into longing; he was afraid even when his mother went with him. In the meantime indications appeared of what it was to which his libido (now changed into anxiety) had become attached. He gave expression to the quite specific fear that a white horse would bite him.

Disorders of this kind are called 'phobias', and we might classify Hans's case as an agoraphobia if it were not for the fact that it is a characteristic of that complaint that the locomotion of which the patient is otherwise incapable can always be easily performed when he is accompanied by some specially selected person – in the last resort, by the physician. Hans's phobia did not fulfil this condition; it soon ceased having any relation to the question of locomotion and became more and more clearly concentrated upon horses. In the early days of his illness, when the anxiety was at its highest pitch, he expressed a fear that 'the horse'll come into the room' [p. 187], and it was this that helped me so much towards understanding his condition.

In the classificatory system of the neuroses no definite position has hitherto been assigned to 'phobias'. It seems certain that they should only be regarded as syndromes which may form part of various neuroses and that we need not rank them as an independent pathological process. For phobias of the kind to which little Hans's belongs, and which are in fact the most common, the name of 'anxiety hysteria' seems to me not inappropriate; I suggested the term to Dr W. Stekel when he was undertaking a description of neurotic anxiety-states,[1] and I hope it will come into general use. It finds its justification in the similarity between the psychological structure of these phobias and that of hysteria – a similarity which is complete except upon a single point. That point, however, is a decisive

1. Stekel (1908). [Freud wrote a preface for the first edition of this work (1908f).]

one and well adapted for purposes of differentiation. For in anxiety hysteria the libido which has been liberated from the pathogenic material by repression is not *converted* (that is, diverted from the mental sphere into a somatic innervation), but is set free in the shape of *anxiety*. In the clinical cases that we meet with, this 'anxiety hysteria' may be combined with 'conversion hysteria' in any proportion. There exist cases of pure conversion hysteria without any trace of anxiety, just as there are cases of simple anxiety hysteria, which exhibit feelings of anxiety and phobias, but have no admixture of conversion. The case of little Hans is one of the latter sort.

Anxiety hysterias are the most common of all psychoneurotic disorders. But, above all, they are those which make their appearance earliest in life; they are *par excellence* the neuroses of childhood. When a mother uses such phrases as that her child's 'nerves' are in a bad state, we can be certain that in nine cases out of ten the child is suffering from some kind of anxiety or from many kinds at once. Unfortunately the finer mechanism of these highly significant disorders has not yet been sufficiently studied. It has not yet been established whether anxiety hysteria is determined, in contradistinction to conversion hysteria and other neuroses, solely by constitutional factors or solely by accidental experiences, or by what combination of the two.[1] It seems to me that of all neurotic disorders it is the least dependent upon a special constitutional disposition and that it is consequently the most easily acquired at any time of life.

One essential characteristic of anxiety hysterias is very easily pointed out. An anxiety hysteria tends to develop more and

1. (*Footnote added* 1923:) The question which is raised here has not been pursued further. But there is no reason to suppose that anxiety hysteria is an exception to the rule that both disposition and experience must co-operate in the aetiology of a neurosis. Rank's view of the effects of the trauma of birth seems to throw special light upon the disposition to anxiety hysteria which is so strong in childhood. [See, however, Freud's later criticism of this view of Rank's in *Inhibitions, Symptoms and Anxiety* (1926*d*), *P.F.L.*, **10**, 292 f.]

more into a 'phobia'. In the end the patient may have got rid of all his anxiety, but only at the price of subjecting himself to all kinds of inhibitions and restrictions. From the outset in anxiety hysteria the mind is constantly at work in the direction of once more psychically binding the anxiety which has become liberated; but this work can neither bring about a retransformation of the anxiety into libido, nor can it establish any contact with the complexes which were the source of the libido. Nothing is left for it but to cut off access to every possible occasion that might lead to the development of anxiety, by erecting mental barriers in the nature of precautions, inhibitions, or prohibitions; and it is these protective structures that appear to us in the form of phobias and that constitute to our eyes the essence of the disease.

The treatment of anxiety hysteria may be said hitherto to have been a purely negative one. Experience has shown that it is impossible to effect the cure of a phobia (and even in certain circumstances dangerous to attempt to do so) by violent means, that is, by first depriving the patient of his defences and then putting him in a situation in which he cannot escape the liberation of his anxiety. Consequently, nothing can be done but to leave the patient to look for protection wherever he thinks he may find it; and he is merely regarded with a not very helpful contempt for his 'incomprehensible cowardice'.

Little Hans's parents were determined from the very beginning of his illness that he was neither to be laughed at nor bullied, but that access must be obtained to his repressed wishes by means of psychoanalysis. The extraordinary pains taken by Hans's father were rewarded by success, and his reports will give us an opportunity of penetrating into the fabric of this type of phobia and of following the course of its analysis.

I think it is not unlikely that the extensive and detailed character of the analysis may have made it somewhat obscure to the reader. I shall therefore begin by giving a brief résumé of it, in which I shall omit all distracting side-issues and shall draw attention to the results as they came to light one after the other.

The first thing we learn is that the outbreak of the anxiety-state was by no means so sudden as appeared at first sight. A few days earlier the child had woken from an anxiety-dream to the effect that his mother had gone away, and that now he had no mother to coax with [p. 186]. This dream alone points to the presence of a repressive process of ominous intensity. We cannot explain it, as we can so many other anxiety-dreams, by supposing that the child had in his dream felt anxiety arising from some somatic cause and had made use of the anxiety for the purpose of fulfilling an unconscious wish which would otherwise have been deeply repressed.[1] We must regard it rather as a genuine punishment and repression dream, and, moreover, as a dream which failed in its function, since the child woke from his sleep in a state of anxiety. We can easily reconstruct what actually occurred in the unconscious. The child dreamt of exchanging endearments with his mother and of sleeping with her; but all the pleasure was transformed into anxiety, and all the ideational content into its opposite. Repression had defeated the purpose of the mechanism of dreaming.

But the beginnings of this psychological situation go back further still. During the preceding summer Hans had had similar moods of mingled longing and apprehension, in which he had said similar things; and at that time they had secured him the advantage of being taken by his mother into her bed. We may assume that since then Hans had been in a state of intensified sexual excitement, the object of which was his mother. The intensity of this excitement was shown by his two attempts [pp. 182 and 186] at seducing his mother (the second of which occurred just before the outbreak of his anxiety); and he found an incidental channel of discharge for it by masturbating every evening and in that way obtaining gratification. Whether the sudden change-over of this excitement into anxiety took place spontaneously, or as a result of his

1. See my *Interpretation of Dreams* [1900a, P.F.L., 4, 333].

mother's rejection of his advances, or owing to the accidental revival of earlier impressions by the 'precipitating cause' of his illness (about which we shall hear presently) – this we cannot decide; and, indeed, it is a matter of indifference, for these three alternative possibilities cannot be regarded as mutually incompatible. The fact remains that his sexual excitement suddenly changed into anxiety.

We have already described the child's behaviour at the beginning of his anxiety, as well as the first content which he assigned to it, namely, that a *horse* would bite him. It was at this point that the first piece of therapy was interposed. His parents represented to him that his anxiety was the result of masturbation, and encouraged him to break himself of the habit [p. 187]. I took care that when they spoke to him great stress was laid upon his affection for his mother, for that was what he was trying to replace by his fear of horses [p. 191]. This first intervention brought a slight improvement, but the ground was soon lost again during a period of physical illness. Hans's condition remained unchanged. Soon afterwards he traced back his fear of being bitten by a horse to an impression he had received at Gmunden [p. 192]. A father had addressed his child on her departure[1] with these words of warning: 'Don't put your finger to the horse; if you do, it'll bite you.' The words, 'don't put your finger to', which Hans used in reporting this warning, resembled the form of words in which the warning against masturbation had been framed. It seemed at first, therefore, as though Hans's parents were right in supposing that what he was frightened of was his own masturbatory indulgence. But the whole nexus remained loose, and it seemed to be merely by chance that horses had become his bugbear.

I had expressed a suspicion that Hans's repressed wish might now be that he wanted at all costs to see his mother's widdler. As his behaviour to a new maid fitted in with this hypothesis, his father gave him his first piece of enlightenment, namely,

1. [Before 1924 this read: 'A father, on his departure, had addressed his child . . .' See footnote 1, p. 270.]

that women have no widdlers [p. 194]. He reacted to this first effort at helping him by producing a phantasy that he had seen his mother showing her widdler.[1] This phantasy and a remark made by him in conversation, to the effect that his widdler was 'fixed in, of course', allow us our first glimpse into the patient's unconscious mental processes. The fact was that the threat of castration made to him by his mother some fifteen months earlier [p. 171] was now having a deferred effect upon him. For his phantasy that his mother was doing the same as he had done (the familiar *tu quoque* repartee of inculpated children) was intended to serve as a piece of self-justification; it was a protective or defensive phantasy. At the same time we must remark that it was Hans's parents who had extracted from the pathogenic material operating in him the particular theme of his interest in widdlers. Hans followed their lead in this matter, but he had not yet taken any line of his own in the analysis. And no therapeutic success was to be observed. The analysis had passed far away from the subject of horses; and the information that women have no widdlers was calculated, if anything, to increase his concern for the preservation of his own.

Therapeutic success, however, is not our primary aim; we endeavour rather to enable the patient to obtain a conscious grasp of his unconscious wishes. And this we can achieve by working upon the basis of the hints he throws out, and so, with the help of our interpretative technique, presenting the unconscious complex to his consciousness *in our own words*. There will be a certain degree of similarity between that which he hears from us and that which he is looking for, and which, in spite of all resistances, is trying to force its way through to consciousness; and it is this similarity that will enable him to discover the unconscious material. The physician is a step in front of him in knowledge; and the patient follows along his

1. The context enables us to add: 'and touching it' (p. 194). After all, he himself could not show his widdler without touching it. [This footnote was added in 1924. Previously the word 'touching' appeared in the text instead of 'showing'.]

own road, until the two meet at the appointed goal. Beginners in psychoanalysis are apt to assimilate these two events, and to suppose that the moment at which one of the patient's unconscious complexes has become known to *them* is also the moment at which the patient himself recognizes it. They are expecting too much when they think that they will cure the patient by informing him of this piece of knowledge; for he can do no more with the information than make use of it to help himself in discovering the unconscious complex *where it is anchored* in his unconscious.[1] A first success of this sort had now been achieved with Hans. Having partly mastered his castration complex, he was now able to communicate his wishes in regard to his mother. He did so, in what was still a distorted form, by means of the *phantasy of the two giraffes*, one of which was calling out in vain because Hans had taken possession of the other [p. 199]. He represented the 'taking possession of' pictorially as 'sitting down on'. His father recognized the phantasy as a reproduction of a bedroom scene which used to take place in the morning between the boy and his parents; and he quickly stripped the underlying wish of the disguise which it still wore. The boy's father and mother were the two giraffes. The reason for the choice of a giraffe-phantasy for the purposes of disguise was fully explained by a visit that the boy had paid to those same large beasts at Schönbrunn a few days earlier, by the giraffe-drawing, belonging to an earlier period, which had been preserved by his father, and also, perhaps, by an unconscious comparison based upon the giraffe's long, stiff neck.[2] It may be remarked that the giraffe, as being a large animal and interesting on account of its widdler, was a possible competitor with the horse for the role of bugbear; moreover, the fact that both his father and his mother appeared as giraffes

1. [Cf. the closing paragraphs of Section II of 'The Unconscious' (1915e), *P.F.L.*, **11**, 178.]

2. Hans's admiration of his father's neck later on would fit in with this. [This is probably a condensation of the episodes on pp. 202 and 215.]

offered a hint which had not yet been followed up, as regards the interpretation of the anxiety-horses.

Immediately after the giraffe story Hans produced two minor phantasies: one of his forcing his way into a forbidden space at Schönbrunn, and the other of his smashing a railway-carriage window on the Stadtbahn [pp. 202-3]. In each case the punishable nature of the action was emphasized, and in each his father appeared as an accomplice. Unluckily his father failed to interpret either of these phantasies, so that Hans himself gained nothing from telling them. In an analysis, however, a thing which has not been understood inevitably reappears; like an unlaid ghost, it cannot rest until the mystery has been solved and the spell broken.

There are no difficulties in the way of our understanding these two criminal phantasies. They belonged to Hans's complex of taking possession of his mother. Some kind of vague notion was struggling in the child's mind of something that he might do with his mother by means of which his taking possession of her would be consummated; for|this elusive thought he found certain pictorial representations, which had in common the qualities of being violent and forbidden, and the content of which strikes us as fitting in most remarkably well with the hidden truth. We can only say that they were symbolic phantasies of intercourse, and it was no irrelevant detail that his father was represented as sharing in his actions: 'I should like', he seems to have been saying, 'to be doing something with my mother, something forbidden; I do not know what it is, but I do know that you are doing it too.'

The giraffe phantasy strengthened a conviction which had already begun to form in my mind when Hans expressed his fear that 'the horse'll come into the room' [p. 187]; and I thought the right moment had now arrived for informing him that he was afraid of his father because he himself nourished jealous and hostile wishes against him – for it was essential to postulate this much with regard to his unconscious impulses. In telling him this, I had partly interpreted his fear of horses for him: the horse must be his father – whom he had good internal reasons for fearing. Certain details of which Hans had shown he was afraid, the black on horses' mouths and the things in front of their eyes (the moustaches and eyeglasses which are the privilege of a grown-up man), seemed to me to have been directly transposed from his father on to the horses [p. 204].

By enlightening Hans on this subject I had cleared away his most powerful resistance against allowing his unconscious thoughts to be made conscious; for his father was himself acting as his physician. The worst of the attack was now over; there was a plentiful flow of material; the little patient summoned up courage to describe the details of his phobia, and soon began to take an active share in the conduct of the analysis.[1]

It was only then that we learnt what the objects and impressions were of which Hans was afraid. He was not only afraid of horses biting him – he was soon silent upon that point – but also of carts, of furniture-vans, and of buses (their common quality being, as presently became clear, that they were all heavily loaded), of horses that started moving, of horses that looked big and heavy, and of horses that drove quickly. The meaning of these specifications was explained by Hans himself: he was afraid of horses *falling down*, and consequently incorporated in his phobia everything that seemed likely to facilitate their falling down [pp. 208–9].

It not at all infrequently happens that it is only after doing a certain amount of psychoanalytic work with a patient that an analyst can succeed in learning the actual content of a phobia, the precise form of words of an obsessional impulse, and so on.

1. Even in analyses in which the physician and the patient are strangers, fear of the father plays one of the most important parts as a resistance against the reproduction of the unconscious pathogenic material. Resistances are sometimes in the nature of [stereotyped] 'motifs'. But sometimes, as in the present instance, one piece of the unconscious material is capable from its actual *content* of operating as an inhibition against the reproduction of another piece. [The issue involved in this footnote seems to be analogous to the question of the innateness of 'primal phantasies'. See above, p. 172 *n.* 2.]

Repression has not only descended upon the unconscious complexes, but it is continually attacking their derivatives as well, and even prevents the patient from becoming aware of the products of the disease itself. The analyst thus finds himself in the position, curious for a doctor, of coming to the help of a disease, and of procuring it its due of attention.[1] But only those who entirely misunderstand the nature of psychoanalysis will lay stress upon this phase of the work and suppose that on its account harm is likely to be done by analysis. The fact is that you must catch your thief before you can hang him, and that it requires some expenditure of labour to get securely hold of the pathological structures at the destruction of which the treatment is aimed.

I have already remarked in the course of my running commentary on the case history [p. 213] that it is most instructive to plunge in this way into the details of a phobia, and thus arrive at a conviction of the secondary nature of the relation between the anxiety and its objects. It is this that accounts for phobias being at once so curiously diffuse and so strictly conditioned.[2] It is evident that the material for the particular disguises which Hans's fear adopted was collected from the impressions to which he was all day long exposed owing to the Head Customs House being situated on the opposite side of the street. In this connection, too, he showed signs of an impulse – though it was now inhibited by his anxiety – to play with the loads on the carts, with the packages, casks and boxes, like the street-boys.

It was at this stage of the analysis that he recalled the event, insignificant in itself, which immediately preceded the outbreak of the illness and may no doubt be regarded as the precipitating cause of its outbreak. He went for a walk with his mother, and saw a bus-horse fall down and kick about with its feet [p. 211]. This made a great impression on him. He was

1. [Similarly with obsessional neuroses: cf. the case of the 'Rat Man' (1909d), P.F.L., 9, 103.]

2. [This point is elaborated by Freud in a discussion of 'systems' in his Totem and Taboo (1912–13), P.F.L., 13, 154–6.]

terrified, and thought the horse was dead; and from that time on he thought that all horses would fall down. His father pointed out to him that when he saw the horse fall down he must have thought of him, his father, and have wished that he might fall down in the same way and be dead. Hans did not dispute this interpretation; and a little while later he played a game consisting of biting his father, and so showed that he accepted the theory of his having identified his father with the horse he was afraid of [p. 213 f.]. From that time forward his behaviour to his father was unconstrained and fearless, and in fact a trifle overbearing. Nevertheless his fear of horses persisted; nor was it yet clear through what chain of associations the horse's falling down had stirred up his unconscious wishes.

Let me summarize the results that had so far been reached. Behind the fear to which Hans first gave expression, the fear of a horse biting him, we had discovered a more deeply seated fear, the fear of horses falling down; and both kinds of horses, the biting horse and the falling horse, had been shown to represent his father, who was going to punish him for the evil wishes he was nourishing against him. Meanwhile the analysis had moved away from the subject of his mother.

Quite unexpectedly, and certainly without any prompting from his father, Hans now began to be occupied with the 'lumf' complex, and to show disgust at things that reminded him of evacuating his bowels [p. 216 f.]. His father, who was reluctant to go with him along that line, pushed on with the analysis through thick and thin in the direction in which he wanted to go. He elicited from Hans the recollection of an event at Gmunden, the impression of which lay concealed behind that of the falling bus-horse. While they were playing at horses, Fritzl, the playmate of whom he was so fond, but at the same time, perhaps, his rival with his many girl friends, had hit his foot against a stone and had fallen down, and his foot had bled [p. 220]. Seeing the bus-horse fall had reminded him of this accident. It deserves to be noticed that Hans, who was at the moment concerned with other things, began by denying that Fritzl had fallen down (though this was the event which formed the connection between the two scenes) and only admitted it at a later stage of the analysis [p. 242]. It is especially interesting, however, to observe the way in which the transformation of Hans's libido into anxiety was projected on to the principal object of his phobia, on to horses. Horses interested him the most of all the large animals; playing at horses was his favourite game with the other children. I had a suspicion – and this was confirmed by Hans's father when I asked him – that the first person who had served Hans as a horse must have been his father; and it was this that had enabled him to regard Fritzl as a substitute for his father when the accident happened at Gmunden. When repression had set in and brought a revulsion of feeling along with it, horses, which had till then been associated with so much pleasure, were necessarily turned into objects of fear.

But, as we have already said, it was owing to the intervention of Hans's father that this last important discovery was made of the way in which the precipitating cause of the illness had operated. Hans himself was occupied with his lumf interests, and thither at last we must follow him. We learn that formerly Hans had been in the habit of insisting upon accompanying his mother to the W.C. [p. 224], and that he had revived this custom with his friend Berta at a time when she was filling his mother's place, until the fact became known and he was forbidden to do so [p. 222]. Pleasure taken in looking on while some one one loves performs the natural functions is once more a 'confluence of instincts', of which we have already noticed an instance in Hans [p. 265]. In the end his father went into the lumf symbolism, and recognized that there was an analogy between a heavily loaded cart and a body loaded with faeces, between the way in which a cart drives out through a gateway and the way in which faeces leave the body, and so on [pp. 226–8].

By this time, however, the position occupied by Hans in the analysis had become very different from what it had been at an earlier stage. Previously, his father had been able to tell him in advance what was coming, while Hans had merely followed his lead and come trotting after; but now it was Hans who was forging ahead, so rapidly and steadily that his father found it difficult to keep up with him. Without any warning, as it were, Hans produced a new phantasy: the plumber unscrewed the bath in which Hans was, and then stuck him in the stomach with his big borer [p. 226]. Henceforward the material brought up in the analysis far outstripped our powers of understanding it. It was not until later that it was possible to guess that this was a remoulding of a *phantasy of procreation*, distorted by anxiety. The big bath of water, in which Hans imagined himself, was his mother's womb; the 'borer', which his father had from the first recognized as a penis, owed its mention to its connection with 'being born'. The interpretation that we are obliged to give to the phantasy will of course sound very curious: 'With your big penis you "bored" me' (i.e. 'gave birth to me') 'and put me in my mother's womb.' For the moment, however, the phantasy eluded interpretation, and merely served Hans as a starting-point from which to continue giving information.

Hans showed fear of being given a bath in the big bath [p. 227]; and this fear was once more a composite one. One part of it escaped us as yet, but the other part could at once be elucidated in connection with his baby sister having her bath. Hans confessed to having wished that his mother might drop the child while she was being given her bath, so that she should die [p. 233]. His own anxiety while he was having his bath was a fear of retribution for this evil wish and of being punished by the same thing happening to him. Hans now left the subject of lumf and passed on directly to that of his baby sister. We may well imagine what this juxtaposition signified: nothing less, in fact, than that little Hanna was a lumf herself – that all babies were lumfs and were born like lumfs. We can now recognize that all furniture-vans and drays and buses were only stork-box carts, and were only of interest to Hans as being symbolic representations of pregnancy; and that when a heavy or heavily loaded horse fell down he can have seen in it only one thing – a childbirth, a delivery ['*ein Niederkommen*'].[1] Thus the falling horse was not only his dying father but also his mother in childbirth.

And at this point Hans gave us a surprise, for which we were not in the very least prepared. He had noticed his mother's pregnancy, which had ended with the birth of his little sister when he was three and a half years old, and had, at any rate after the confinement, pieced the facts of the case together – without telling any one, it is true, and perhaps without being able to tell any one. All that could be seen at the time was that immediately after the delivery he had taken up an extremely sceptical attitude towards everything that might be supposed to point to the presence of the stork [p. 174]. *But that – in complete contradiction to his official speeches – he knew in his unconscious where the baby came from and where it had been before,* is proved beyond a shadow of doubt by the present analysis; indeed, this is perhaps its most unassailable feature.

The most cogent evidence of this is furnished by the phantasy (which he persisted in with so much obstinacy, and embellished with such a wealth of detail) of how Hanna had been with them at Gmunden the summer before her birth, of how she had travelled there with them, and of how she had been able to do far more then than she had a year later, after she had been born [p. 230 ff.]. The effrontery with which Hans related this phantasy and the countless extravagant lies with which he interwove it were anything but meaningless. All of this was intended as a revenge upon his father, against whom he harboured a grudge for having misled him with the stork fable. It was just as though he had meant to say: 'If you really thought I was as stupid as all that, and expected me to believe that the stork brought Hanna, then in return I expect *you* to accept *my*

1. [See footnote, p. 255. – Further discussion of this particular symbolism will be found near the end of Freud's paper on a childhood memory of Goethe's (1917*b*).]

inventions as the truth.' This act of revenge on the part of our young enquirer upon his father was succeeded by the clearly correlated phantasy of teasing and beating horses [p. 239]. This phantasy, again, had two constituents. On the one hand, it was based upon the teasing to which he had submitted his father just before; and, on the other hand, it reproduced the obscure sadistic desires directed towards his mother, which had already found expression (though they had not at first been understood) in his phantasies of doing something forbidden. Hans even confessed consciously to a desire to beat his mother [p. 241].

There are not many more mysteries ahead of us now. An obscure phantasy of missing a train [p. 241f.] seems to have been a forerunner of the later notion of handing over Hans's father to his grandmother at Lainz, for the phantasy dealt with a visit to Lainz, and his grandmother appeared in it. Another phantasy, in which a boy gave the guard 50,000 florins to let him ride on the truck [p. 243], almost sounds like a plan of buying his mother from his father, part of whose power, of course, lay in his wealth. At about this time, too, he confessed, with a degree of openness which he had never before reached, that he wished to get rid of his father, and that the reason he wished it was that his father interfered with his own intimacy with his mother [p. 242]. We must not be surprised to find the same wishes constantly reappearing in the course of an analysis. The monotony only attaches to the analyst's interpretations of these wishes. For Hans they were not mere repetitions, but steps in a progressive development from timid hinting to fully conscious, undistorted perspicuity.

What remains are just such confirmations on Hans's part of analytical conclusions which our interpretations had already established. In an entirely unequivocal symptomatic act, which he disguised slightly from the maid but not at all from his father, he showed how he imagined a birth took place [p. 244]; but if we look into it more closely we can see that he showed something else, that he was hinting at something which was not alluded to again in the analysis. He pushed a small penknife which belonged to his mother in through a round hole in the body of an india-rubber doll, and then let it drop out again by tearing apart the doll's legs. The enlightenment which he received from his parents soon afterwards [p. 247], to the effect that children do in fact grow inside their mother's body and are pushed out of it like a lumf, came too late; it could tell him nothing new. Another symptomatic act, happening as though by accident, involved a confession that he had wished his father dead; for, just at the moment his father was talking of this death-wish, Hans let a horse that he was playing with fall down – knocked it over in fact. Further, he confirmed in so many words the hypothesis that heavily loaded carts represented his mother's pregnancy to him, and the horse's falling down was like having a baby. The most delightful piece of confirmation in this connection – a proof that, in his view, children were 'lumfs' – was his inventing the name of 'Lodi' for his favourite child. There was some delay in reporting this fact, for it then appeared that he had been playing with this sausage child of his for a long time past [p. 253].[1]

We have already considered Hans's two concluding phantasies, with which his recovery was rounded off. One of them [p. 257], that of the plumber giving him a new and, as his father guessed, a bigger widdler, was not merely a repetition of the earlier phantasy concerning the plumber and the bath. The new one was a triumphant, wishful phantasy, and with it he overcame his fear of castration. His other phantasy [p. 256], which confessed to the wish to be married to his mother and to have many children by her, did not merely exhaust the content

1. I remember a set of drawings by T. T. Heine in a copy of *Simplicissimus*, in which that brilliant illustrator depicted the fate of the pork-butcher's child, who fell into the sausage machine, and then, in the shape of a small sausage, was mourned over by his parents, received the Church's blessing, and flew up to Heaven. The artist's idea seems a puzzling one at first, but the Lodi episode in this analysis enables us to trace it back to its infantile root.

of the unconscious complexes which had been stirred up by the sight of the falling horse and which had generated his anxiety. It also corrected that portion of those thoughts which was entirely unacceptable; for, instead of killing his father, it made him innocuous by promoting him to a marriage with Hans's grandmother. With this phantasy both the illness and the analysis came to an appropriate end.

While the analysis of a case is in progress it is impossible to obtain any clear impression of the structure and development of the neurosis. That is the business of a synthetic process which must be performed subsequently. In attempting to carry out such a synthesis of little Hans's phobia we shall take as our basis the account of his mental constitution, of his governing sexual wishes, and of his experiences up to the time of his sister's birth, which we have given in an earlier part of this paper.

The arrival of his sister brought into Hans's life many new elements, which from that time on gave him no rest. In the first place he was obliged to submit to a certain degree of privation: to begin with, a temporary separation from his mother, and later a permanent diminution in the amount of care and attention which he had received from her and which thenceforward he had to grow accustomed to sharing with his sister. In the second place, he experienced a revival of the pleasures he had enjoyed when he was looked after as an infant; for they were called up by all that he saw his mother doing for the baby. As a result of these two influences his erotic needs became intensified, while at the same time they began to obtain insufficient satisfaction. He made up for the loss which his sister's arrival had entailed on him by imagining that he had children of his own; and so long as he was at Gmunden – on his second visit there – and could really play with these children, he found a sufficient outlet for his affections. But after his return to Vienna he was once more alone, and set all his hopes upon his mother. He had meanwhile suffered another privation, having been exiled from his parents' bedroom at the age of four and a half.[1] His intensified erotic excitability now found expression in phantasies, by which in his loneliness he conjured up his playmates of the past summer, and in regular auto-erotic satisfaction obtained by a masturbatory stimulation of his genitals.

But in the third place his sister's birth stimulated him to an effort of thought which, on the one hand, it was impossible to bring to a conclusion, and which, on the other hand, involved him in emotional conflicts. He was faced with the great riddle of where babies come from, which is perhaps the first problem to engage a child's mental powers,[2] and of which the riddle of the Theban Sphinx is probably no more than a distorted version. He rejected the proffered solution of the stork having brought Hanna. For he had noticed that months before the baby's birth his mother's body had grown big, that then she had gone to bed, and had groaned while the birth was taking place, and that when she got up she was thin again. He therefore inferred that Hanna had been inside his mother's body, and had then come out like a 'lumf'. He was able to imagine the act of giving birth as a pleasurable one by relating it to his own first feelings of pleasure in passing stool; and he was thus able to find a double motive for wishing to have children of his own: the pleasure of giving birth to them and the pleasure (the compensatory pleasure, as it were) of looking after them. There was nothing in all of this that could have led him into doubts or conflicts.

But there was something else, which could not fail to make him uneasy. His father must have had something to do with little Hanna's *birth*, for he had declared that Hanna and Hans himself were his children. Yet it was certainly not his father

---

1. [In the earlier editions 'four', which was altered to 'four and a half' in 1924. See, however, Hans's father's remark (3) on p. 258. The sleeping-arrangements may have been changed at the time of the move into the new flat (p. 179).]

2. [Freud emended this view, as regards girls, in a footnote to his paper on the distinction between the sexes (1925j), *P.F.L.*, 7, 336 n.2.]

who had brought them into the world, but his mother. This father of his came between him and his mother. When he was there Hans could not sleep with his mother, and when his mother wanted to take Hans into bed with her, his father used to call out. Hans had learnt from experience how well-off he could be in his father's absence, and it was only justifiable that he should wish to get rid of him. And then Hans's hostility had received a fresh reinforcement. His father had told him the lie about the stork and so made it impossible for him to ask for enlightenment upon these things. He not only prevented his being in bed with his mother, but also kept from him the knowledge he was thirsting for. He was putting Hans at a disadvantage in both directions, and was obviously doing so for his own benefit.

But this father, whom he could not help hating as a rival, was the same father whom he had always loved and was bound to go on loving, who had been his model, had been his first playmate, and had looked after him from his earliest infancy: and this it was that gave rise to the first conflict. Nor could this conflict find an immediate solution. For Hans's nature had so developed that for the moment his love could not but keep the upper hand and suppress his hate – though it could not kill it, for his hate was perpetually kept alive by his love for his mother.

But his father not only knew where children came from, he actually performed it – the thing that Hans could only obscurely divine. The widdler must have something to do with it, for his own grew excited whenever he thought of these things – and it must be a big widdler too, bigger than Hans's own. If he listened to these premonitory sensations he could only suppose that it was a question of some act of violence performed upon his mother, of smashing something, of making an opening into something, of forcing a way into an enclosed space – such were the impulses that he felt stirring within him. But although the sensations of his penis had put him on the road to postulating a vagina, yet he could not solve the problem, for within his experience no such thing existed as his widdler required. On the contrary, his conviction that his mother possessed a penis just as he did stood in the way of any solution. His attempt at discovering what it was that had to be done with his mother in order that she might have children sank down into his unconscious; and his two active impulses – the hostile one towards his father and the sadistic-tender one towards his mother – could be put to no use, the first because of the love that existed side by side with the hatred, and the second because of the perplexity in which his infantile sexual theories left him.

This is how, basing my conclusions upon the findings of the analysis, I am obliged to reconstruct the unconscious com-plexes and wishes, the repression and reawakening of which produced little Hans's phobia. I am aware that in so doing I am attributing a great deal to the mental capacity of a child between four and five years of age; but I have let myself be guided by what we have recently learned, and I do not consider myself bound by the prejudices of our ignorance. It might perhaps have been possible to make use of Hans's fear of the 'making a row with the legs' for filling up a few more gaps in our adjudication upon the evidence. Hans, it is true, declared that it reminded him of his kicking about with his legs when he was compelled to leave off playing so as to do lumf; so that this element of the neurosis becomes connected with the problem whether his mother liked having children or was compelled to have them. But I have an impression that this is not the whole explanation of the 'making a row with the legs'. Hans's father was unable to confirm my suspicion that there was some recol-lection stirring in the child's mind of having observed a scene of sexual intercourse between his parents in their bedroom. So let us be content with what we have discovered.

It is hard to say what the influence was which, in the situation we have just sketched, led to the sudden change in Hans and to the transformation of his libidinal longing into anxiety – to say from what direction it was that repression set in. The question could probably only be decided by making a comparison between this analysis and a number of similar ones. Whether the scales were turned by the child's *intellectual* inability to solve the difficult problem of the begetting of children and to cope with the aggressive impulses that were liberated by his approaching its solution, or whether the effect was produced by a *somatic* incapacity, a constitutional intolerance of the masturbatory gratification in which he regularly indulged (whether, that is, the mere persistence of sexual excitement at such a high pitch of intensity was bound to bring about a revulsion) – this question must be left open until fresh experience can come to our assistance.

Chronological considerations make it impossible for us to attach any great importance to the actual precipitating cause of the outbreak of Hans's illness, for he had shown signs of apprehensiveness long before he saw the bus-horse fall down in the street.

Nevertheless, the neurosis took its start directly from this chance event and preserved a trace of it in the circumstance of the horse being exalted into the object of his anxiety. In itself the impression of the accident which he happened to witness carried no 'traumatic force'; it acquired its great effectiveness only from the fact that horses had formerly been of importance to him as objects of his predilection and interest, from the fact that he associated the event in his mind with an earlier event at Gmunden which had more claim to be regarded as traumatic, namely, with Fritzl's falling down while he was playing at horses, and lastly from the fact that there was an easy path of association from Fritzl to his father. Indeed, even these connections would probably not have been sufficient if it had not been that, thanks to the pliability and ambiguity of associative chains, the same event showed itself capable of stirring the second of the complexes that lurked in Hans's unconscious, the complex of his pregnant mother's confinement. From that moment the way was clear for the return of the repressed; and it returned in such a manner that *the pathogenic material was remodelled and transposed on to the horse-complex, while the accompanying affects were uniformly turned into anxiety.*

It deserves to be noticed that the ideational content of Hans's phobia as it then stood had to be submitted to one further process of distortion and substitution before his consciousness took cognizance of it. Hans's first formulation of his anxiety was: 'the horse will bite me'; and this was derived from another episode at Gmunden, which was on the one hand related to his hostile wishes towards his father and on the other hand was reminiscent of the warning he had been given against masturbation. Some interfering influence, emanating from his parents perhaps, had made itself felt. I am not certain whether the reports upon Hans were at that time drawn up with sufficient care to enable us to decide whether he expressed his anxiety in this form *before* or not until *after* his mother had taken him to task on the subject of masturbating. I should be inclined to suspect that it was not until afterwards, though this would contradict the account given in the case history. [See p. 187.] At any rate, it is evident that at every point Hans's hostile complex against his father screened his lustful one about his mother, just as it was the first to be disclosed and dealt with in the analysis.

In other cases of this kind there would be a great deal more to be said upon the structure, the development, and the diffusion of the neurosis. But the history of little Hans's attack was very short; almost as soon as it had begun, its place was taken by the history of its treatment. And although during the treatment the phobia appeared to develop further and to extend over new objects and to lay down new conditions, his father, since he was himself treating the case, naturally had sufficient penetration to see that it was merely a question of the emergence of material that was already in existence, and not of fresh productions for which the treatment might be held responsible. In the treatment of other cases it would not always be possible to count upon so much penetration.

Before I can regard this synthesis as completed I must turn to yet another aspect of the case, which will take us into the

very heart of the difficulties that lie in the way of our understanding of neurotic states. We have seen how our little patient
was overtaken by a great wave of repression and that it caught
precisely those of his sexual components that were dominant.[1]
He gave up masturbation, and turned away in disgust from
everything that reminded him of excrement and of looking on
at other people performing their natural functions. But these
were not the components which were stirred up by the
precipitating cause of the illness (his seeing the horse fall down)
or which provided the material for the symptoms, that is, the
content of the phobia.

   This allows us, therefore, to make a radical distinction. We
shall probably come to understand the case more deeply if
we turn to those other components which *do* fulfil the two
conditions that have just been mentioned. These other components were tendencies in Hans which had already been
suppressed and which, so far as we can tell, had never been able
to find uninhibited expression: hostile and jealous feelings
towards his father, and sadistic impulses (premonitions, as it
were, of copulation) towards his mother. These early suppres-
sions may perhaps have gone to form the predisposition for his
subsequent illness. These aggressive propensities of Hans's
found no outlet, and as soon as there came a time of privation
and of intensified sexual excitement, they tried to break their
way out with reinforced strength. It was then that the battle
which we call his 'phobia' burst out. During the course of it a
part of the repressed ideas, in a distorted form and transposed
on to another complex, forced their way into consciousness as
the content of the phobia. But it was a decidedly paltry success.
Victory lay with the forces of repression; *and they made use of
the opportunity to extend their dominion over components other than
those that had rebelled.* This last circumstance, however, does not

---

   1. Hans's father even observed that simultaneously with this repression a certain amount of sublimation set in. From the time of the
beginning of his anxiety Hans began to show an increased interest in
music and to develop his inherited musical gift.

in the least alter the fact that the essence of Hans's illness was entirely dependent upon the nature of the instinctual components that had to be repulsed. The content of his phobia was such as to impose a very great measure of restriction upon his freedom of movement, and that was its purpose. It was therefore a powerful reaction against the obscure impulses to movement which were especially directed against his mother. For Hans horses had always typified pleasure in movement ('I'm a young horse', he had said as he jumped about [p. 219]); but since this pleasure in movement included the impulse to copulate, the neurosis imposed a restriction on it and exalted the horse into an emblem of terror. Thus it would seem as though all that the repressed instincts got from the neurosis was the honour of providing pretexts for the appearance of the anxiety in consciousness. But however clear may have been the victory in Hans's phobia of the forces that were opposed to sexuality, nevertheless, since such an illness is in its very nature a compromise, this cannot have been all that the repressed instincts obtained. After all, Hans's phobia of horses was an obstacle to his going into the street, and could serve as a means of allowing him to stay at home with his beloved mother. In this way, therefore, his affection for his mother triumphantly achieved its aim. In consequence of his phobia, the lover clung to the object of his love – though, to be sure, steps had been taken to make him innocuous. The true character of a neurotic disorder is exhibited in this twofold result.

Alfred Adler, in a suggestive paper[1], has recently developed the view that anxiety arises from the suppression of what he calls the 'aggressive instinct', and by a very sweeping synthetic process he ascribes to that instinct the chief part in human events, 'in real life and in the neuroses'. As we have come to the conclusion that in our present case of phobia the anxiety is to be explained as being due to the repression of Hans's aggressive propensities (the hostile ones against his father and the

1. (1908). This is the same paper from which I have borrowed the term 'confluence of instincts'. (See above [pp. 265 and 284].)

sadistic ones against his mother), we seem to have produced a most striking piece of confirmation of Adler's view. I am nevertheless unable to assent to it, and indeed I regard it as a misleading generalization. I cannot bring myself to assume the existence of a special aggressive instinct alongside of the familiar instincts of self-preservation and of sex, and on an equal footing with them.[1] It appears to me that Adler has mistakenly promoted into a special and self-subsisting instinct what is in reality a universal and indispensable attribute of *all* instincts – their instinctual and 'pressing' character, what might be described as their capacity for initiating movement. Nothing would then remain of the other instincts but their relation to an aim, for their relation to the means of reaching that aim would have been taken over from them by the 'aggressive instinct'. In spite of all the uncertainty and obscurity of our theory of instincts I should prefer for the present to adhere to the usual view, which leaves each instinct its own power of becoming aggressive;[2] and I should be inclined to recognize the two instincts which became repressed in Hans as familiar components of the sexual libido.

1. (*Footnote added* 1923:) The above passage was written at a time when Adler seemed still to be taking his stand upon the ground of psychoanalysis, and before he had put forward the masculine protest and disavowed repression. Since then I have myself been obliged to assert the existence of an 'aggressive instinct', but it is different from Adler's. I prefer to call it the 'destructive' or 'death instinct'. See *Beyond the Pleasure Principle* (1920g) and *The Ego and the Id* (1923b). [*P.F.L.*, **11**, 316 and 381 ff.] Its opposition to the libidinal instincts finds an expression in the familiar polarity of love and hate. My disagreement with Adler's view, which [as explained later in the paragraph] results in a universal characteristic of instincts in general being reduced to be the property of a single one of them, remains unaltered. – [A detailed account of Freud's differences with Adler will be found in the latter part of his 'History of the Psycho-Analytic Movement' (1914d).]

2. [In the earlier editions the words 'without being directed towards an object' occurred at this point. They were omitted in 1924.]

3

I shall now proceed to what I hope will be a brief discussion of how far little Hans's phobia offers any contribution of general importance to our views upon the life and upbringing of children. But before doing so I must return to the objection which has so long been held over, and according to which Hans was a neurotic, a 'degenerate' with a bad heredity, and not a normal child, knowledge about whom could be applied to other children. I have for some time been thinking with pain of the way in which the adherents of 'the normal person' will fall upon poor little Hans as soon as they are told that he can in fact be shown to have had a hereditary taint. His beautiful mother fell ill with a neurosis as a result of a conflict during her girlhood. I was able to be of assistance to her at the time, and this had in fact been the beginning of my connection with Hans's parents. It is only with the greatest diffidence that I venture to bring forward one or two considerations in his favour.

In the first place Hans was not what one would understand, strictly speaking, by a degenerate child, condemned by his heredity to be a neurotic. On the contrary, he was well formed physically, and was a cheerful, amiable, active-minded young fellow who might give pleasure to more people than his own father. There can be no question, of course, as to his sexual precocity; but on that point there is very little material upon which a fair comparison can be based. I gather, for instance, from a piece of collective research conducted in America[1], that it is by no means such a rare thing to find object-choice and feelings of love in boys at a similarly early age; and the same may be learnt from studying the records of the childhood of men who have later come to be recognized as 'great'. I should therefore be inclined to believe that sexual precocity is a cor-

1. [Sanford Bell (1902).]

relate, which is seldom absent, of intellectual precocity, and that it is therefore to be met with in gifted children more often than might be expected.[1]

Furthermore, let me say in Hans's favour (and I frankly admit my partisan attitude) that he is not the only child who has been overtaken by a phobia at some time or other in his childhood. Troubles of that kind are well known to be quite extraordinarily frequent, even in children the strictness of whose upbringing has left nothing to be desired. In later life these children either become neurotic or remain healthy. Their phobias are shouted down in the nursery because they are inaccessible to treatment and are decidedly inconvenient. In the course of months or years they diminish, and the child seems to recover; but no one can tell what psychological changes are necessitated by such a recovery, or what alterations in character are involved in it. When, however, an adult neurotic patient comes to us for psychoanalytic treatment (and let us assume that his illness has only become manifest after he has reached maturity), we find regularly that his neurosis has as its point of departure an infantile anxiety such as we have been discussing, and is in fact a continuation of it; so that, as it were, a continuous and undisturbed thread of psychical activity, taking its start from the conflicts of his childhood, has been spun through his life – irrespective of whether the first symptom of those conflicts has persisted or has retreated under the pressure of circumstances. I think, therefore, that Hans's illness may perhaps have been no more serious than that of many other children who are not branded as 'degenerates'; but since he was brought up without being intimidated, and with as much consideration and as little coercion as possible, his anxiety dared to show itself more boldly. With him there was no place for such motives as a bad conscience or a fear of punishment, which with other children must no doubt contribute to making the anxiety less.

1. [This question is touched on in a paragraph on 'Precocity' near end of Freud's *Three Essays* (1905*d*, P.F.L., **7**, 166).]

It seems to me that we concentrate too much upon symptoms and concern ourselves too little with their causes. In bringing up children we aim only at being left in peace and having no difficulties, in short, at training up a model child, and we pay very little attention to whether such a course of development is for the child's good as well. I can therefore quite imagine that it may have been to Hans's advantage to have produced this phobia. For it directed his parents' attention to the unavoidable difficulties by which a child is confronted when in the course of his cultural training he is called upon to overcome the innate instinctual components of his mind; and his trouble brought his father to his assistance. It may be that Hans now enjoys an advantage over other children, in that he no longer carries within him that seed in the shape of repressed complexes which must always be of some significance for a child's later life, and which undoubtedly brings with it a certain degree of deformity of character if not a disposition to a subsequent neurosis. I am inclined to think that this is so, but I do not know if many others will share my opinion; nor do I know whether experience will prove me right.

But I must now inquire what harm was done to Hans by dragging to light in him complexes such as are not only repressed by children but dreaded by their parents. Did the little boy proceed to take some serious action as regards what he wanted from his mother? or did his evil intentions against his father give place to evil deeds? Such misgivings will no doubt have occurred to many doctors, who misunderstand the nature of psychoanalysis and think that wicked instincts are strengthened by being made conscious. Wise men like these are being no more than consistent when they implore us for heaven's sake not to meddle with the evil things that lurk behind a neurosis. In so doing they forget, it is true, that they are physicians, and their words bear a fatal resemblance to Dogberry's, when he advised the Watch to avoid all contact with any thieves they might happen to meet: 'for such kind of men, the less you meddle or make with them, why, the more is for your honesty.'[1]

On the contrary, the only results of the analysis were that Hans recovered, that he ceased to be afraid of horses, and that he got on to rather familiar terms with his father, as the latter reported with some amusement. But whatever his father may have lost in the boy's respect he won back in his confidence: 'I thought,' said Hans, 'you knew everything, as you knew that about the horse.' For analysis does not undo the *effects* of repression. The instincts which were formerly suppressed remain suppressed; but the same effect is produced in a different way. Analysis replaces the process of repression, which is an automatic and excessive one, by a temperate and purposeful control on the part of the highest agencies of the mind. In a word, *analysis replaces repression by condemnation.* This seems to bring us the long-looked-for evidence that consciousness has a biological function, and that with its entrance upon the scene an important advantage is secured.[2]

1. [*Much Ado about Nothing*, Act III, Scene 3.] At this point I cannot keep back an astonished question. Where do my opponents obtain their knowledge, which they produce with so much confidence, on the question whether the repressed sexual instincts play a part, and if so what part, in the aetiology of the neuroses, if they shut their patients' mouths as soon as they begin to talk about their complexes or their derivatives? For the only alternative source of knowledge remaining open to them are my own writings and those of my adherents.

2. (*Footnote added* 1923:) I am here using the word 'consciousness' in a sense which I later avoided, namely, to describe our normal processes of thought – such, that is, as are capable of consciousness. We know that thought processes of this kind may also take place *preconsciously*; and it is wiser to regard their actual 'consciousness' from a purely phenomenological standpoint. By this I do not, of course, mean to contradict the expectation that consciousness in this more limited sense of the word must also fulfil some biological function. [See *The Ego and the Id* (1923b), *P.F.L.*, **11**, 351 ff. Cf. also the early discussion of the biological function of 'consciousness' in *The Interpretation of Dreams* (1900a), *P.F.L.*, **4**, 776 ff.]

If matters had lain entirely in my hands, I should have ventured to give the child the one remaining piece of enlightenment which his parents withheld from him. I should have confirmed his instinctive premonitions, by telling him of the existence of the vagina and of copulation; thus I should have still further diminished his unsolved residue, and put an end to his streams of questions. I am convinced that this new piece of enlightenment would have made him lose neither his love for his mother nor his own childish nature, and that he would have understood that his preoccupation with these important, these momentous things must rest for the present – until his wish to be big had been fulfilled. But the educational experiment was not carried so far.

That no sharp line can be drawn between 'neurotic' and 'normal' people – whether children or adults – that our conception of 'disease' is a purely practical one and a question of summation, that disposition and the eventualities of life must combine before the threshold of this summation is overstepped, and that consequently a number of individuals are constantly passing from the class of healthy people into that of neurotic patients, while a far smaller number also make the journey in the opposite direction, – all of these are things which have been said so often and have met with so much agreement that I am certainly not alone in maintaining their truth. It is, to say the least of it, extremely probable that a child's upbringing can exercise a powerful influence for good or for evil upon the disposition which we have just mentioned as one of the factors in the occurrence of 'disease'; but what that upbringing is to aim at and at what point it is to be brought to bear seem at present to be very doubtful questions. Hitherto education has only set itself the task of controlling, or, it would often be more proper to say, of suppressing, the instincts. The results have been by no means gratifying, and where the process has succeeded it has only been to the advantage of a small number of favoured individuals who have not been required to suppress their instincts. Nor has any one enquired by what means and at what cost the suppression of the inconvenient instincts has been achieved. Supposing now that we substitute another task for this one, and aim instead at making the individual capable of becoming a civilized and useful member of society with the least possible sacrifice of his own activity; in that case the information gained by psychoanalysis, upon the origin of pathogenic complexes and upon the nucleus of every nervous affection, can claim with justice that it deserves to be regarded by educators as an invaluable guide in their conduct towards children. What practical conclusions may follow from this, and how far experience may justify the application of those conclusions within our present social system, are matters which I leave to the examination and decision of others.[1]

I cannot take leave of our small patient's phobia without giving expression to a notion which has made its analysis, leading as it did to a recovery, seem of especial value to me. Strictly speaking, I learnt nothing new from this analysis, nothing that I had not already been able to discover (though often less distinctly and more indirectly) from other patients analysed at a more advanced age. But the neuroses of these other patients could in every instance be traced back to the same infantile complexes that were revealed behind Hans's phobia. I am therefore tempted to claim for this neurosis of childhood the significance of being a type and a model, and to suppose that the multiplicity of the phenomena of repression exhibited by neuroses and the abundance of their pathogenic material do not prevent their being derived from a very limited number of processes concerned with identical ideational complexes.

1. [Freud returned to the question of psychoanalysis and the upbringing of children in his prefaces to books by Pfister and Aichhorn (Freud, 1913b and 1925f) and in Part II (H) of his contribution to Scientia (1913j). He also devoted some pages to the same subject in Lecture 34 of his New Introductory Lectures (1933a, P.F.L., 2, 181-6).]

POSTSCRIPT
(1922)

A FEW months ago – in the spring of 1922 – a young man introduced himself to me and informed me that he was the 'little Hans' whose infantile neurosis had been the subject of the paper which I published in 1909. I was very glad to see him again, for about two years after the end of his analysis I had lost sight of him and had heard nothing of him for more than ten years. The publication of this first analysis of a child had caused a great stir and even greater indignation, and a most evil future had been foretold for the poor little boy, because he had been 'robbed of his innocence' at such a tender age and had been made the victim of a psychoanalysis.

But none of these apprehensions had come true. Little Hans was now a strapping youth of nineteen. He declared that he was perfectly well, and suffered from no troubles or inhibitions. Not only had he come through his puberty without any damage, but his emotional life had successfully undergone one of the severest of ordeals. His parents had been divorced and each of them had married again. In consequence of this he lived by himself; but he was on good terms with both of his parents, and only regretted that as a result of the breaking-up of the family he had been separated from the younger sister he was so fond of.

One piece of information given me by little Hans struck me as particularly remarkable; nor do I venture to give any explanation of it. When he read his case history, he told me, the whole of it came to him as something unknown; he did not recognize himself; he could remember nothing; and it was only when he came upon the journey to Gmunden that there dawned on him a kind of glimmering recollection that it might have been he himself that it happened to. So the analysis had not preserved the events from amnesia, but had been overtaken by amnesia itself. Any one who is familiar with psychoanalysis may occasionally experience something similar in sleep. He will be woken up by a dream, and will decide to analyse it then and there; he will then go to sleep again feeling quite satisfied with the result of his efforts; and next morning dream and analysis will alike be forgotten.[1]

1. [This phenomenon was discussed by Freud in a passage added in 1911 to his *Interpretation of Dreams* (1900a), Chapter VII, Section A (*P.F.L.*, 4, 666–7).]

BIBLIOGRAPHY
AND AUTHOR INDEX

Titles of books and periodicals are in italics, titles of papers are in inverted commas. Abbreviations are in accordance with the *World List of Scientific Periodicals* (London, 1963–5). Further abbreviations used in this volume will be found in the List at the end of this bibliography. Numerals in bold type refer to volumes, ordinary numerals refer to pages. The figures in round brackets at the end of each entry indicate the page or pages of this volume on which the work in question is mentioned.

In the case of the Freud entries, only English translations are given. The initial dates are those of the German, or other, original publications. (The date of writing is added in square brackets where it differs from the latter.) The letters attached to the dates of publication are in accordance with the corresponding entries in the complete bibliography of Freud's writings included in Volume 24 of the *Standard Edition*. Details of the original publication, including the original German (or other) title, are given in the editorial introduction to each work included in the *Pelican Freud Library*.

For non-technical authors, and for technical authors where no specific work is mentioned, see the General Index.

ABRAHAM, K. (1909) *Traum und Mythus: eine Studie zur Völker-psychologie*, Leipzig and Vienna. (257)
   [*Trans.:* 'Dreams and Myths: A Study in Folk-Psychology', *Clinical Papers and Essays on Psycho-Analysis*, London and New York, 1955, Part III: Essays, I.]
   (1965) With FREUD, S. *See* FREUD, S. (1965*a*)
ADLER, A. (1908) 'Der Aggressionstrieb im Leben und in der Neurose', *Fortschr. Med.*, **26**, 577. (265, 296–7)
ALEXANDER, F. (1922) 'Kastrationskomplex und Charakter', *Int. Z. Psychoanal.*, **8**, 121. (172)
   [*Trans.:* 'The Castration Complex in the Formation of Character', *Int. J. Psycho-Analysis*, **4**, (1923), 11.]

ANDREAS-SALOMÉ, L. (1916) '"Anal" und "Sexual"', *Imago*, **4,** 249. (172)

(1966) With FREUD, S. *See* FREUD, S. (1966*a*)

BELL, J. SANFORD (1902) 'A Preliminary Study of the Emotion of Love between the Sexes', *Am. J. Psychol.*, **13,** 325. (298)

BLOCH, I. (1902–3) *Beiträge zur Ätiologie der Psychopathia sexualis* (2 vols), Dresden. (85)

BREUER, J., and FREUD, S. (1893) *See* FREUD, S. (1893*a*)

(1895) *See* FREUD, S. (1895*d*)

DEUTSCH, F. (1957) 'A Footnote to Freud's "Fragment of an Analysis of a Case of Hysteria"', *Psychoanal. Q.*, **26,** 159. (43)

FINGER, E. (1900) *See* MEDICAL CONGRESS

FREUD, M. (1957) *Glory Reflected*, London. (22)

FREUD, S. (1891*b*) *On Aphasia*, London and New York, 1953. (14, 26)

(1893*a*) With BREUER, J., 'On the Psychical Mechanism of Hysterical Phenomena: Preliminary Communication', in *Studies on Hysteria, Standard Ed.*, **2,** 3; *P.F.L.*, **3,** 53. (26, 57)

(1895*b* [1894]) 'On the Grounds for Detaching a Particular Syndrome from Neurasthenia under the description "Anxiety Neurosis"', *Standard Ed.*, **3,** 87; *P.F.L.*, **10,** 31. (117)

(1895*d*) With BREUER, J., *Studies on Hysteria*, London, 1956; *Standard Ed.*, **2**; *P.F.L.*, **3.** (26, 35, 40–41, 54, 57–8, 62, 159)

(1896*a*) 'Heredity and the Aetiology of the Neuroses', *Standard Ed.*, **3,** 143. (50)

(1896*c*) 'The Aetiology of Hysteria', *Standard Ed.*, **3,** 189. (35, 58)

(1900*a*) *The Interpretation of Dreams*, London and New York, 1955; *Standard Ed.*, **4–5**; *P.F.L.*, **4.** (8, 21, 26, 32–3, 39, 44, 47, 59, 90, 103, 123–6, 131, 137, 140, 172, 175, 184, 220, 269, 272, 276, 301, 305)

(1901*b*) *The Psychopathology of Everyday Life, Standard Ed.*, **6**; *P.F.L.*, **5.** (21, 26, 31, 57, 113, 163)

(1905*d*) *Three Essays on the Theory of Sexuality*, London, 1962; *Standard Ed.*, **7,** 125; *P.F.L.*, **7,** 31. (26, 32, 33, 84, 85, 86, 90, 118, 155, 170, 176, 203, 260, 267, 268, 269, 299)

(1905*e* [1901]) 'Fragment of an Analysis of a Case of Hysteria', *Standard Ed.*, **7,** 3; *P.F.L.*, **8,** 29. (168, 171)

(1906*a* [1905]) 'My Views on the Part played by Sexuality in the Aetiology of the Neuroses', *Standard Ed.*, **7,** 271; *P.F.L.*, **10,** 71. (155)

(1907c) 'The Sexual Enlightenment of Children', *Standard Ed.*, **9**, 131; *P.F.L.*, **7**, 171. (167)

(1908c) 'On the Sexual Theories of Children', *Standard Ed.*, **9**, 207; *P.F.L.*, **7**, 183. (168, 172, 176, 268)

(1908f) Preface to Stekel's *Nervöse Angstzustände und ihre Behandlung*, *Standard Ed.*, **9**, 250. (273)

(1909a [1908]) 'Some General Remarks on Hysterical Attacks', *Standard Ed.*, **9**, 229; *P.F.L.*, **10**, 95. (76)

(1909b) 'Analysis of a Phobia in a Five-Year-Old Boy', *Standard Ed.*, **10**, 3; *P.F.L.*, **8**, 165. (27, 43, 76, 86)

(1909d) 'Notes upon a Case of Obsessional Neurosis', *Standard Ed.*, **10**, 155; *P.F.L.*, **9**, 31. (43, 47, 282)

(1910a [1909]) *Five Lectures on Psycho-Analysis*, *Standard Ed.*, **11**, 3; in *Two Short Accounts of Psycho-Analysis*, Penguin Books, Harmondsworth, 1962. (16, 27)

(1910i) 'The Psycho-Analytic View of Psychogenic Disturbance of Vision', *Standard Ed.*, **11**, 211; *P.F.L.*, **10**, 103. (73)

(1911c [1910]) 'Psycho-Analytic Notes on an Autobiographical Account of a Case of Paranoia (Dementia Paranoides)', *Standard Ed.*, **12**, 3; *P.F.L.*, **9**, 129. (27, 43, 198)

(1912–13) *Totem and Taboo*, London, 1950; New York, 1952; *Standard Ed.*, **13**, 1; *P.F.L.*, **13**, 43. (27, 168, 198, 282)

(1913b) Introduction to Pfister's *Die psychanalytische Methode*, *Standard Ed.*, **12**, 329. (303)

(1913j) 'The Claims of Psycho-Analysis to Scientific Interest', *Standard Ed.*, **13**, 165; *P.F.L.*, **15**, 27. (303)

(1914d) 'On the History of the Psycho-Analytic Movement', *Standard Ed.*, **14**, 7; *P.F.L.*, **15**, 57. (27, 58, 247)

(1915d) 'Repression', *Standard Ed.*, **14**, 143; *P.F.L.*, **11**, 139. (59)

(1916–17 [1915–17]) *Introductory Lectures on Psycho-Analysis*, New York, 1966; London, 1971; *Standard Ed.*, **15–16**; *P.F.L.*, **1**. (8, 27, 76, 168, 172, 261)

(1917b) 'A Childhood Recollection from *Dichtung und Wahrheit*', *Standard Ed.*, **17**, 147; *P.F.L.*, **14**, 321. (286)

(1918b [1914]) 'From the History of an Infantile Neurosis', *Standard Ed.*, **17**, 3; *P.F.L.*, **9**, 225. (27, 43, 168, 169, 172)

(1920g) *Beyond the Pleasure Principle*, London, 1961; *Standard Ed.*, **18**, 7; *P.F.L.*, **11**, 269. (27, 59, 297)

(1921c) *Group Psychology and the Analysis of the Ego*, London and

FREUD, S. (*cont.*)

New York, 1959; *Standard Ed.*, **18**, 69; *P.F.L.*, **12**, 91. (27)

(1922c) 'Postscript to the "Analysis of a Phobia in a Five-Year-Old Boy"', *Standard Ed.*, **10**, 148; *P.F.L.*, **8**, 304.

(1923b) *The Ego and the Id*, London and New York, 1962; *Standard Ed.*, **19**, 3; *P.F.L.*, **11**, 339. (27, 79, 297, 301)

(1923e) 'The Infantile Genital Organization', *Standard Ed.*, **19**, 141; *P.F.L.*, **7**, 303. (268–9)

(1924d) 'The Dissolution of the Oedipus Complex', *Standard Ed.*, **19**, 173; *P.F.L.*, **7**, 313. (172)

(1925d [1924]) *An Autobiographical Study*, *Standard Ed.*, **20**, 3; *P.F.L.*, **15**, 183. (12)

(1925f) Preface to August Aichhorn's *Wayward Youth*, *Standard Ed.*, **19**, 273. (303)

(1925h) 'Negation', *Standard Ed.*, **19**, 235; *P.F.L.*, **11**, 435. (92)

(1925j) 'Some Psychical Consequences of the Anatomical Distinction between the Sexes', *Standard Ed.*, **19**, 243; *P.F.L.*, **7**, 323. (290)

(1926d [1925]) *Inhibitions, Symptoms and Anxiety*, London, 1960; *Standard Ed.*, **20**, 77; *P.F.L.,*. **10**, 227. (27, 59, 76, 117, 168, 169, 274)

(1927a) 'Postscript to *The Question of Lay Analysis*', *Standard Ed.*, **20**, 251; *P.F.L.*, **15**, 355. (12)

(1927c) *The Future of an Illusion*, London, 1962; *Standard Ed.*, **21**, 3; *P.F.L.*, **12**, 179. (27–8)

(1930a) *Civilization and its Discontents*, New York, 1961; London, 1963; *Standard Ed.*, **21**, 59; *P.F.L.*, **12**, 243. (28, 63)

(1932a) 'The Acquisition and Control of Fire', *Standard Ed.*, **22**, 185; *P.F.L.*, **13**, 225. (107)

(1933a [1932]) *New Introductory Lectures on Psycho-Analysis*, New York, 1966; London, 1971; *Standard Ed.*, **22**; *P.F.L.*, **2**. (8, 303)

(1935a) Postscript (1935) to *An Autobiographical Study*, new edition, London and New York; *Standard Ed.*, **20**, 71; *P.F.L.*, **15**. (12)

(1939a [1934–38]) *Moses and Monotheism*, *Standard Ed.*, **23**, 3; *P.F.L.*, **13**, 237. (28, 199)

(1940a [1938]) *An Outline of Psycho-Analysis*, New York, 1968; London, 1969; *Standard Ed.*, **23**, 141; *P.F.L.*, **15**, 369. (28)

(1950a [1887–1902]) *The Origins of Psycho-Analysis*, London and New York, 1954. (Partly, including 'A Project for a Scientific

Psychology', in *Standard Ed.*, **1**, 175.) (15–16, 24, 25, 26, 31–2 63, 115)

(1960a) *Letters 1873–1939* (ed. E. L. Freud) (trans. T. and J. Stern), New York, 1960; London, 1961. (22, 23–4)

(1963a [1909–39]) *Psycho-Analysis and Faith. The Letters of Sigmund Freud and Oskar Pfister* (ed. H. Meng and E. L. Freud) (trans. E. Mosbacher), London and New York, 1963. (24)

(1965a [1907–26]) *A Psycho-Analytic Dialogue. The Letters of Sigmund Freud and Karl Abraham* (ed. H. C. Abraham and E. L. Freud) (trans. B. Marsh and H. C. Abraham), London and New York, 1965. (24)

(1966a [1912–36]) *Sigmund Freud and Lou Andreas-Salomé: Letters* (ed. E. Pfeiffer) (trans. W. and E. Robson-Scott), London and New York, 1972. (24)

(1968a [1927–39]) *The Letters of Sigmund Freud and Arnold Zweig* (ed. E. L. Freud) (trans. W. and E. Robson-Scott), London and New York, 1970. (24)

(1970a [1919–35]) *Sigmund Freud as a Consultant. Recollections of a Pioneer in Psychoanalysis* (Letters from Freud to Edoardo Weiss, including a Memoir and Commentaries by Weiss, with Foreword and Introduction by Martin Grotjahn), New York, 1970. (24)

(1974a [1906–23]) *The Freud/Jung Letters* (ed. W. McGuire) (trans. R. Manheim and R. F. C. Hull), London and Princeton, N.J., 1974. (24)

JANET, PIERRE (1894) *État mental des hystériques*, Vol. 2, Paris. (156)

JONES, E. (1953) *Sigmund Freud: Life and Work*, Vol. 1, London and New York. (23)

    (1955) *Sigmund Freud: Life and Work*, Vol. 2, London and New York. (Page reference is to the English edition.) (23, 33)

    (1957) *Sigmund Freud: Life and Work*, Vol. 3, London and New York. (23)

JULLIEN, L. (1900) *See* MEDICAL CONGRESS

JUNG, C. G., and FREUD, S. (1974) *See* FREUD, S. (1974a). (24)

KRAFFT-EBING, R. VON (1893) *Psychopathia Sexualis* (8th ed.), Stuttgart. (1st ed., 1886.) (84)

    [*Trans.: Psychopathia Sexualis*, New York, 1922.]

KRIS, E. (1950) Introduction to S. Freud's *Aus den Anfängen der Psychoanalyse*, London. (115)

KRIS, E. (cont.)

[Trans.: In FREUD, S. (1950a) The Origins of Psycho-Analysis, London and New York, 1954.]

MANTEGAZZA, P. (1875) Fisiologia dell'amore, 2nd ed., Milan. (56, 97)

MEDICAL CONGRESS (1900) Thirteenth International Medical Congress, Paris. (XIII. Congrès International de Médecine, Paris, 1900), Vol. 9: Section de Dermatologie et de Syphiligraphie. Contributions by E. Finger, L. Jullien and B. Tarnowsky on 'La descendance des hérédo-syphilitiques'. (50)

MOLL, A. (1898) Untersuchungen über die Libido sexualis, Vol. 1, Berlin. (269)

PFISTER, O. (1913) Die psychanalytische Methode, Leipzig and Berlin. (303)

[Trans.: The Psychoanalytic Method, New York and London, 1917.]

(1963) With FREUD, S. See FREUD, S. (1963a)

RANK, O. (1909) Der Mythus von der Geburt des Helden, Leipzig and Vienna. (230)

[Trans.: The Myth of the Birth of the Hero, New York, 1914.]

SADGER, I. (1908) 'Fragment der Analyse eines Homosexuellen', Jb. sex. Zwischenstufen, 9, 339. (267)

(1909) 'Zur Ätiologie der konträren Sexualempfindung', Medsche Klinik, Nr 2. (267)

SCHMIDT, R. (1902) Beiträge zur indischen Erotik, Leipzig. (37–8)

STÄRCKE, A. (1921) 'Der Kastrationskomplex', Int. Z. Psychoanal., 1, 9. (172)

[Trans.: 'The Castration Complex', Int. J. Psycho-Analysis, 2 (1921), 179.]

STEKEL, W. (1908) Nervöse Angstzustände und ihre Behandlung, Berlin and Vienna. (273)

TARNOWSKY, B. (1900) See MEDICAL CONGRESS

WEININGER, O. (1903) Geschlecht und Charakter, Vienna. (198)

WEISS, E., and FREUD, S. (1970) See FREUD, S. (1970a)

WERNICKE, C. (1900) Grundriss der Psychiatrie, Leipzig. (88)

ZWEIG, A., and FREUD, S. (1968) See FREUD, S. (1968a)

LIST OF ABBREVIATIONS

Gesammelte Schriften	= Freud, *Gesammelte Schriften* (12 vols.) Vienna, 1924–34.
Gesammelte Werke	= Freud, *Gesammelte Werke* (18 vols.), Vols. 1–17 London, 1940–52, Vol. 18 Frankfurt am Main, 1968. From 1960 the whole edition published by S. Fischer Verlag, Frankfurt am Main.
S.K.S.N.	= Freud, *Sammlung kleiner Schriften zur Neurosenlehre* (5 vols.), Vienna, 1906–22.
Vier Krankengeschichten	= Freud, *Vier psychoanalytische Krankengeschichten*, Vienna, 1932.
Collected Papers	= Freud, *Collected Papers* (5 vols.), London, 1924–50.
Standard Edition	= *The Standard Edition of the Complete Psychological Works of Sigmund Freud* (24 vols.), Hogarth Press and The Institute of Psycho-Analysis, London, 1953–74.
P.F.L.	= *Pelican Freud Library* (15 vols.), Penguin Books, Harmondsworth, from 1973.

GENERAL INDEX

This index includes the names of non-technical authors. It also includes the names of technical authors where no reference is made in the text to specific works. For references to specific technical works, the Bibliography should be consulted. The index is based on originals compiled by Mrs R. S. Partridge.

Busch, Wilhelm, 179 n. 1

Cart as symbol, 207–11, 216,
226, 228, 249–50, 255, 281,
284, 288
Cases (see also 'Dora';
'Little Hans')
of 'Anna O', 14–15
of 'Rat Man', 43 n., 47 n.
of Schreber, 27, 42 n.
of 'Wolf Man', 27, 43 n.,
169 n., 172 n. 2
Castration complex, 27, 171, 198
and n. 2, 264, 279, 288
use of term, 172 nn. 1 and 2
Castration threat, 171, 172 n. 2,
195 and n. 2, 198, 265, 278
Cathartic method, 14–15, 26
Charcot, J.-M., 13–14, 25, 71,
156
Chemistry, sexual, 113–14
Childhood
experiences, 58, 107, 125–8,
130–31, 143–4
memories and phantasies of,
172 n. 2, 281 n.
neuroses, 274, 298, 300
Children (see also Infantile;
Infantile sexuality; Parents
and children; Seduction)
education of, 101, 262, 298,
299–300, 302
psychoanalysis of, 169, 260–
61, 263, 304
punishment of, 299
sexual curiosity of (see
Infantile sexual curiosity)
suggestibility of, 261

tu quoque arguments of, 67,
278
unreliability of assertions of,
261–2
Circumcision, 198 n. 2
Cleanliness, obsessional, 50,
118 n., 129
Clitoris, 61
Coitus interruptus, 116
Collateral flow, perverse
sexuality and, 84–5
Component instincts, 267, 295,
297, 300
Compulsive behaviour, 51
Condensation, 130, 243,
279 n. 2
'Confluence of instincts', 265,
284, 296 n.
Confusional states, 48, 145 n.
Consciousness, 44, 47, 89, 93,
156
biological function of, 301
relation to the unconscious,
263, 278
repression and, 278, 301
Wundt's view of, 175 n.
Constipation (see also Faeces,
retention of, in infancy),
141, 217, 258, 270 n. 2
Constitutional factors (see
Heredity and experience)
Contrectation (Moll), 269
Conversion, hysterical, 87–8,
274
Convulsions, hysterical, 53 n. 2
Cow's udder connects ideas of
penis and breast, 171
Creusa, 96
Cruelty, 152 n., 162

FOR THE BEST IN PAPERBACKS, LOOK FOR THE

In every corner of the world, on every subject under the sun, Penguin represents quality and variety – the very best in publishing today.

For complete information about books available from Penguin – including Pelicans, Puffins, Peregrines and Penguin Classics – and how to order them, write to us at the appropriate address below. Please note that for copyright reasons the selection of books varies from country to country.

In the United Kingdom: Please write to *Dept E.P., Penguin Books Ltd, Harmondsworth, Middlesex, UB7 0DA*

In the United States: Please write to *Dept BA, Penguin, 299 Murray Hill Parkway, East Rutherford, New Jersey 07073*

In Canada: Please write to *Penguin Books Canada Ltd, 2801 John Street, Markham, Ontario L3R 1B4*

In Australia: Please write to the *Marketing Department, Penguin Books Australia Ltd, P.O. Box 257, Ringwood, Victoria 3134*

In New Zealand: Please write to the *Marketing Department, Penguin Books (NZ) Ltd, Private Bag, Takapuna, Auckland 9*

In India: Please write to *Penguin Overseas Ltd, 706 Eros Apartments, 56 Nehru Place, New Delhi, 110019*

In Holland: Please write to *Penguin Books Nederland B.V., Postbus 195, NL–1380AD Weesp, Netherlands*

In Germany: Please write to *Penguin Books Ltd, Friedrichstrasse 10–12, D–6000 Frankfurt Main 1, Federal Republic of Germany*

In Spain: Please write to *Longman Penguin España, Calle San Nicolas 15, E–28013 Madrid, Spain*

In France: Please write to *Penguin Books Ltd, 39 Rue de Montmorency, F-75003, Paris, France*

In Japan: Please write to *Longman Penguin Japan Co Ltd, Yamaguchi Building, 2–12–9 Kanda Jimbocho, Chiyoda-Ku, Tokyo 101, Japan*

FOR THE BEST IN PAPERBACKS, LOOK FOR THE 🐧

KARL MARX IN PENGUIN

GRUNDRISSE
Introduction to the Critique of Political Economy

The *Grundrisse* throws light on many obscure corners of Marx's thought and, in this light, the English reader can now assess how far his economic and philosophic outlook changed and how far it has simply been misinterpreted. For here is a major part of Marx's work which was unknown even to Lenin.

THE REVOLUTIONS OF 1848
Political Writings Volume I

The bulk of this volume contains articles from the *Neue Rheinische Zeitung*, a journal in which Marx (or occasionally Engels) interpreted the risings in Vienna, Berlin and Prague. In addition there are reviews, addresses, speeches on Poland and the minute of the London meeting of 1850 when Schapper and others finally left the Communist League.

At the head of these political writings is Marx's most famous text – the *Manifesto of the Communist Party* (1848), in which he outlines the class struggles of history.

SURVEYS FROM EXILE
Political Writings Volume II

After perfecting his English Marx began to interpret, in a series of articles for the American (and German) press, the English political scene and British rule in India, and, on the outbreak of the American Civil War, he wrote at length on that conflict for a liberal paper in Vienna. Samples of these extensive writings, by which Marx earned a scanty living, appear in this volume, along with other reviews, speeches and political statements.

and

EARLY WRITINGS
THE FIRST INTERNATIONAL AND AFTER
CAPITAL (IN 3 VOLS.)
Published in association with New Left Review

FOR THE BEST IN PAPERBACKS, LOOK FOR THE 🐧

THE PENGUIN FREUD LIBRARY

Based on James Strachey's Standard Edition, this collection of fifteen volumes, formerly published as the *Pelican Freud Library*, is the first full paperback edition of Freud's works in English. The first eleven volumes have been edited by Angela Richards, and subsequent volumes by Albert Dickson.